Samuel Watson

A Memphian's Trip to Europe with Cook's Educational Party

Samuel Watson

A Memphian's Trip to Europe with Cook's Educational Party

ISBN/EAN: 9783744794251

Printed in Europe, USA, Canada, Australia, Japan

Cover: Foto ©Andreas Hilbeck / pixelio.de

More available books at **www.hansebooks.com**

A MEMPHIAN'S TRIP TO EUROPE

WITH COOK'S EDUCATIONAL PARTY:

TO WHICH IS ADDED

LETTERS FROM REVS. T. W. HOOPER, A. B. WHIPPLE, AND C. W. CUSHING; ALSO, LETTERS FROM SEVERAL LADIES AND GENTLEMEN OF THE PARTY.

BY SAMUEL WATSON.

NASHVILLE, TENN.:
SOUTHERN METHODIST PUBLISHING HOUSE.
PUBLISHED FOR THE AUTHOR.
1874.

Entered, according to act of Congress, in the year 1874, by
SAMUEL WATSON,
in the office of the Librarian of Congress, at Washington.

DEDICATION.

To Mr. THOMAS COOK, Sr., Of London, to whose liberality and kindness the Educational Party are much indebted for favors beyond their agreement, this Book is
Respectfully Dedicated by
THE AUTHOR.

PREFACE.

WHAT! Another book of travels? Yes; and different from every other one that has ever been published.

On the 21st of June, 1873, there sailed from New York the steam-ships Victoria and Canada, with Cook's Educational Party, composed of about one hundred and seventy persons, from over twenty different States. The Victoria was bound for Glasgow, Scotland, the Canada for Liverpool, England. It fell to my lot to go on the Canada, leaving one hour after the Victoria.

Having been solicited by the editor of the *Memphis Avalanche* to write sketches of our trip, I complied with his request, writing hastily, as I only could under the circumstances. Having been requested by many—in whose judgment I have confidence—to publish them in book-form, I concluded to get the letters of several other gentlemen, who wrote for other papers, and publish them all together. They are from prominent ministers of the Presbyterian, Baptist, and Methodist Churches—and some from ladies—all of our party, though belonging to different sections, into which we divided at London. By this arrangement we saw more of the country, thus giving more variety and interest to them. The Presbyterians can see what the Rev. T. W. Hooper, of Lynchburg, Va., has to say of Europe; the Baptists can read what the Rev. A. B. Whipple, of New York, says; while the Methodists can read how Rev. C. W. Cushing, of Massachusetts, tells what he saw. The writer gives a running sketch of how he saw things.

These gentlemen are presidents of institutions of learning, and capable, as will be seen, of presenting what came under their observation in an attractive, instructive, and entertaining style.

Since my return, I have, from very extensive *memoranda* taken at Rome, and Augustus Hare's "Walks in Rome," written up some articles on the "Eternal City." These will come in at their proper place with the entire series, so that there will be all said by each of us about places and things before we leave them. It has been our intention to take the reader along with us, and let him see things as we saw them, without the labor and expense necessarily attending such a trip.

Hoping that those who follow us through will be amply compensated for their time, and learn something more of the *country*, *places*, *things*, and *people* which we visited, that will interest them,

I am truly theirs,

SAMUEL WATSON.

Contents.

CHAPTER I.

A Memphian's trip from New York to Liverpool and London—An ocean voyage—England's great port—London and the Shah—A day among the London churches, and amid the tombs of the great dead—Off for the Continent—Taking a look at London . . 11

CHAPTER II.

Letters from the Rev. T. W. Hooper. 1. From Lynchburg to New York. 2. Life on the ocean. 3. Moville—Giant's Causeway—Glasgow. 4. Edinburgh—Speech-making—Scott's home 39

CHAPTER III.

Letters from the Rev. A. B. Whipple. 1. Adieu—Victoria—Time and keeping speed. 2. Emerald Isle—Cars—Dunluce Castle—Origin of Giant's Causeway. 3. Clyde—Ship-building—Glasgow Cathedral—Monuments—Trosachs. 4. Edinburgh—Route to London—Hospitality—Adventures 56

CHAPTER IV.

Letter from Miss Hattie Stanard—Route to New York—Ship-life—Sabbath services—How time is kept—Londonderry—Portrush—Dunluce Castle—Adam Clarke's monument 71

CHAPTER V.

Letters from the Rev. C. W. Cushing—Scottish preaching, etc.—Contrast between a Sabbath in Edinburgh and in Cologne 78

CHAPTER VI.

The American Educational Party in Edinburgh—Commencement of Cook's tours—Speeches by Dr. Donaldson, Rev. T. D. Witherspoon, Rev. Professor Cushing, Lord Provost, and Mr. Cook 83

CHAPTER VII.

A trip from London to Antwerp—A look about the ancient city—Sights and impressions in Belgium and Germany—Experience in Brussels and Cologne—Habits and occupation of the people—The great Cathedral and other objects of interest—From Cologne to Munich—The Rhine and its marvelous beauties—How railroads are run in Germany—The people and their habits—A day in Mayence—Guttenberg's statue—Munich and its attractions, etc.—From Munich to Vienna—Notes by the wayside—The Austrian capital and the Exposition—Sights and improvements—Condition of the people of Europe—Something for Americans to think about—Some of the features of the great Exposition—Sights and sight-seers 96

CHAPTER VIII.

Letters from the Rev. T. W. Hooper. 1. Zurich—Luther—Calvin—Paintings—Statue of Bavaria. 2. Vienna Exposition—Home things. 3. Tombs of royalty—Gathering rocks, and a hasty retreat. 4. Down the Rhine—Cologne Cathedral—St. Ursula—Brussels lace-factories. 125

CHAPTER IX.

Letters from the Rev. A. B. Whipple. 1. Antwerp—Brussels—Carved pulpit—Royal palace—Parks—Museum—Cologne Cathedral—Sunday. 2. University—Rhine scenery—Castles—Villages—Mayence—Munich—Palace of the king—Statue of Bavaria. 3. Vienna cordiality—Exposition building 143

CHAPTER X.

Letter from the Rev. C. W. Cushing. Vienna—Churches—Exposition—Reflections upon them 158

CHAPTER XI.

Letter from Miss Hattie Stanard. Munich—Vienna—Mayence—Down the Rhine—Cologne—Brussels . . 163

CHAPTER XII.

"Beautiful Venice"—An *Avalanche* correspondent in the City of the Sea—From Austria to Italy—Highly romantic scenery—Sights and impressions in Venice—The art galleries and and the royal palace—Characteristics of the Italians—Among the gondoliers, etc.—From Venice to Florence—Observations by the wayside—The ruins and beauties of Italy—The Eternal City—What a Memphian saw in Rome—Scenes on the banks of the Tiber—The great Cathedral—Statuary, paintings, etc.—Capitol statues—Hall of Emperors—Hall of illustrious men—Historic prison—Palaces of Augustus, Palatine, Nero—Church of St. Clement—The Forums and the Coliseum—The Catacombs—St. Agnes—The Santa Scala—Roman Funeral—The Pantheon—St. Peter's—The Vatican—Sistine Chapel—Michael Angelo—Leaving the city 171

CHAPTER XIII.

Letters from the Rev. A. B. Whipple. 1. Description of Venice—St. Mark's Church. 2. Rome—History—First Basilica—Pantheon—Baths—Latin Rome. Letter from the Rev. C. W. Cushing. Professor Wood—Palaces of the Cesars—Great Circus—Baths—Coliseum—Palace of Nero—Church of St. Clement. 222

CHAPTER XIV.

Switzerland—From Rome to Geneva—Scenes by the wayside—The indescribable splendor of the Alps—On the shores of Lake Geneva—Picturesque Switzerland—The watches and music-boxes of Geneva—Rambles afoot—Beautiful Berne—The Swiss love of home—Life and

habits of the Bernese—The wonderful clock of 1191—
The Lake of Geneva—Three thousand feet high—The
illuminated falls at Interlachen—Seas of ice—The
Bernese Alps—Up among the coolness of Switzerland
in August—Top of the Alps—A view of three hundred
miles from Rigi—One of Nature's grandest displays—
Romantic Switzerland—Impressions of the most interesting country in Europe—An amusing dinner-table
experience—The need of an interpreter—Sketch of
Lucerne—William Tell—A mountain railroad—Farewell, Switzerland—Letters from the Rev. T. W. Hooper
—Letter from the Rev. A. B. Whipple 240

CHAPTER XV.

"Paris is France"—Views in the wicked, beautiful city—
Strolls in historic localities, some of which have been
baptized in the blood of saint and sinner—Lingering in
Paris—Sight-seeing in the finest city in the world—Versailles and its antique remains of royalty—The Tuileries
—Pantheon—St. Cloud—Gobelin—Farewell to France
—Back in London—Dr. Cummings—Billingsgate—The
Tower—The docks and the shipping—Letter from the
Rev. T. W. Hooper—Letter from the Rev. A. B. Whipple 278

CHAPTER XVI.

Loitering in London—Prince Albert's memorial monument—Description of its beauties, its grandeur, and its
sculpture—Letters from the Rev. A. B. Whipple—Letters from the Rev. T. W. Hooper—Homeward bound
—From London to Edinburgh—Interesting sights in
the Scottish capital—Castle Rock—Burns's grave—
Mary Queen of Scots—Dr. Chalmers—Bunyan—The
rolling deep—Leaving Glasgow, the prosperous city on
the Clyde—The pleasures and misfortunes of a life of
ten days on the ocean wave 303

A MEMPHIAN'S TRIP TO EUROPE.

CHAPTER I.

LETTER 1.

Rev. Samuel Watson's trip from New York to Liverpool and London—An ocean voyage—England's great port—London and the Shah.

STEAMER CANADA
(*Approaching Queenstown, Ireland*),
July 2, 1873.

ON THE BILLOWS.

EDITOR AVALANCHE:—Having promised to write you "semi-occasionally" during my European tour, I drop you a few lines, to be mailed at Queenstown.

We left New York on Saturday, 21st of June. The weather has been fine; consequently the sea has been very quiet, except on last Saturday, when we had quite a gale nearly all day. It was the grandest, the most sublime, scene I ever witnessed. The ocean seemed to rise up like hills, while the noble ship rode them like a thing of life, now on the summit, then in the valley between, playing sad havoc with the movables on board. At dinner there was a great deal of commotion, not only among the dishes, but the people were tossed to and fro, to the amusement of all but those who were the sufferers.

There is much less danger than is generally supposed in crossing the ocean. Facts and figures show that there are fewer lives lost at sea, in proportion to the number of passengers, than by any other mode of traveling. Take, for instance, this line, the "National." They have been running for ten years, have twelve ships, have carried over 300,000 passengers, and have never lost a ship or a man. The Cunard line has been in operation for about thirty years, and has never lost a passenger. Where can such safety be found on any of our thoroughfares of travel? A trip across the ocean, with a calm sea, is a very monotonous affair. We eat, and read, and sleep, to rise and eat and read again.

By the way, I don't fancy the English style of eating. They breakfast at $8\frac{1}{2}$, lunch at $12\frac{1}{2}$, dine at 4, which takes one hour and a half, tea at 7. Their roast beef, the boast of the Englishman, has too much blood remaining in it for me. I will inclose a bill of fare, by which you can see the style of English living on the ocean. I would greatly prefer a modification of quantity, quality, and a great reduction in the time consumed in disposing of it. But so it is, in "Rome, we must do as Rome does." The most exciting time we have had has been when a large number of whales were seen. They spout a large stream of water up some distance in the air, then throw themselves nearly out of the water, and seeming to be as anxious to show themselves as we were to see them. We have seen the sea-lions, porpoises, etc., sporting amid the ocean's waves. It has been quite cold for several days, so much so that flannel and winter clothes would not keep us warm on deck.

I am pleasantly located near "midship," close to the Captain's room. My room-mates are Mr. B. A. Rogers, of Verona, Miss.; Capt. John Deering, of Covington, Tenn.; and Mr. A. S. Elliott, of Huntsville, Ala. Our ship is about 400 feet long, 40 wide, and 41 deep. She was 23 feet under water when we left New York, but she is somewhat lighter now, as we consume about forty tons of coal per day. She has the compound engine, or, more properly, two engines—one of the low, the other high pressure. This is a most important discovery for steam navigation. The coal now consumed by this recent discovery is only about one-third of what it was by using only one engine; hence the expense is greatly reduced, besides giving the tonnage for freight previously required for coal. It is to be hoped that Americans will now build ocean steamers and save to our country some of the countless millions paid to other nations for this service. Philadelphia has commenced two lines of steam-ships to Liverpool, and has built her own vessels. The success of the experiment has been of the most satisfactory character. We have seen quite a number of ships, but not near enough to any of them to speak, only by the "signal rocket" sent up, which is a nautical language I have not yet learned.

We have a nice lot of passengers, representing several nationalities and churches. There are six ministers, some of whom will go with us through Europe. We have had services both Sabbaths, the traveling ministers officiating.

We are anxious to see land again. To be out on the "ocean's wave" for ten or twelve days, pent up in a small room, to sleep in a berth but little longer than your body, is not calculated to impress one very favorably with a sea-faring life. Our trip has been a very pleasant one thus far, and we hope to-morrow to arrive at Liverpool, the great "cottonopolis" of the world. I will, from time to time, as I may have opportunity, dot down whatever I may think will interest your readers, as I pass on from place to place with the rapidity indicated by the inclosed programme.

P. S.—We are now sailing along the Irish coast, the hills of "sweet Ireland" coming down to the water's edge, and saying to the surging waves, Thus far shalt thou come and no farther. There was much excitement this morning when the steersman announced land in sight. We all rejoiced, but especially those who had been long absent from their native land. Their joy was manifested in various ways. We will soon be at Queenstown, where this will be mailed. We expect to arrive at Liverpool to-morrow, but remain till next day for the daylight to see over 200 miles of merry Old England to London, from whence you may hear from me again.

ASHORE AT LAST.

LIVERPOOL, July 2, 1873.

We arrived at this great sea-port yesterday, having been twelve days out from New York. Though I wrote you yesterday from Queenstown, I will drop you a few lines before leaving for London, which we will do early in the morning.

It is said that the trade of the whole world concentrates at this, the largest sea-port on the globe. We look to the cotton market here with much interest in the South.

The docks are the most costly and extensive of any in the world. They are six miles in extent, and cost from eighty-five to one hundred millions of dollars. The Sanden docks are immense basins, like those in the navy-yards of Brooklyn and Charleston, for the floating in of vessels for repairs, closing and pumping out till the hulls are left dry for the workmen. The others are commercial docks, rendered necessary from the immense height to which the tide rises—it being from 18 to 30 feet. These docks are constructed out of Scotch granite and iron. They are immense canal locks, with swinging gates, closed so as to retain the water and keep the vessel afloat while discharging. They are moved by machinery. These gates are never allowed to be open except at near high tide.

There are to be seen vessels from all nations lying in dock—each showing its nationality.

The weather to-day has been very cold, with rain and wind, which prevented our seeing as much as I desired while we ascended the river Mersey. The rocky headland of Holyhead of Wales, with its strange clift and bridged rock, its white light-house, and the wonderful breakwater defending the harbor. Then comes the Welsh lands, with thrifty farms, and neat farm-houses and windmills. Behind these the fair Welsh mountains rise, the Snowdon, said to be the highest in the south-west of Great Britain, but they looked small compared to the mountains we pass over coming to New York. Little Welsh villages, nestled at the feet of these highlands, present a beautiful view. Three magnificent steam-ships passed near us, crowded with passengers for America. But I am going back in my scrawl. I must let the ocean trip pass. Though it has been a pleasant one, yet I never wanted to close up one so much as I have this, my first ocean voyage. Long will I remember the Canada and its worthy officers. But other things crowd upon my mind on *terra firma*. Liverpool has been in a state of excitement about the visit of the Shah of Persia. The papers are filled with accounts of his visit here. It is said he had six wives with him, but as he was visiting a nation which did not recognize but one, he only took one of them with him in public.

What folly this man-worship is! I am glad I feel no inclination in that direction. I expect to see much of it before my return, but I have no idea of imbibing any of it, either politically or ecclesiastically.

The buildings for some distance from the wharf are large and fine, and those over the city generally are three stories only, and look rather antiquated; but there are some magnificent buildings here—the largest I ever saw. Most prominent is St. George's Hall, one of the most magnificent structures in the world. We went to see it; and here is the largest organ in the country. In front of it stand the statues of Queen Victoria and Prince Albert, each on a very large horse. On the former is this inscription: "Erected by the Corporation of Liverpool, in the thirty-fourth year of her reign." Over the latter: "This statue of a wise and good prince is erected by the Corporation of Liverpool, October, 1866. Albert, Prince Consort, born 1819; died 1861." At the north end, standing on a high column, is the statue of Wellington, and the battles he fought and won engraved on the base. Inside the hall are the marble statues of quite a number of England's great men. I felt the most interest in Sir Robert Peel and Mr. Gladstone. We have hurried over the city in several directions, and seen most of it, and hasten to take the train for London, of which you shall hear by and by.

LETTER 2.

Another interesting letter from Rev. Samuel Watson—A day among London churches and amid tombs of the great dead— Off for the Continent.

LONDON, July 7, 1873.

We left Liverpool early on the 4th for this city. For many miles we passed through what is properly called the "manufacturing district." The tall chimneys and immense buildings which could be seen all over the country, filled with machinery, told the secret of England's greatness. Those nearest Liverpool, judging from the number of cotton bales and cotton machinery we saw, were for manufacturing cotton goods. Then comes a broken agricultural district, after which silk, hosiery, and other manufactories. I have never seen, nor will I ever see again, such a country as this. All the way, every spot of ground showed the evidences of what man had done for it. Cities, towns, villages, gardens, meadows, cut up in all sorts of shapes and sizes (except large ones), divided by their hawthorn hedges, and covered with herds of cattle, sheep, etc., defy description. I shall not attempt it. Paradise, no doubt, was more lovely, but this excels any thing I have ever seen. Our conductor, Mr. Anderson, who met us at Liverpool, was born here, and pointed out many places of interest. None more so than Derby, where Bunyan was born and imprisoned for twelve years, and where the "Pilgrim's Progress" was written.

England is proverbial for showers. It happened that as we were landing a heavy rain came on, very much to the discomfort of the passengers, who had to embark on another boat to reach the shore. I heard a remark made which I did not then appreciate as much as subsequently: that it was a pity that the first boat for that purpose had not been made with a roof. If it had been, all of them would have been made after that model.

In the Great City.—About 3 o'clock we arrived at London, walked out of the cars (as we call them, but "carriages" here), in the rear entrance of the Midland Grand Hotel. It is the largest, and when completed, will be the most magnificent hotel I ever saw. Dinner over, we go to Cook's, Fleet street, to report ourselves. From here we go to call on the United States Minister to see if we can get into Parliament. He received us kindly, and after some time spent pleasantly, told us he would see by next day, as he was authorized to give but two permits a day, and that there were so many Americans now here that he feared there was no chance for us during our brief stay in the city. St. James's Park was next visited. Something over a mile, at Buckingham Palace (the Queen's present residence), we see a vast crowd of people, and learn that the Shah, of whom I spoke in my last letter, is to attend the Opera, and will, with the royal family, in state, pass out. Notwithstanding my opinion expressed in my last letter, I resolved to see all of it that could be seen, even at some discomfort. We wait. The crowd thickens and spreads over the vast grounds; the police can hardly keep the way open for the carriages. After about two hours out they came. Fortunately, our position was on the margin of the open way. We saw all we could, but did not discover that kings and queens (prospective) are different from other people, only in their external trappings. I was surprised to find the thousands that were gathered there so anxious to see them. There is a magic charm in royalty to those who are governed by it. As this was my first, and may be my last chance, to be a "looker-on," I was glad to embrace it in this best phase of monarchy. Saturday we visit the financial portion of the city. Wall street seems but a small affair compared to this world's heart of money-power. The Bank of England covers eight acres, while other moneyed institutions cover over a large portion of this part of the city.

On the Rounds.—The Westminster Abbey, the place where sleeps the remains of the sovereigns and great men of the nation for hundreds of years, is the most solemn, grand, and impressive place I ever entered. We paid our fee to go round with one of the guides, who gave a synopsis of many who rest there, embracing an epitome of England's history for hundreds of years.

We got permission, and go through the Parliament

buildings and look at the statues of many men whom the nation delight to honor. Of some of these I may speak at some future time; also of the Abbey. We go to the office of the United States Legation—but one ticket to the House of Lords can be given, and I am the fortunate recipient. I go on Tuesday, at 5 P.M., when they meet.

After dinner we take a trip on the underground railroad. Notwithstanding the millions on the surface, traveling, they seem to be as crowded on the cars under the ground. At the crossing of some of the streets steps go down, and regular stations for passengers to get on and off. There are many of these running through and around the city; others traverse it in the air. On our return we take the top of a street-car, and go several miles to its terminus, and walk several more to London Cemetery, overlooking the city—said to be the highest point in the vicinity. The monuments are of a previous age, mostly. The prospective is grand for many miles around.

This has been a busy day of intense interest, to which I shall look back with pleasure, and may at some time say something more about it.

Hearing and Seeing Spurgeon.—Mr. Spurgeon is the great attraction here. Every one of our party, indeed all the Americans at the hotel, go to hear him. He is a truly great man. I took notes of his sermon, but this is not the place for them. The sermon was one of the plainest, most evangelical, and spiritual, I ever listened to. He had been absent about a month, as he said, in the only forest in England. He seems to be over forty; but one of his members told me he was only thirty-three, and that he was about five feet six or eight inches in height. He opened his service with prayer, then singing, he giving out a verse at a time; then read and commented on several passages of Scripture;

then singing and prayer; singing and sermon. His church is of a circular form, with two galleries extending all around, he standing on a circular platform about the height of the first gallery. It holds between 7,000 and 8,000 people, and was filled, as usual.

Among the Tombs.—We then went to Wesley Chapel and to City Road Methodist Church, where lie the remains of John Wesley and Dr. Adam Clarke, side by side. On the monument erected to the former is this inscription: "To the memory of the venerable John Wesley, A.M., late Fellow of Lincoln College, Oxford; died March 2, 1791, aged 88 years." On the latter: "Sacred to the memory of Adam Clarke, LL.D., A.S., who rested from his labors August 26, 1832." Then comes the tomb of Richard Watson, with this: "Sacred to the memory of Rev. Richard Watson, who died in the Lord January 8, 1833, in the 52d year of his age—a man no more distinguished for admirable endowment of his mind than for the depth of his piety, the fervor of his zeal, and the constancy of his powerful genius to the service of God in His sanctuary, and the spiritual interests of mankind." Here sleep the remains of many distinguished Methodist preachers. Dr. Bunting was the last one buried here—June 16, 1858. I copy the inscription of Wesley's mother:

"Here lies the body of Mrs. Susanna Wesley, widow of Rev. Samuel Wesley, M. A., late Rector of Epworth, in Lincolnshire, who died July 23, 1742, aged 72 years. She was the youngest daughter of the Rev. Samuel Annesley, D.D., ejected by the Act of Uniformity from the Rectory of St. Giles's Cripplegate, August 24, 1662. She was the mother of nineteen children, of whom the most eminent were the Revs. John and Charles Wesley, the former of whom was, under God, founder of the Society called Methodists.

"In sure and certain hope to rise,
And claim her mansion in the skies;
A Christian here, her flesh laid down,
The cross exchanging for a crown."

There, on the opposite side of the street, are many whose names are as household words with us. Prominent among these is John Bunyan, whose "Pilgrim's Progress" has perhaps been more extensively read than any book except the Bible. In marble he lies on top of his tomb, on one side of which his sins press on his back, as a large weight. On the other side they are gone—very impressive.

John Wesley.—It was here, in this chapel, that John Wesley preached, and near it he lived and died. It was, and is, the center of Methodism. There are now two parsonages here, in which the preachers live who are on this circuit; for this is still their plan. In one of these Benson wrote his "Commentary." They have a number of class-rooms in the basement, in which they were having meetings when we were there. They still adhere to the plan of small classes. The chapel is one of the largest, with a box pulpit hung up, I know not how far, though it has been lowered five feet. I felt that I was standing in a holy place, where Mr. Wesley had so often preached, and where he commenced an organization now more numerous than any other Protestant Church. After spending a long time with the preachers and people there, learning all I could, we went to hear the same preacher who preached there in the "*Goshetten.*" I judge it to be a hard vicinity, from what I saw. Street-singing and exhortation, perhaps preaching, is kept up here as in olden times. We stopped a while at several such places, day and night. But I must not dwell longer in this detail.

London's Immensity.—London overwhelms me with its immensity: just think of ten miles, some say twelve by twelve miles, of houses filled up, and filled with human beings, numbering between three and four million! To see it all would require weeks instead of days. There are several important places we will visit in the next three days, after which we are to be off for the Continent. Then we shall feel our dependence on our conductor, as we shall be barbarians to each, as the Shah has been to all here. He has gone to France, and royalty is quiet again. The weather is still cool, alternating often between sunshine and shower, as usual here. They have very little night here; but they make it up by sleeping late. Our company are learning the same fashion of getting up at 9 and 10 o'clock. I rise and write this hasty scrawl while some of them are quietly folded in the arms of Morpheus. I will sketch our pathway briefly as I may have time.

LETTER 3.

Rev. Samuel Watson taking a look at London—Westminster Abbey—St. Paul's—Tower of London.

LONDON, July 8, 1873.

Zoölogical Gardens. — On Monday evening we went to the Zoölogical Gardens, as they are called, though they contain over two hundred acres. Here are collected the plants, flowers, shrubs, animals, etc., of the world. Though they are exceedingly interesting, they do not come up to the Central Park, of New York.

Westminster Abbey.—No one who visits London would ever think of leaving there without one or more visits to Westminster Abbey. Who has not read of that little island of thorns around which, in the days of the Druids, the Thames threw an arm, on which the Roman colonists erected a temple to Apollo? The Christian faith, advancing from the East, began to fulfill the prophet's declaration that the wilderness and the solitary place shall blossom as the rose. Sebert, King of the East Saxons, cleared away the thorns, and erected in the midst of the temple a rude church, which he dedicated to St. Peter, and received his remains. A neat monument still marks the place of his remains. Three hundred years afterward King Edgar established a priory, consisting of twelve monks of the Benedict order. One hundred and fifty years later Edward the Confessor elevated the priory to an abbey, within whose enlarged borders he found an honorable tomb. It was not, however, till 1220 that the present church was commenced by Henry III., to whom is ascribed the chapels of the virgin and of the confession, the transepts, and the choir. The building was carried on by twelve successive abbots and kings, but is not yet finished, and perhaps never will be. It is like many we see over Europe, that mock the pride of man, whose foundations crumble before the capstone of the last tower can be put on. It was called Westminster—that is, the minster or monastery church west of London. It consists—first, of Henry VII.'s chapel, the exterior of which has been restored at an expense of two hundred thousand dollars; second, Edward the Confessor's chapel and shrine, with the chapels of St. Nicholas, St. Benedict, St. Edmund, St. John the Baptist, St. Paul, St. Erasmus; third, the transepts; fourth, the choir; fifth, the nave; sixth, Blaze chapel; seventh, Jerusalam Chamber; eighth, chapter-house; ninth, pise; tenth, little cloisters; eleventh, dark cloisters; twelfth, area cloisters; thirteenth, Dean's Yard. Exteriorly, the church measures 532 feet by 220. I have always had a great desire to see the Westminster Abbey; hence it was one of the first places I visited. I was there several times. There is no other such place in the world. There is an epitome of England's history in the monuments and epitaphs of the men and women she has delighted to honor. Passing through the general entrance on the east side of the south transept, I found myself in the "poet's corner." The eye is at once riveted on the distinguished dead —Chaucer, Spenser, Dryden, Milton, Shakspeare, Addison, etc. In the center transept of the largest gothic structure of Great Britain you may attend worship. Around and beneath you are the monuments of the mighty dead, while every thing you cast your eye upon is associated with the history of the past. Here Druids once offered bloody sacrifices. Here a long line of priests lived and died. Here kings and queens of Great Britain, from Edward the Confessor to the present popular queen, Victoria, were crowned. The old chair is there still; but those who have occupied it on those important occasions live there only in the history of the past. Here, from the days of Henry III. to those of George II., they were entombed. To this altar princes brought their incense, and crusaders consecrated their victorious swords. The gorgeous buildings, the solemn associations, were calculated to inspire feelings of grandeur, solemnity, and reverence. For a small fee a guide directs you through the seven chapels. The center of these is Edward the Confessor's, the floor of which is several feet above the general level of the Abbey. Around it are the tombs of royal personages. Some of these tombs, though considerably damaged, are very rich. In this chapel are two large chairs. One of them is the coronation chair, brought from Scotland by Edward I., underneath which is suspended the large, rough stone on which the kings of Scotland had previously been crowned, and which, in the superstition of England, is associated with the sovereignty of this realm; the other, the chair which was provided for Mary, wife of William III., when she was crowned jointly with her husband. From this chapel you pass into the ambulatory and the chapels opening into it, all of which are surrounded by tombs and monuments, ancient and modern; the oldest, that of William de Valence, is dated 1226. From here we ascend a small flight of stairs into Henry VII.'s chapel of the Virgin Mary. This is the gem of the whole structure. The roof is most beautifully wrought into circles, which are carved in elegant fan-tracery, each circle having a pendent boss in the center. The pillars and arches by which it is supported are adorned with ornamental carving, and the walls decorated with statues of patriarchs, apostles, and martyrs. In this chapel are several royal tombs, the most sumptuous of which is that of Henry VII. and his queen, Elizabeth. Those in which I felt most interest were Queen Elizabeth, and Queen Mary, and Mary Queen of Scots, in much closer proximity, and with much more apparent friendship than they manifested toward each other in their lives. Thus I felt, and so expressed myself to the guide. As we pass among these tombs one can but reflect on the desolations of time and the weakness of humanity. Vanity of vanities is earthly glory; yet those monuments to the dead may inspire the British youths with virtuous heroism. Pitt stands speaking with commanding grace; Newton sits in lofty contemplation of the laws of nature, which he discovered by the falling of an apple.

St. Paul's.—We then visited St. Paul's Cathedral. This is said to be the most prominent object in the city. We went up to the dome, and took a fine view of the city. The whispering gallery, at the bottom of the inner dome, renders audible the slightest whisper from side to side. The great bell here is only tolled when a member of the royal family dies. This is the largest church in the world, except St. Peter's, at Rome; cost between seven and eight millions, and was finished in 1710. But notwithstanding the superior size of St. Peter's, this is a grander and more magnificent building. I like its style of architecture much better. From whatever point it is viewed it presents a more imposing appearance. St. Peter's is divided up into chapels; St. Paul's has an immense audience-room, capable of seating several thousand people. Like Mount Zion, it is beautiful for situation—elevated, central, the joy of all London. The ground on which it stands has been the site of a cathedral ever since the sixth century, and has been a place of sepulture ever since the Roman conquest. In digging the foundations of the present structure, in 1674, the workmen pierced, at different distances, the graves of four different peoples. Old St. Paul's was 690 feet by 130, with a nave 102 feet, and a choir 88 feet high. The great fire of 1666 swept over it. In 1765 Sir Christopher Wren laid the first stone of the present cathedral, and in 1710 laid the last of the lantern of the cupola. The building is in the form of a cross, having naves and transepts. Its entire length is 500 feet, 285 feet in breadth of nave, and transept 107; average height of the wall 90 feet; two towers, 220 feet; that of the summit of the cross, 404 feet. Over the northern portico are carved the royal arms, supported by angels; eight Corinthian columns of blue-veined marble support the organ and gallery, beautiful in themselves, rendered more so by the carved work. Near the gallery is a plain slab, bearing the name of Christopher Wren. The organ contains thirty-three stops and two thousand one hundred and twenty-two pipes. Its effects are grand. I attended church there one Sabbath while in London, and the church, the congregation, the service, pulpit, and preacher, were all on the grandest scale I ever witnessed. The stalls of the choir are enriched with the most elegant carving. The altarpiece is adorned with four fluted pilasters, painted, and veined with gold. Within the choir and aisles the floor is white; in the body and west end it consists of bodies of black and white marble, alternately; within the altar-rails, of porphyry, polished and placed in geometrical forms. The pulpit is elegantly carved, and occupies a central position. I went up to the whispering gallery; the entire ascent to the ball is six hundred and sixteen steps. From this place you have the finest view of London and for miles around of any place I visited. Away in the distance is seen the Crystal Palace, the various parks and palaces of which I have written—grand, beautiful, and sublime. The bell is ten inches thick, and weighs 11,474 pounds; the clapper weighs 180 pounds, and is moved only on the death of a member of the royal family, the Archbishop of Canterbury, the Bishop of London, or mayor of the city. The clock strikes the hour, and is heard twenty miles; the hammer weighs 145 pounds.

The Tower of London.—This is one of the most interesting places to visit in this great city. Much of the history of the nation is connected with the events which have transpired here. It is a group of structures, a cluster of houses, towers, barracks, armories, warehouses, and prison-like edifices near the River Thames, separated from the crowded streets of the city by an open space called Tower Hill. It was founded by William the Conqueror, on the site of an old fortress, to secure his authority over the people of London; but it has been greatly extended by the subsequent monarchs. It was surrounded in the twelfth century by a large ditch or canal, to prevent the escape of prisoners. This was drained in 1842. Within the center wall the ground measures upward of twelve acres. Next to the river was a water entrance called the "Traitor's Gate." The interior of the Tower is an irregular assemblage of short streets and courtyards. The "White Tower" is the oldest, and the chapel a fine specimen of a small Norman church. The "Lion Tower" is near the principal entrance. The "Bloody Tower" nearly opposite the "Traitor's Gate." These old towers are very curious. The principal objects of interest are a collection of cannon, trophies of war. The "Horse Armory" is a long gallery, built in 1826, has an extensive collection of cannon, consisting of almost every thing in that line for ages past, venerable for the antiquity. There are about twenty suits of armor complete, placed on stuffed men and stuffed horses. Four of the suits belonged to Henry VIII. Queen Elizabeth's armory is in the "White Tower," the walls of which are thirteen feet thick, and still contain inscriptions of state prisoners in troubled times. The instruments of torture looked horrible. The beheading ax and block where royal blood has been spilt makes one shudder to behold. The lions in the Tower were among the sights of the place for six hundred years, but they have been given to the Zoölogical Society. The English people hold the lion as the king of beasts, and the emblem of their own superiority; so Switzerland regards Bruin as their emblem. The jewel house is a well-guarded room to the east of the armories, contains the valuable collection of state jewels. Among them St. Edward's crown, used at all the coronations from Charles II. to William IV. The new state crown, made for the coronation of Queen Victoria, and valued at more than five hundred thousand dollars; the Prince of Wales and the queen consort's crowns, and many others, are here to be seen. The famous "mountain of light," the wonderful diamond, the property of Queen Victoria, is kept here. It was an object of great interest at the two exhibitions. You are guided through these places by wardens who wear a curious costume of Henry VIII.'s time.

Here are the works of the great masters of the world who nobly represent the Roman, Bolognese, Venetian, Paduan, Flemish, Dutch, French, and English schools of painting, which seem to give visibility to things not seen. Francias's *Dead Christ*, with his head reposing on his mother's lap, while angels hover over his face and feet, is very impressive, and seems to

> Dissolve the heart in tenderness
> And melt the eyes to tears.

At the south-west angle we come to the bell-tower, which suspends the garrison alarm-bell, and is celebrated as the mission-house of the brave old Bishop of Rochester, who persisted in denying the legality of Henry VIII.'s divorce, even to death. Here, in this apparently small matter, we see how much often depends upon a single event. If Henry's divorce had been acknowledged by the bishop, England might have continued a Catholic country. God only knows. The walls of the Beauchamp Tower are fifteen feet thick, where he was imprisoned in the reign of Richard III. As we proceed, we pass the church of St. Peter. On the right we see another tower suggestive of painful recollections. Here we are reminded of the rashness and ruin of Elizabeth's great favorite, the meanness and perfidy of her bosom friend; the struggle between revenge and love in the breast of the man over her doomed friend, and the history of that reign; the death-bed confession of Lady Harard; the violence of her sovereign, who shook the dying countess in her bed, screaming, "May God forgive you, I never can;" and the gloom that thenceforward settled down upon that sovereign's great but guilty soul. How vivid these things come into one's mind when viewing the places where these things occurred! Facing the east, and passing on the right of the barracks, and on the left of the "little hell," or "Flint Tower," and on to the brick tower, where the beautiful, the beloved, the good, and the accomplished Lady Jane Grey found her last earthly home, and from which she passed to her heavenly mansion. Among my boyhood memories cluster the history of this deeply interesting woman, and I still love to read any thing of her and her sad end. Through that window she could see the palace in which she had been hailed as queen, amid the rejoicings of the metropolis. Through the same dungeon-window she bade farewell to her young and innocent loving husband as he passed to execution, and soon after saw his headless body, wrapped in a linen cloth dripping with blood, conveyed to the chapel. Through that door she herself passed to the block, saying: "Lord Jesus, receive my spirit." Such has been royal life. This place, so remarkable in English history, being near a half mile in circumference, is a subject of long and interesting study and reflection upon "man's inhumanity to man." Time swallows the ordinary labors of man, but these towers, prisons, and monuments, which for near a thousand years have stood marking the generations of men as they pass by on the stage of action, bear a few landmarks of their history as a great abstract of the past and index to the future. These have witnessed generation after generation marching on as one vast funeral procession to the tomb of Norman, Saxon, Briton, Scot; white rose and red, royalist and rebel, cavalier and roundhead, protestant and papist, marching to mortal combat. New consecrations and fetes, processions and tournaments; then the doomed prisoner, muffled in his cloak, following the ax, with a few weeping friends, clad in black, and here we stand and behold the ax-block and the instruments of death around. How sad and sickening! But these days are past, never, I presume, to return. Pagan, Jew, Christian, Papist and Protestant, Puritan and Churchman, have worshiped in these courts, and all can now worship God in this glorious land and be protected by its laws. These mouths of death are forever closed. These bloody towers look peacefully upon, perhaps, the "best government in the world." These dungeons are empty. These instruments of torture are objects of curiosity, as relics of the darker ages. These subterranean passages are closed, and England presents the brightest history of the world.

London Parks, Palaces, etc.—Whether we consider this great city as the metropolis of a great and mighty empire, upon the dominion of whose sovereign the sun never sets, or the home of between three and four millions of people, and the richest city in the world, it is an intensely interesting place to visit. The Romans, after conquering the ancient British inhabitants, about A. D. 61, rebuilt and walled it in about 301. Roman remains, and some fragments of the old wall, are still found when making excavations. London, in the Anglo-Norman times, though originally confined by the walls, grew up a dense mass of brick and wooden houses. The city stands from twelve to sixteen feet higher than it did in the early part of its history. From a city hemmed within a wall London expanded in all directions, and thus gradually formed a connection with various clusters of dwellings in the neighborhood. It has, in fact, absorbed towns and villages for a considerable distance around. This is the main reason why it is so difficult to comprehend. It is an assemblage of towns, the intervening spaces having been built up. Some of the streets are very long and straight, being, I suppose, originally the roads between the towns. City Road, I presume, was one of these connecting links, but now one of the finest streets in the city. The growth of London, to its present enormous size, may readily be accounted for, from the fact that for ages it has been the capital of England, and the seat of her court and legislature; and that since the union with Scotland and Ireland it has become a center for those two countries. It is the residence of the nobility, landed gentry, and other families of wealth. It has a fine natural position, lying, as it does, upon the banks of what they consider a great river (but only about the size of White River), some sixty miles from the sea. The great central thoroughfare of Cheapside is one of the oldest and most famous streets in the city, intimately associated with the municipal glories of London for centuries past. Many of the business houses here are magnificent. Some small plots of ground here have been sold as high as five millions of dollars per acre. On each side of Cheapside narrow streets diverge into the dense mass behind. The greater part of these back streets, with the lanes adjoining, are occupied by the offices or warehouses of wholesale dealers in cloth, silk, hosiery, lace, etc., and are resorted to by London and country shop-keepers for supplies. The Strand, so called because it lies along the bank of the river, now hidden by houses, is a long and somewhat irregular built street. In the seventeenth century the Strand was a country road connecting the city with Westchester, and on its southern side a number of noblemen's residences, with gardens toward the river. The eastern half of the Strand is thickly surrounded by theaters and places of amusement. The residences of the nobility and gentry are chiefly in the western part of the metropolis. In this quarter there have been large additions of handsome streets, squares, and terraces, within the past few years. Much has been done recently toward adorning the metropolis with health-giving parks and grounds, freely open to the public. St. James's Park was the first one I visited. It was near our minister's residence, whom I called to see about getting a ticket to parliament soon after our arrival. This is a grand, picturesque, lovely place, though once a marshy waste, which was drained and otherwise improved by Henry VIII. Charles II. improved the gardens by planting avenues of lime-trees on the north and south sides of the park, and by forming the mall, which was a hollowed, smooth graveled space half a mile long, skirted with a wooden border, for playing ball. It is nearly a mile and a half in circumference, and covers ninety acres, and the avenues form delightful shady promenades. In the center is a fine lake of water, interspersed with islands, and dotted with swans and water-fowl. A bridge was built across this water in 1857. On each side are spacious lawns encircled with lofty trees and flowering shrubs. There are nine or ten entrances to the park, the queen's guard doing duty each day and night. At the east side is a large graveled space, called the parade, on which, about ten o'clock every morning, the body-guards required for the day are mustered, and here the regimental bands perform. At the western end is Buckingham Palace, around and about which we visited, with thousands of others, some hours, to see the Shah of Persia with the royal family accompanying him to the opera. This park, all things considered, is regarded as one of the greatest ornaments of the city. Green Park contains only about sixty acres, rising with a gentle slope to the north of Buckingham Palace, and is bounded on the east side by many mansions of the nobility. The largest equestrian statue in England, that of the Duke of Wellington, stands on a triumphal arch of the reign of George IV. Hyde Park has three hundred and ninety acres, part of which is considerably elevated. The whole is intersected with noble roads, paths, and luxuriant trees, planted singly or in groups, presenting a very diversified prospect of beauty and grandeur. Near the south-east corner, on an elevated pedestal, stands a colossal bronze statue of Achilles, cast from the cannon taken at the battles of Salamanca and Waterloo, weighing thirty tons, and, as the inscription informs us, erected to the Duke of Wellington and his companions in arms by their countrymen, at a cost of fifty thousand dollars. The great Exhibition of 1851, the first of its kind, was held in Crystal Palace, near the south-west corner of this park. The exhibition building of 1862 was beyond the limits of the park. The Albert Memorial is at the Remington end of Hyde Park, of which I have written. Passing through this park one may almost suppose they are far away from human habitation. You can hear the roar of the great city in the distance, but see no habitation. Large flocks of sheep are grazing; policemen are seen scattered along the roads, but you feel like you were in the woods, made paradisical by man's art and taste. We visited no place where such preparations had been made as in this vast city and its surroundings for country recreations. All that nature, art, and genius can do seems to have been done to make these parks attractive to the millions toiling in the city for their maintenance. Near Prince's Gate of Hyde Park is the London International Exhibition of 1873. This we visited, and was much interested. Among the many objects of interest are shown selected specimens, as follows: Pictures, oil and water color; sculpture, decorative furniture, plate designs, Mosaics, etc.; stained glass, architecture and models, engravings, lithography, photography as a fine art, porcelain, earthenware, *terra cotta*, and stoneware; machinery used for pottery of all kinds, willow manufactories, machinery in motion, used in woolen and worsted manufactories; live alpacas, scientific inventions and discoveries, horticulture, etc. Victoria Park has about two hundred and seventy acres. Having been formed only a few years, the trees have not yet grown to the full size, but it is becoming a pleasant place, with flower-beds, lakes, walks, and shady avenues. This park is distinguished by the most magnificent public fountain yet constructed in the metropolis. Battersea Park has about one hundred and eighty acres, on which fifteen thousand dollars have been spent. Until recently it was a miserable swamp—now it is a fine park. A beautiful suspension-bridge connects this park with Chelsea, on the other side of the river. There are a number of other parks, but I did not visit them, and have said enough to let the reader know that this great city has also immense lungs, and breathes freely from them. Besides these there are the Zoölogical Gardens, containing about two hundred acres, at the northern extremity of Regent's Park. Here they have the vegetable and the animal kingdom well represented. Captain Deering and myself accepted an invitation from a London friend to go with him to see them. I will here say, by way of parenthesis, that English people, women as well as men, are the greatest walkers I ever saw. Ask any one how far to such a place, and they will tell you so many minutes; then multiply by two or three, and you will get the time it will take you to get there. I was walked around in these gardens, so-called, until I was tired down. The collection of animals is unquestionably the finest in England. The sea-lions and the sea-bears were rare specimens of the inhabitants of the briny deep blue sea. The polar-bear, or ice-bear, measures eight feet seven inches, and weighs sixteen hundred pounds.

Palaces.—The palaces of London are places of great interest. Buckingham Palace stands at the west end of St. James's Park. It does not present a very magnificent appearance. The ground on which it stands is too low. I was not favorably impressed with the buildings for the sovereign of this great nation's residence. The park and royal gardens were grand, but the palace fell far below my expectations as to its appearance. Marlborough House, the residence of the Prince and Princess of Wales, is immediately east of St. James's Palace, separated only by a carriage road. It was built by Christopher Wren, for the great Duke of Marlborough. The house was bought from him for the Princess Charlotte. It was afterward occupied in succession by Leopold (the late King of the Belgians). St. James's Palace is an elegant brick structure, built by Henry VIII., in 1530, on the site of what was once the hospital for lepers. The fine bands of the foot-guards play daily at eleven in the color-court, or in another quadrangle on the east side. Lambeth Palace is said to be about four hundred years old.

Houses of Parliament.—This is the name usually given to the new Palace of Westminster. It is close to the river. It is said to be the finest modern Gothic structure in the world, at least for civil purposes. The entire building covers about eight acres. The chief public entrance is by Westminster Hall, which forms a vestibule to the houses of parliament and their numerous committee-rooms. The rooms and staircases are inconceivably numerous, and there are said to be two miles of passages and corridors. The river-front, raised upon a fine terrace of Aberdeen granite, is nine hundred feet in length, and profusely adorned with statues, heraldic shields, and tracers covered with stone. It is a gorgeous structure, which has cost over ten millions of dollars. A farther cost of near a million for frescoes and statuary had been incurred up to March, 1860. The two chambers in which parliament meets are ill-adapted for a great nation's legislature to meet.

The house of peers is ninety-seven feet long, forty-five wide, and forty-five high. It is profusely painted and gilt, and the windows are so darkened by deep-tinted stained-glass that the eye can with difficulty make out the details. At the southern end is the gorgeous gilt and canopied throne. Near the center is the wool-sack on which the lord chancellor sits; at the end and sides are the galleries for the peeresses, reporters, and strangers. The poorest accommodations I ever saw. Even in our state-house they are far superior. There are some twelve or fifteen comfortable seats for reporters, and room, perhaps, for some thirty or forty more persons to sit on—hard seats, patched up at the far end. The seats remind one of an old-field school-house—long benches with not a desk or any convenience for writing, which they do not need, as they write their speeches, I presume, before they come there. This house of lords fell greatly below my expectations in several respects. I heard, perhaps, some fifteen or twenty of them speak, and, with one or two exceptions, they fell, I think, below our members of our legislatures as speakers. In the house of commons it is very different. There the members are chosen by the people, and the best talent of the nation is chosen to represent them. Their room is sixty-two feet long, by forty-five wide, and forty-five high, and is much less elaborate than the house of peers. The speaker's chair is in the north end, with galleries along the sides and ends. In a gallery behind the speaker's chair the reporters for the newspapers sit. Over them is the ladies' gallery, where the view is obstructed by the grating. One might suppose from the name that these two chambers—the house of peers and commons—constitute nearly the whole of the building, but they occupy only a small part of the area. There are many large, fine libraries, committee-rooms, halls, lobbies, offices, corridors, princes' chamber, peers' corridor, commoners' lobby, and corridente. The Victoria, at the south-west angle of the entire structure, is one of the finest in the world. It is seventy-five feet square, and three hundred and forty feet high. The "Clock Tower," in the north end, is forty feet square, three hundred and twenty feet high, profusely gilt mantel top. The clock is by far the largest and finest in this country. There are four dials on the face of the tower, each twenty-two and a half feet in diameter; the hour figures are two feet high, twenty-six feet apart; minute marks fourteen inches apart; the hands weigh two hundred and forty pounds, the minute-hand sixteen feet long. There are about five hundred carved stone statues in the building. The Royal Gallery is being filled, illustrative of English history. There, among others specially noted, is a picture forty-five feet long by twelve high, representing "The meeting of Wellington and Blucher" after the battle of Waterloo, and the companion frescoe, "The Death of Nelson." Yesterday morning we went out to the Crystal Palace. This surpassed my highest expectations. In many respects it is the most remarkable structure in the world. It was built for the great Exhibition in 1851. It is sixteen hundred feet long, three hundred and eighty wide. There are two arcades, forty-five feet long by one hundred. I cannot say any thing now, only that, if one has but two days in London, one of them should be spent at the Crystal Palace by all means. The Italian section of the Educational party arrived last night, and join ours. We now number fifty, mostly teachers. We leave at 4:25 for Antwerp. You shall hear from me again when I can find time to drop a few lines as we pass rapidly on to Vienna and Rome.

CHAPTER II.

Letters from the Rev. F. W. Hooper, of Lynchburg, Virginia, written for the *News*.

Astor House, New York, June 20, 1873.

Dear "News:"—According to promise, I now commence a series of letters to you, in which, I trust by the providence of God, to take your readers to many points in foreign lands.

We started from the "Hill City" on yesterday, amid the hearty Godspeed of many a loving friend, whose kindly faces will beam around us in all our journeyings. After an hour or so the blues and the headache both wore away, and by the time we reached Charlottesville we were ready to give a hearty greeting to several new companions. One of these was a brilliant young lady, who at once put herself under my care with the joyous self-congratulation that "unmarried ladies could use other people's husbands on such voyages." I replied to this in a jovial allusion to an old bachelor who was present, suggesting that a bridal party would lend a romantic interest to our excursion. But both of these birds were too old to be caught with such chaff, and the younger gentlemen of the party looked as if they might be singing internally, "The girl I left behind me."

Of course we had a merry discussion about seasickness, and some of them commenced eating lemons before we reached Alexandria. Various remedies were discussed—among them a blue-mass pill to rectify the liver, whereupon a solemn divine suggested "Simmons's liver *exterminator.*" As it was evident that his brain was confusing bile and bed-bugs, his suggestion was treated with scorn. Well, we came on to Washington, where we had time to loaf around the Capitol and admire its splendid architecture. But I was amused at the quaint criticism of one of the party, on the Goddess of Liberty. He said "she looked like she was holding up her skirts," which at once reminded him of "Cousin Sally Dillard." During the night we had nothing of special interest, except that we must have met about fifty trains, and it seemed to me that every engineer sounded his steam-whistle right at my window. Arriving here this morning, we determined to start out with this hotel, which is now kept on the European plan. We found the excursion party rapidly filling up, and I have never seen a better business man than Mr. Jenkins, of the firm of Cook, Son & Jenkins, under whose auspices we are to travel. He seemed to know every member of the party as soon as his name was mentioned, and evidently intends to satisfy all, if such a thing is possible where there are one hundred and fifty persons concerned and one-half of them of the *gentler* sex.

I went aboard the Victoria this evening, and met a cordial greeting from Captain Munroe, to whom I had a letter of introduction from Captain Cumminger, of your city. But I was amused at his exhibition of nautical perversity, when he told me he remembered Captain Cumminger's ship, but did not remember him. It reminded me of General Buck Terry's ostler, who, at the surrender, told me he knew General Lee was near Spout Spring, "Because," said he, "I seen his stock." Captain Munroe says that so many parsons are sure to cause bad weather, and I may just as well make up my mind to be sea-sick—which I have n't.

Your readers may form some idea of the size of the Victoria, if they will imagine her extending across Church street, from the Washington House to Dudley Hall, and in such a predicament my state-room would be about where the Baptist Church is, but high enough above the water-line, I trust, to prevent any danger of immersion. It is said to be the largest, newest, and best of the "Anchor Line;" and Captain Munroe is not only a most competent commander, but is also said to be a devoted Christian.

I think, from what I have seen of our party, that we will have a most delightful voyage; but about that I can write more fully hereafter.

This evening I went out to Central Park, and though wearied and sleepy, I enjoyed the lively scene presented by the Gothamites driving their fast horses, and showing off the tinsel of a shoddy aristocracy. I want to see some genuine aristocracy, out of a laudable curiosity—not to compare it with the mere sham which I have witnessed this evening.

Well, you are not the only one to whom I must write before retiring to rest, and I will therefore close, with the best wishes for all of you who are toiling while I am resting, and with the humble hope that I shall be spared to inflict many a note of correspondence before I return, about the first of September, to my family and charge. God help us all!

———

STEAMER VICTORIA, June 23, 1873.

John Phœnix wrote that on leaving San Diego, on a certain occasion, he felt mortified at having no friend to bid him farewell; so, walking to the side of the boat, he took off his hat and sung out, "Good-bye, Colonel!" when twelve or fourteen gentlemen at once replied in the most graceful manner imaginable. On leaving New York Saturday, we were in a similar predicament; but, taking off our hats and waving our handkerchiefs, about five hundred persons on shore waved us a most hearty farewell, supposing that we were acquaintances and friends.

And now we are out on the ocean, and, much to my surprise, it has been all the time calmer than Chesapeake Bay. The ship is a screw propeller, and moves as smoothly as a Pullman car on steel rails. There is scarcely a jar, and the engines are as regular as a pulse-beat in their great throbbing, which gives us motion as a thing of life. Our excursion party is composed of one hundred and forty-eight persons, embracing thirteen ministers of various denominations, and any number of college professors and school-marms. But while there is such a promiscuous assemblage, all seem inclined to minister to each other's comfort, and to add as much as possible to the pleasure of the excursion.

Mr. Cook sent over a conductor to meet us and escort us across the great waters. His name is A. H. Plagge, a German; and if all his conductors are as competent and attentive, I am sure we shall have a most delightful time.

I had supposed that life on ship-board was monotonous and wearisome; but, so far from that being so, it is really a treat to me to shut myself up in the smoking-room to write these few lines. It is interesting to look out upon the waves of the restless ocean, and while it is the same old ocean, there is a constant change in the movement of its waters. At times its surface seems as smooth and placid as a mirror, and then, as the breeze starts up, there will be a gentle ripple, and by and by the spray will begin to plash and gleam in all its snowy whiteness; and at night, too, we love to stand at the stern and watch the seething caldron which rises from the screw, while phosphorescent sparks fly off as if from a nautical sky-rocket. Then, too, we watch other ships that are floating near us, and feel, at fifteen miles off, a nearness and companionship which landsmen cannot appreciate.

Yesterday, being our first Sunday on board, was devoted almost entirely to religious exercises. We had preaching on deck at 10:30 A.M., by the Rev. Dr. Witherspoon, of the Presbyterian Church; service at 4:30 P.M., by the Rev. Mr. Cosh, of the Episcopal Church; and at 7:30 P.M., in the saloon, by the Rev. Mr. Pierce, of the Methodist Church.

I find that my appetite is steadily improving, and at night I sleep as soundly as I ever did in all my life. Last night we had quite a stiff breeze after I had retired, and some of our party had a little touch of sea-sickness; but, with that exception, we have all been perfectly well.

Two of our young men got caught in a trap by the sailors, in the bow of the boat. It seems that they draw a chalk-line, and when any one passes over it he has to pay a fine. These young gents were, of course, anxious to see every thing, and asked if they would be permitted to go to the bow. They were politely invited to do so; but on their return they were headed off by the jolly tars, who informed them that while they might pass to the bow, they could not return except on condition of paying the usual tax of a bottle of whisky. This they did as gracefully as possible, and tried to keep it a secret; but such things will leak out on ship-board.

While I write, a gentleman is looking over a list of our excursion, and discovers that twenty-one States are represented, and yet, so far, all has been pleasant — politically, socially, and religiously. I think at least half of us are correspondents for some newspaper; so Messrs. Cook & Son will have to keep the best terms with all, or take the worst journalistic pop-gun stinging that a naughty boy ever received. In regard to the ship, I will only say it is splendid, beyond all my previous conceptions. The officers are very polite and gentlemanly, and the tables are loaded at every meal with the greatest profusion. We have also the privilege of a bathroom, where at any hour we can take a hot or cold bath of fresh sea-water, and every thing around us seems to be *pro bono publico.*

Wednesday, 25th.—I wrote the above on Monday, and have been so busy ever since doing nothing, that I have not had time or inclination to continue it. We have now been four days out, and are more than twelve hundred miles from New York, making over three hundred miles a day. We have passed the Banks of New Foundland, and are now "out on the ocean sailing." The small darkey who "rocks this cradle of the deep," finished his nap night before last, and since that time he has been rocking us most vigorously fore and aft, as well as from starboard to larboard. Some of us rather enjoy it, but two or three of our party have settled their fare with Old Neptune most generously. I have not been sick at all, but am more and more confirmed in laziness. We have been dressed in our thickest winter clothing, with our coats and blankets, and still we cannot keep warm. I have seen two whales, and grampuses innumerable. The grampuses went jumping along over the waves, reminding me of old hares in the broom-sedge fields of the "free State." I only saw the tails of the whales, and these seemed to be about eighteen inches across. We also passed this morning through a fishing squadron, and passed near enough to one of the boats to see the cod-fish— the aristocracy we have on our own vessel. We have continued the usual amusements of rope-quoits, horse-billiards, leap-frog, chess, draughts, etc. At night we have family worship in the saloon, conducted by the various ministers in succession. Then we have music, recitations, readings, etc. We had a fine entertainment Monday night—being a tale of "Tildy's first visit to the show," rendered by a Scotchman, with the broadest kind of an accent.

The fare is admirable, consisting of all sorts of meats and vegetables, and then pastry, fruits, nuts. There are so many passengers that we have to provide two tables at every meal, and to save trouble they only give us three meals a day—breakfast at eight bells, *alias* 8 A.M.; dinner at four bells, *alias* 2 P.M.; and supper at six bells, *alias* 7 P.M. There is a fine piano in the saloon, and quite a number of excellent performers. Just above this there is a fine library of choice literature; but the most of the party are too much occupied with watching ships and talking to read. There are some rich specimens of the school-marm on board, and to see one of these keel over with sea-sickness, and hear the nasal twang mixing with incidental guttural sounds, is a richer show than a circus to a Lynchburg school-boy. But more anon.

Saturday, 28th.—This morning I was aroused at 3:30 o'clock by the water pouring into my berth from the deck, and looking out by broad daylight, I found what I would call a heavy sea rolling, and now and then a wave would break over the deck, from stem to stern. Composing myself as well as I could, I went to sleep again, and slept until breakfast-time. We have had fine fun on deck this morning, as it is very slippery, and the ship is rocking fearfully. I found one lady of giant proportions sliding across the deck, and she never brought up until she hung to the ropes at the side. Stepping forward as gallantly as I could, I offered my arm, when, starting back, I found we had too much material aboard, and before I had time to consider clerical dignity, we were walking to the other side, and came to anchor against a boat, my head furnishing the point of contact. I then steered her for the gang-way, which, with the assistance of a Scotchman, we reached in safety; and plunging her in, I hung on to the door while she glided all the way across—taking in her furious course several old gentlemen and ladies who were quietly watching the storm. This is to be my last attempt at voluntary gallantry. Yesterday, and part of last night, we had all the sails up and a full head of steam, and have been making fifteen knots an hour —add one-seventh if you wish to reduce it to miles.

Mr. Plagge has divided our company into sections, and while some of our party will go to Italy, the most of us are in the fourth section, and will spend the additional ten days in England and Ireland. Several of the party have been so sick, that "Carry me back to Old Virginny" would have awakened a flood of tears, but so far I have not missed a meal, a smoke, or a chew. I will now leave this until I get in sight of land.

Monday, June 30th.—Yesterday was pleasant, and we had a spread-eagle sermon on deck by Rev. Mr. Barrows, Congregationalist, at 10 A.M. At 4 P.M. Mr. Cook read "the sermon," and a Baptist preacher preached on "the ark," a suggestive sermon. At night we had a capital sermon from Rev. Prof. Cushing (a Methodist), on "You are laborers together with God"—most too much "free agency" for me, but a capital sermon. We expect to land this evening or to-night, so if you ever receive this, you may take it for granted we are safe.

EDINBURGH, July 5, 1873.

I did not expect to let so many days glide by without writing you a line, but we have been on the wing ever since we landed, and even now I must write hastily.

At Moville we embarked on a steam-tug under the escort of Mr. John Cook, and on landing were met by Mr. Thos. Cook and a grandson, so that, as we have been several times informed, there are three generations of Cooks escorting us. Passing up Loch Foyle, which soon lessened to River Foyle, we passed by the old Culmore Castle and church, which were standing in 1688, at the siege of Derry. There too, we were told, the cable was stretched to prevent the Protestants from receiving supplies. It was in this siege that two thousand persons perished from famine, after eating all kinds of food to keep off starvation.

Luckily, leaping into the cars, we were whirled along at a rapid rate to Portrush. The scenery is wild and beautiful. Bold headlands pushing out into the sea and then sloping off into fertile fields, intersected everywhere with hedges, and dotted with farm-houses. The houses of the farmers are larger and handsomer than we had supposed, while the thatched cottages of the peasants, with their piles of peat, are scarcely equal to the negro cabins which our slaves once occupied. Flitting through a long tunnel on the lands of Sir Harvey Bruce, we soon brought up at Portrush, a small town on the coast, and were escorted to the town-hall, where a cold lunch awaited us. Standing around the table were fine-looking "old Irish gentlemen," dressed in swallow-tail coats, white ties, and black pants, and some of our party thought that the mayor and aldermen of the town had turned out to serve us at the table. But it turned out that these were the ordinary waiters, who would put Ned Pryor to the blush in politeness, and are more handsomely dressed than any clergyman in Lynchburg. Passing out of the hall as a gazing stock for the whole populace, we had our first experience in an Irish "jaunting-car." They are two-wheeled vehicles, with seats over the wheels sideways, and will accommodate four persons besides the driver. Jumping on to one at the head of the column, we trotted out ten miles to the Giant's Causeway, passing the Castle of Dunbece, now in ruins. This was the seat of the old feuds between the O'Donnells and the McQuillians, in other days, and was demolished, along with thousands of other places, by Oliver Cromwell. We also passed through "Bush Mills," famous for its "Irish poteen," or whisky, and then through the lands of Sir E. McFadden, whose name our driver called out to me half a dozen times without my understanding him. At last we reached the hotel, and dismounting, had a rush down the cliff for the boats. Reaching the first one, we jumped in, and three stalwart oarsmen pulled us out to the mouth of the cave, washed by the breakers, while our guide kept up an incessant gibberish, retailing old jokes to our infinite disgust, and preventing such sentimentalism as the grandeur of the scene is calculated to inspire.

This causeway must be seen on the spot to be appreciated, and when you sit in a skiff half a mile out on the heaving tide, or stand upon its solid rocks, you must be impressed with its magnificence, as well as wonder at its geological formation. Millions of stones in triangles, pentagons, hexagons, and cut in the most accurate mathematical precision, form a solid mass that even the ocean itself in ages has not disturbed. The rock is black, and of a basaltic character, and as to who put it there, and why it was put there, and when, I leave to those geologists who know all about fossils and creation. If these rocks have grown any since the creation, they have preserved their proportions most marvelously, and as far as we can see they are of no more practical value than which I hold were created *as fossils* when God said, "Let there be light." But I have too much to write about to moralize. Returning to Portrush, we were met by an amateur band of boys playing fifes and drums, who escorted us in style to the "Antrim Arms," playing "Dixie," and "The Bonny Blue Flag," to the evident disgust of the "Maroons."

At twelve o'clock that night we reached the Victoria, and soon after steamed up for Greenock, on the Clyde. Passing the "Isle of Bute," and various places of interest, we anchored, and as quietly as possible waited until 4 P. M. for the coming in of the tide. When this time arrived two tug-boats were attached to the steamer, one at each end, to help guide her up the narrow stream, which is nothing but a ship canal at Glasgow, and slowly and cautiously we glided up the stream, past old Dumbarton, and thousands of iron ships in process of construction. The scenery on both sides is beautiful. The trees, as well as the houses, are larger than those we saw in Ireland, and cattle were grazing in herds along the shore that would have made Major Cloyd break the commandment. Well, after running aground several times, we at last landed at our wharf and scattered like a flock of sheep all over the city. Climbing to the top of an omnibus, we paid our fare, and rode through several splendid streets to George's Square, where there is a fine monument to Sir Walter Scott, and several splendid statues, among them Queen Victoria and Prince Albert on horseback.

The next day Mr. Cook brought around omnibuses enough to accommodate the whole party, and although it was raining we started out, and visited first the Cathedral. This is a splendid structure, as any guide-book will inform your readers, and abounds in hundreds of the most magnificent stained windows, and is still used as a place for public worship by the Established Presbyterian Church. It has no organs, and they still sing Rome's version of the Psalms. Overlooking this is a beautiful cemetery, where are buried some of the noblest scholars that have made Scotland famous in literature. There too is a beautiful monument to John Knox, surmounted by a splendid statue of this bold reformer. I gathered some daisies at its base, and we then passed on to the Botanical Gardens, West End Park, etc., and that night we slept our last sleep (for the present) on the steamer. Yesterday we started at 7:20 A. M., and stopped for our breakfast at Stirling. It was hard to eat amid such surroundings, but appetite will get the better of romance, and I am sorry to say that, sitting amid all these memories of Wallace, Bruce, and the beautiful Mary, we ate as heartily as if we had been at home in America. Then lighting our pipes, we strolled along the streets that had rumbled with the chariots of kings and queens, until we climbed the heights of old Stirling, from which we had a magnificent view of the surrounding country. On one side was the battle-field of Bannockburn, on the other Stirling Bridge, over which on a beetling crag was a fine monument to Wm. Wallace, while stretching out beyond were the "blinks" of Stirling, formed by the windings of the river. Gazing for some time from the very spot Mary Queen of Scots had so often and so sadly stood and gazed and sighed, was well calculated to bring out all the poetry that a man has, and I could have sat there for hours musing upon the past. But when I went up to the room where Duncan was stabbed, and saw the very window out of which he was thrown, and the very pulpit in which John Knox preached to the queen, and the communion-table on which he celebrated the Lord's Supper not as a mass, but as a memorial of our Lord, memory, fancy, imagination, reason, were all clashing in their several spheres, and I came away with a confused, but hallowed, memory of that eventful morning.

Starting again, we went on to the Collender, where we took the spring-wagons called "wagonettes," and drove rapidly through the Trossocks, a rough gorge in the mountains, to Loch Katrine, immortalized by Scott's "Lady of the Lake." Darting through this in a little steamer called the Rob Roy, with a Scotch Highlander screeching through a bagpipe, we rode five miles farther in the "van," and at "Inversnaid," under care of Rob Roy, and on his land, we took the steamer on "Loch Lomond," and steaming around the base of "Ben Lomond," we landed near the Castle of Balloch, where we took the train again, and at about 9 o'clock we reached this beautiful city.

London, July 11, 1873.

I left your kind readers at Edinburgh, where we had just arrived and were pleasantly quartered at the Cockburn hotel. The next day our party went down to a public garden and had ourselves photographed. We then branched out, and some of us went first to Holyrood Palace, where are clustered many of the sweetest as well as most painful memories of Scottish history. We went into the audience-chamber of the faithless but beautiful Queen of Scots; saw the bed on which she slept, the chairs, and furniture, so queer and antique, that well graced those gilded halls. But we also saw the fatal private supper-room where Rizzio was stabbed, and the bed-chamber through which he was dragged. We also saw the old chapel where she pretended to worship God, and memory was busy as we stood among these enchanting scenes. But leaving this spot we rode on and saw the old Tolbooth, the original pillory, the cross of Edinburgh, the spot where so many were executed, the grave of John Knox and his former home, the "Heart of Midlothian," and the old Grayfriars Church, where the solemn "League and Covenant" was signed by our Presbyterian Fathers. You can, perhaps, imagine, but I cannot describe, the feelings that gushed forth at all these strange scenes of the hoary past. And then when I stood in the old castle where Mary spent so many years, and looked out of the very window of which she looked so longingly until her son was born, I seemed to be drifting back out of the present into the centuries that are gone. But we must leave this guide-book strain and come back to our own eventful history. This was Saturday, and soon after leaving the castle, whom should I meet but Mr. Stuart Robinson, whose greeting was: " Why, Hooper, where did you spring from?" This speedily explained, and we cracked many a joke together before he left us at Melrose Abbey on Monday. He was coming out of an old bookstore, and had been reveling in various discoveries he had made, with which to sting the Northern brethren when he comes back from Palestine, whither he is bound. I had made up my mind to hear him preach the next day, but the Lord had some of that kind of work for me to do at the same hour. That night we had a "grand conversazione," which means, being interpreted, a dinner of speeches and a dessert of music. The Lord Provost presided and made a lame attempt at a welcome, and Dr. Witherspoon made one of the grandest speeches of the kind that I ever heard. Dr. Davidson also gave us a good task, and Professor Cushing replied. We then went into the museum building, and were entertained by a magnificent band from the Castle, whose revelry was interspersed by singing by a lady, and what they called music on bagpipes.

That night Rev. Dr. Arndt invited me to preach

for him, and as I could not well decline, I did so to the best of my ability. He is one of the most distinguished men in Scotland, and is pastor of the "Free High Church" of Edinburgh, where he wears a gown. They have no organ, and use Rome's version of the Psalms. The congregation was large, and in the morning I was delighted with his plain, simple, beautiful expository style. The second service is held at 2:15 p. m., when I preached, and the old gentleman afterward kindly presented me with one of the numerous volumes which he himself has written. I never felt smaller than when standing in his pulpit, and preaching to his immense audience, who came, no doubt, through curiosity to hear an American preacher.

The next morning, all too soon, we started out for Melrose. There at the little inn some of us took breakfast, while others went on at once to Abbotsford, the home of Sir Walter Scott. After breakfast we started down to Melrose Abbey, which is said to be the best preserved ruin in Scotland, and which Scott has immortalized by his writings. It must have been a grand affair in the olden time, but the sparrows now build upon its walls, and there is no sound but the bleating of sheep in the ancient churchyard to disturb the slumbers of its sleeping dead. There we saw the spot where is said to be buried the heart of Robert Bruce, and here also the grave of the Black Douglas, and I felt strongly as I gathered daisies from above them, and thought how appropriately when we bury the dead, "Earth to earth, ashes to ashes, dust to dust." But leaving the old Abbey, we rode on a "van" with the driver to Abbotsford, one of the grandest old places in Scotland. The whole house is literally crowded with remnants of Scottish history. There is a chapter from some old castle, there the door out of the old Tolbooth, and here a statue or a stone ornament which this wizard of romance gathered from all quarters of the kingdom, and then when we went inside, here we saw his chain and desk, his pipes and canes, his clothes and guns, until we felt as if he would himself come out to do honors to erect an occasion. But I must hurry on. Leaving Melrose, we passed a long day, and reached Derby, a small town of sixty thousand inhabitants, where we had another grand reception, so-called. The dinner was good, but most of the speeches were bores, and especially that of a Yankee "chasm," who had been a missionary to the colored people in the foreign State of Texas. She piously asked for the prayers of the English, and so did Uncle Mike Connell ask me to remember him when we prayed in a cathedral. I hope all of us will remember these two subjects, for they both need them. That night, as you may imagine, I slept without rocking, at a most delightful hotel, called the St. James, and the next day we spent at Alton Towers, owned by the Earl of Shrewsbury. He and the bounties were necessarily absent (and I do n't blame them), but we had a singing of the Episcopal service in the chapel, and then walked through the palace and grounds, visited the flowery shore, lunched on the green with his son, Lord Somebody, and a very fine-looking boy he is, about the size of Lewis Mosby, and the exact image of his sister.

That evening we came on to London, and the first man I met was Mr. A. McDonald, and we have been together almost all the time since, have visited the Museum, the Tower, the Crystal Palace, Hyde Park, Buckingham Palace, Bank of England, St. Paul's, and Westminster Abbey. We have also dined, as well as lunched, with Mr. J. C. Muller, to whom I had an introduction from Capt. C. W. Statham. He and his kind lady showed us every attention, and evinced a hearty hospitality, which I am sure will wipe out all scores that are against him among his and our friends in Lynchburg. He is engaged in the tobacco business, and being familiar with this great metropolis, it seems to have been his delight to go with us from one place to another that he thought would interest us. If he is as good at business as he is at entertaining strangers, he is certainly deserving of success.

But I must close now by adding two more places of interest to which we have gone with intense satisfaction. One is the old Crosby House, once the property of Richard III., mentioned by Shakspeare, and the other Madame Tussaud's wax-work exhibition, which is so natural and life-like that I almost shuddered as I looked at some of the familiar personages that have figured in history.

CHAPTER III.

Letters from the Rev. A. B. Whipple, President of Lansingburgh College, New York.

On the Steamer Victoria, Saturday, June 28, 1873.

A week to-day we saw an acre—more or less—of kerchiefs waving us a kind adieu as, without parade or cannonade, we quietly glided away from pier No. 20 down the harbor, leaving New York and its thousand spires to sink behind the receding waters. A good dinner at 2 o'clock lessened the pangs of hunger and the pangs of parting, and prepared us to part with our pilot off Sandy Hook Light, some twenty-two miles from the city. The day was very fair, and so were the following days, till Friday afternoon. A storm came on, which is still continuing to keep most of the passengers below, penning, as I am, to "friends in America."

Every moment, thus far, has been one of pleasure, and now, twenty-five hundred miles on my way, I, with most of the others, can say the God of the Sea has dealt kindly with us, and not turned our stomachs into heaving notions. To describe an ever-changing sea — its grand sunset and sunrise scenery — its changing, real and reflected, colors, in all their marine varieties—the myriad sea-fowl that swim or skim its surface—the schools of whale, porpoise, and grampus, that seem to be having a short recess, and sporting near us for our observation—the beautiful sail-spread *nautili* as they, catching the sunset glow, sail by us toward the sunset—the passing ships that greet us kindly with national flag—the ocean steamers that ere this have reported us—the northern lights that make our northern sky aglow with dancing twilight—or the little ripples that simply ruffle the surface—or the mighty waves that just now dash against the cabin-light, and break in, striking on the deck above my head—to describe all this, I say, to appreciating friends, can be far better done in the drawing-room, with the voyager in your very midst.

Some of the dryer details connected with the ship Victoria may not, however, be devoid of interest as mere matters of nautical history. I came as a student to learn what I could, without asking questions, and after that to seek information under the not always pleasant privilege of questioning. Unlike most of the party, I came without a supply of guide-books, choosing to use my own eyes, and so not copy what I do not see; in other words, I want my own impression. Let me, then, confine the rest of this letter to the Victoria—370 feet in length, 43 in breadth, and 32 from deck to keel, drawing just now $22\frac{1}{2}$ feet of water, with an engine of 2,200 horse-power, the propeller $18\frac{3}{4}$ feet in diameter. She is steered by steam-power, her sails hoisted and lowered by steam, as well as cargo taken in and out by steam—3,600 tons, a ton being forty cubic feet of space; has on board three thousand tons of cargo, exclusive of seven hundred tons of coal, using about sixty tons per day; cargo mostly provisions; officers and crew, one hundred and thirty; souls on board, about four hundred; built last year at Glasgow, costing $500,000—being one of thirty-six belonging to the same company, perhaps the largest ship-owning company in the world; insure themselves. So far, we go about three hundred miles per day. Their ways of determining the rate of motion are three—one by solar observation, made at noon, by means of a sextant; a second way, by a patent log, so-called, towed astern, consisting of a long tube of brass, with four flanges set at right angles with the tube; when drawn through the water it revolves like a turbine water-wheel; within is a clock-work, with discs like a gasometer, and indices to tell how many revolutions have been made in twenty-four hours—a known number indicating a mile, or knot, which is about one-seventh more than a mile. The third way is by the old-fashioned log, used every two hours. It is a cord wound on a reel, with knots every forty-three and one-half feet; at the end is a cone-shaped canvas sac, which, when thrown overboard, fills with water and holds back, drawing the cord from the reel. A sailor stands with a sand-glass of twenty-eight seconds duration; from the moment of dropping the log till the sand-glass is empty the line pays out; then it is stopped and hauled in, and the number of knots counted is the number of knots per hour. Yesterday, most of the time, we made fifteen.

This must suffice for the mathematics of the ship. Kind readers, please fancy me writing this, leaning against my berth, feet well braced, swaying to and fro through at least forty-five degrees of a circle north and south, and half as many east and west, and you will excuse me from more.

GREENOCK, ON THE CLYDE, July 2, 1873.

Since last the pen was laid aside I have traversed the northern coast of Ireland, and am now waiting a favorable tide to Glasgow to-night. Let me tell you of yesterday's doings, and you shall judge whether a day of sight-seeing may not also be a day of hard work. At about 3:15 o'clock the sun rose, and yet before it most of us were up to catch the first glimpse of land, and that land the far-famed Emerald Isle.

A few rocky islands first appeared, then a "sterile and rock-bound coast;" soon a few green patches, with here and there low houses. At 8 o'clock we entered Loch Foyle, famous where we entered for a huge chain stretched across its entrance during the historic siege of Londonderry by King James, in 1689. Lovers of history will remember the story. The Earl of Mount Alexander received an anonymous letter that on a certain day the Protestants of Ireland were to be murdered by the Catholics. He gave the alarm, and some dozen apprentice-boys seized the keys from the guard, just as Lord Antrim's troops reached the ferry-gate, and drew it up. Thus began a siege lasting one hundred and five days, compelling the eating of dogs and rats. The chain or boom spoken of above was to prolong the siege. One of the supply-frigates, however, commanded by Admiral Kirk, dashed with great force, and broke the barrier, but in the rebound was thrown on the beach. The enemy, rejoicing, prepared to board her, when, firing a broadside at them, she righted herself and sailed up the Foyle to Londonderry, where nearly two thousand had died of starvation. Taking a small steamer — the Heron — we reach this same Londonderry at 12 o'clock. It is a city of twenty thousand inhabitants. The bridge connecting Uxtuside, on the opposite side of the river, is a fine structure, and made worthy of note by the fact that it was built by an American in 1789. We took cars to Portrush, forty miles away, and thence by Irish jaunting-cars to the Giant's Causeway, a distance of eight miles. A brief description of these cars is needed, being unlike any thing we have at home. I call them side-saddle carry-alls. They are two-wheeled, with side-seats toeing outward. We sit two on a side, back to back, outside the wheels, which are small, and the driver immediately behind the horse. When not in use the side-seats can be folded up upon top—the whole on easy springs. With some forty of these, each with four besides the driver in it, formed an American procession seldom seen on such a line of march. The roads are all excellent, and kept so by pounded stones. The whole country presents attractions particularly pleasing. Turf fences, with ditches behind, and many of them overgrown with hawthorn hedges, everywhere interlaced the fields. Low stone houses, all neatly whitewashed, are the homes of the laborers. The land is owned by the nobility, and let to the tenants. It is everywhere carefully tilled. Oats, peas, beans, barley, and potatoes, are abundant; saw no orchards. It is haying time, and men and women are together in the fields at work, with equal rights. They looked hale, happy, and hearty. For eight miles we ride through such scenery, with a good driver, who gladly tells us the places of most interest and their history. For instance, we pass Dunluce Castle, in ruins, the most picturesque ruins in Ireland, and perhaps in the kingdom. It stands on an isolated rock, one hundred feet above the sea, and only reached from the mainland by a bridge—a natural bridge—eighteen inches wide. It was built as the residence of the McQuillians, and afterward of the McDonalds, of Scotland, he having married into the former family. The Scottish family are still lords of Antrim and Dunluce. This castle is the subject of endless tradition, and has been the scene of many romantic as well as horrible events.

At length we reach the object of our day's trip—the Giant's Causeway—quite unlike my anticipation. All the way from Portrush we have been near the sea, on bluffs two and three hundred feet high, mostly of limestone, here and there deeply washed into, and forming many wild caverns, through which the roaring sea makes wild music. When we reached the terminus we found the bluff increased to five hundred feet somewhat back, leaving ample room to go down among the basaltic rocks which, in their regular arrangement and structure, give it its name. To get a full view, we take a guide and boat, and go out among the rocks and coves at some risk, as the swells are constantly tossing us among the rocks; indeed, one corpulent lady fell into the sea, and was with some difficulty rescued by two sailors, who jumped in to aid her. The basaltic promontory reaches some one thousand feet into the sea. Man's art could hardly rival the nicety with which the prisms fit each other. We can easily believe when told we walk over some forty thousand of these polished columns. We cannot tell all the legends connected with the Giant's Well, the Portoon Cave, the Dunkerry Cave, the Giant's Amphitheater, Chimney Tops, and Gateway, which our broguish guide told us, to say nothing of his second eighteen-year-old wife and his seventeen children. Here cometh the legend of the origin of the Giant's Causeway, or cause-why: The giant, Finn McCoul, was the champion of Ireland, and felt very much aggrieved at the insolent boasting of a certain Caledonian giant, who offered to beat all who came before him, and even dared to tell Finn that if it were not for the wetting of himself, he would swim over and give him a drubbing. Finn at last applied to the king, who not, perhaps, daring to question the doings of such a mighty man, gave him leave to construct a causeway right across to Scotland, on which the Scot walked over and fought the Irishman. Finn turned out victor, and, with an amount of generosity quite becoming his Hibernian descent, kindly allowed his former rival to marry and settle in Ireland, which the Scot was nothing loth to do, seeing that at that time living in Scotland was none of the best; and everybody knows that Ireland is the richest country in the world. Since the death of the giants, the causeway, being no longer wanted, has sunk under the sea, only leaving a portion of itself visible here, and a trifle at the Island of Rathlin and the portals of the grand gate on Staffa. After six we retraced our course to Portrush, where we stopped awhile to look at a nice granite monument reared in memory of Dr. Adam Clarke, the great Methodist preacher, and author of those commentaries so long the authority of Bible students. We shall have occasion to remember Portrush, for, on our arrival, at 2 P. M., and before going to the Causeway, we were met by a band of music, and escorted to the town-hall, where a sumptuous banquet was in store for us, though we were one day ahead of time. Englishmen, in white vests and aprons, aided us beyond what we were able to help ourselves to good things. We had new potatoes, grown here this summer—this nearly fifty-five degrees north. Amusement mingled with the dinner at the expense of a few more greedy for the good things than the others. By way of amusement, on the table was a new something shaped like an inverted bowl, with a tea saucer on the top filled with candies and goodies; the whole structure was white, like frosted cake. Our eager gourmands cut into it; it was white and hard like tallow; visions of something good and new whetted the appetites of the tasters. A sudden elevation of nose, and upturning of lips, with a look around to see if anybody was watching them, plainly indicated that they had sold themselves for naught—but tallow; that it was, and nothing more.

At twelve, midnight, we reached the Victoria, found supper waiting, and at one, after twenty-two hours of day, sought our berths.

GLASGOW, SCOTLAND, July 3, 1873.

We reached this place yesterday, coming up the

Clyde—for the most part man made the river, for, said a Scotchman as we were sailing up, "My grandmother when a girl could step across it at Glasgow." It has been dug and deepened like a canal, till now it is the second shipping port in Great Britain, as well as the second city of commercial importance. Our approach to it was interesting; among other places passing the death and burial-place of Robert Bruce, and the famous Dumbarton Castle, where for a long time Wallace, of Scottish history, had his dwelling-place. It is five hundred and sixty feet high, and a mile in circumference, a huge double-peaked rock rising, almost completely surrounded, from the river, or rather from the junction of the Clyde and Leven Rivers. It is entered by a gate at the bottom, and within among the relics is Wallace's two-handed sword, five and one-half feet in length. Its history is part of that of this country. A little farther up the river we pass the remains of an old tower, ivy-clad, from the midst of which rises a lofty monumental shaft, on which we read as we passed, "Henry Bell." He was the builder of the first steam-boat on the Clyde, now a river on which more iron steam-boats are made than in all the world beside. Held in memory, beside a wharf just above the monument, was the "Industry," the second steam-boat built here; the first was called the "Comet." On and on we sailed, looking right and left upon some of those beautiful farms and lawns of which we have read; mansions, parks, and surroundings indicating wealth, culture, and age. Our winding way was somewhat new, and perhaps worthy of description. As the Clyde is very narrow, we had a steam-tug ahead and one astern of us, so that when the Victoria would turn in some of the windings, one tug would pull the prow of the great ship one way, and the one at the stern pull the other way. Thus we entered the city, passing ship-yard after ship-yard, where the building of the ocean steamers gives employment to many thousand men. Iron steamers we could see in all stages of structure, from iron keels, and iron ribs, and iron lungs, iron sides and iron decks, iron wheels and iron ropes; and the clatter and clangor of ten thousand iron hammers, mingled with the puffing and piping steam-boats, and the oft-repeated cheers of merry passengers on outward-bound ships, all served to fill the mind with new delights.

Glasgow is the most prosperous city in Scotland; and in wealth, population, and commercial importance is now the second in the United Kingdom; in external appearance elegant and impressive, substantially built and regular in arrangement. It is in the vicinity of extensive coal-fields, and has ready access by the Clyde and the canal to the Atlantic and German Oceans. Its present harbor, called the Broomielaw, is a basin of about fifty acres, with fine quays, and deep enough for the largest vessels. Glasgow first grew wealthy in the tobacco trade, and the prosperous men were called tobacco lords. This trade failing, the cotton trade took its place, and prosperity made this city master of the cotton situation. Competition withdrew the trade after awhile; and then, turning attention to iron ship-building, she now rules the world in this line of manufactures, and more than one-half a million people occupy her dwellings. The one great object of interest to the tourist here is the Cathedral, founded more than seven hundred years ago. So far it is the grandest structure I have entered—massive, well-proportioned, and beautiful. Sixteen years ago all the windows were put in anew, richly colored, and enough of them to give a pictorial history of Bible scenes commencing with Adam and coming down through all subsequent sacred history far this side of our Saviour's death and ascension. As works of art, and specimens of beautiful coloring, they can hardly be surpassed; the perfection and richness of the colors can hardly be surpassed; the perfection and richness of the colors is worthy of all praise; but as true representations of Bible facts they are not trustworthy. For instance, the prodigal son has a richer coloring to his robes than the silks and satins of to-day, and the poor widow dropping her mites into the treasury has an elegance of drapery that the greatest devotee of modern fashion might envy; and our Saviour, the man without comeliness, and the poor he came to help, all are clothed in bright and shining garments. Pictorial truth and history here disagree, and yet the colored tracing on the windows is strikingly beautiful. Adjoining the Cathedral is the Necropolis, a cemetery, in which are many beautiful monuments of men renowned in history. Take that of John Knox, whose power as a reformer the world well knows. Here also is a monument to John Dick, the Christian philosopher; through such men Scotland became Protestant, and the Cathedral is now Presbyterian, as this is the Established Church of Scotland. As elsewhere, so here, Cromwell meant to destroy this cathedral, and but for the determined resistance of one man it would have been accomplished. Perhaps the most attractive building in Glasgow is the Royal Exchange, built in 1829, noted for its decorative architecture; and in front of it is an equestrian statue in bronze of the Duke of Wellington, costing, by subscription, fifty thousand dollars. George's Square, the largest in the city, incloses many monuments; one to Sir Walter Scott is a Doric column, eighty feet in height, with his statue on the top. At one corner of the square is a bronze statue of James Watt; in another corner, one to Sir Robert Peel, while within the square are bronze statues to Sir John Moore and Lord

Clyde, both natives of Glasgow. But I may not dwell on the works of man in the city. We take cars and stages for mountain and lake scenery; and it will not be uninteresting to your readers who have read "The Lady of the Lake," to know that we followed in the very track of Fitz James, in his chase along the shores of Loch Achray and Loch Katrine, through the Trossachs, and among the bold mountain peaks of Ben Nevis and Ben Lomond. Such mountains, piled in confused grandeur around such beautiful lakes, and such charming islands as Ellen's Isle, have never before made such pleasing impressions on my eyes, or called forth such sublime emotion from my heart. The whole region round about is made classic by the genius of Scott, whose stories have their truth and illustration in these wild mountains and lovely lakes. It was amid such scenery as this we spent the Fourth of July, and many a hearty cheer went echoing along the lakes and up the mountains as from time to time we caught sight of some little American flag that friends waved to us as we passed their pleasure parties or their wild mountain homes; for our coming is known in advance along the whole journey. It was a glorious *Fourth*, though we wore overcoats all the day. We have seen the glory of the natural Scotland.

BRUSSELS, July 11, 1873.

Kind readers, once more I take up the pen to record some of the scenes through which I have passed in the last few days. At Edinburgh we spent two days — Saturday and Sunday. On Saturday we visited the castle overlooking the city. Here a bird's-eye view of the capital city amply repays the toil of climbing to it. Only those who have visited castles on the eminences of Scotland can form a very clear conception of its size and strength. It is one of four kept in repair and use in Scotland. In this one are kept the crown and crown-jewels of Scotland. Here are the rooms occupied by kings and queens. We were shown the rooms down from the window of which, in a basket, descended the infant James, afterward king. Lovers of such remnants of royalty may gaze with wonder at them if they will. I am interested in them only so far as they help to give history of the past a greater freshness and reality. We pass to the occupied palace of Holyrood, where we see the massive walls required to preserve the sacred persons of royalty. We see where kings and queens have been born and murdered—where queens were kept as prisoners, or danced in rooms adorned with paintings of royal ancestors. We see a splendid fountain, where a few years since stood a statue of Queen Victoria, so poorly executed that Prince Albert had it buried six feet under the horse-stable, to be dug up by some future generation, with as much wonder as the Cardiff Giant.

We gaze with admiration on the splendid monuments of Sir Walter Scott, Robert Burns, and others whom man delights to honor. We go to church on the Lord's day, and hear a good, sound sermon in the Tron Church, from Rev. Mr. McGregor, D.D., in true Scottish Presbyterian style, as to dress reforms.

Monday morning we start for Abbotsford, the home of Sir Walter Scott. Here we spent some hours looking through armorial halls, halls of paintings, and his library of twenty thousand volumes; saw the many presents from time to time given him by fond admirers of his genius; then, without, we walked through ample grounds made beautiful by his own genius, and left with a pleasant picture in the mind of the palace of Abbotsford, on the Tweed.

Next, Melrose Abbey took an hour of our time in

looking at its still wonderful ruins, once the finest cathedral in all Scotland. Within it is buried the heart of Bruce; for they have a strange way over here of satisfying the Cathedral's desire for royal remains, by giving part of the body to one, and another to another—and parts or the whole of still earlier kings. Besides a burial-place of royalty, it is remarkable for its architecture, beautiful in its ruins —the fine sculpture in stone, and the climbing ivy to the very top, here and there adorning it with living green.

Taking the cars, we are hurried along through garden-like fields, where every rod is well tilled, and grain-fields yellow with wild mustard, and red with the poppy—here a troublesome weed. Next we pass into an uncultivated region — the Downs — huge sheep-pastures, where for miles we see neither tree, nor fence, nor house; only sheep-cotes, and shepherds watching their flocks far away on the plain, or up the mountain sides. Hours pass, and we find ourselves in the coal regions. Hillsides and valleys are black with bituminous coal, and busy thousands are engaged in bringing it to the surface. We skip the city of Manchester, and pass through Sheffield, noted for its cutlery manufactories. All along the country is darkened by the smoke of so many iron-making furnaces, that, as I gaze at all this—the mere outside—I am inclined to think that, as an agricultural people, they are busily engaged in raising— coal; and in like manner, their chief manufacture is—smoke.

At 7:30 P. M. we enter Derby, to find the streets and depot crowded with thousands of men, women, and children, gathered there to see "the Americans." We are a hundred and fifty, and our coming is known; for in the spacious halls of the Midland Railroad Station has been provided our dinner. His Honor the Mayor presides, surrounded by other dignitaries of the city. Here we have a real English test of hospitality — good things in abundance to eat, beautiful flowers to adorn the table, English and American flags to embellish the room, and English men and women to eat and drink with us in friendly cheer. Drinking toasts to the Queen and the President, and the others, with speeches of welcome and the replies, filled up the time till 11 o'clock, when we, tired, sought our beds.

Next morning we were borne onward by cars — an especial train of twelve cars, which, thus far, has been at our disposal — to Alton Towers. Here is the palatial home of the Earl of Shrewsbury — the premier or first Earl in rank in England, though not the wealthiest, having an income of only £50,000, or $250,000 — the owner of several estates like this, some twenty-five miles in length by five or more in breadth. His income is from the rental of his lands, averaging about five dollars an acre for what is good enough to let. We were met by his private brass band, and escorted by them to the chapel, where for an hour we gazed on the rich adornments of the spacious room, or listened to the true English style of service. After this we were guided through splendid halls, made so by paintings of ancestors and royal personages, sculpture such as only the wealthy can purchase, and furniture massive and elegant. Room after room was shown to us, though at every door stood a soldier on guard. Next we wandered through sixty acres of the prettiest garden scenery I ever saw. Flowers of every kind, in all conceivable places — in dells, caverns, or terraces, in ponds, in hot-houses, with towers, Swiss cottages, Chinese towers — all extremely beautiful, and not easily described. A great flower-show was held at the same time, in tents within the garden, to which all the people from the country round had gathered. This show is like our fair, in this: the show is limited to flowers and plants, for which prizes are offered. So on gathered and skillfully-arranged flowers we gazed in pleasure. Next, in a tent with our flag above it, the Earl gave us a dinner, followed, as at Derby, with toasts and speeches. At 9 o'clock we were in London.

CHAPTER IV.

Letter from Miss Hattie Stanard, Des Moines, Iowa.

GLASGOW, SCOTLAND, July 3, 1873.

EDITOR IOWA SCHOOL JOURNAL:—Yes, at last we have realized our fondest hopes—we have been tossed on the mountain waves of the broad Atlantic—we are in Europe. And yet with all *that*, we would not forget our promise to the *Iowa School Journal;* for we have pleasant recollections of the past, and do not wish to be forgotten by our Iowa friends. After tearing ourselves away from them on that memorable Wednesday afternoon, we went into the car, and after watering a bouquet that had been pressed into our hand at the last moment with a few tears—not from any sense of duty, but because we had a cinder in our eye, for our thoughts were really too sad to find the relief that tears bring—we concluded that we had been as miserable as we could, so we ended that scene and have had a good time ever since.

We spent one day in Cleveland, Ohio; and right here let me say, if any of our friends ever stop in that beautiful city, be sure to ride out on Euclid street. We think it one of the handsomest streets to be found in America.

At Niagara we spent one day listening to the "Thunder of Waters," and the everlasting "Have your picture taken? Do it cheaper than any one else; only three dollars and a-half." We could enjoy it for fifty or sixty times, but there was a great deal of sameness about it when we heard it at every step (we refer to the latter). We could listen to Niagara forever, and it would always remind us of the power and greatness of Him who hath made all things, the small as well as the great, and who careth for all.

We enjoyed the day very much, and especially when we were done up in an oil-cloth hood and frock, accompanied by some high rubber boots, and went under the falls, helped along by a good-natured guide, who every once in a while said, "How do you like it as far as you have gone?" At half-past five P. M. we left for New York by way of the Hudson River. Were somewhat disappointed with the scenery on the Hudson; having heard so much in its favor, we expected more than we saw. Arrived in the metropolis about noon, Friday. Spent the afternoon in Central Park; would have liked a week to spend there, but no, the time had come, the most eventful day, thus far, of our lives, when we were to sail on our first ocean voyage; and it was with every hope inspired that we were carried out of the hotel in the arms of the accommodating porter, loaded into a hack, and driven to pier number twenty, where we went aboard the Victoria, our home for the next nine days.

We have a fine steamer, and every thing more than meets our expectations. A jolly company of one hundred and forty-five, representing twenty-three states of the Union, good state-rooms, obliging officers, stewards, and stewardesses; nice things to eat, and O such an appetite! We think the Anchor Line will not make very much off this company, we are too regular at meals, and there has been so little sea-sickness. What we miss most at table is the bread. When we asked a pensive-looking steward, "Why is this thus?" his eyes brightened (they like to tell stories), and straightening himself back, he said, "Once we had a baker, we trusted him, but away back in New York he got angry, went off on a spree, and just as the vessel was about to leave he rushed aboard, seized the yeast, and yeast nor man has ever been heard of since, madam." Then drawing a long sigh, he walked slowly back to the regions of cookerydom, in a way that would cause us to never mention bread again. We have heard of some who doubted the story, but we believe it; we feel sure that that steward "cannot tell a lie, pa."

This is the first time crossing the ocean for the most of our party, and life on ship-board is so different from what we had thought, that with all our guide-books and kind advice from friends, we find that one needs to make one trip across in order to know how to go and what to take. I think, however, that the most of us remembered to leave our formality at home, as well as our Sunday clothes. For amusements we have occasionally a shark, whale, or porpoise, and in the evening, after devotional exercises, we usually have something literary, and then games of all sorts, "and yet we are not happy," for we have not been sea-sick, and are afraid we may die without ever knowing what the feeling is. It is quite amusing to see the different kinds of sea-sick people. Some went to their berths at once, even before the steamer sailed, though for two days the sea was very calm—no more motion than on a river—but they were afraid they *might* be sick. Others kept several kinds of remedies on hand, and would take a sip of each every once in a while. The only wonder to me is that there is as much left of them as there is. Some lie whining in their state-rooms, and their friends take them huge plates of raisins, figs, nuts, etc. Their only wish is that they were back on land again, and I think it is all the wish their fellow-passengers have for them. Others look cross, and grumble. We think their only wish is to be let alone. This latter class is composed mostly of the stronger-minded. We saw one of them, a man (they are mostly men), dragged about the deck in spite of himself for nearly an hour, by two large females. The majority belong to a more sensible class, who stay as much as possible in the pure air, enjoy every thing there is to be enjoyed, and forget to be sick. Perhaps it is the novelty, but we think the two Sabbaths spent on the ocean among the pleasantest of our lives. Of all places, there seems to be no place more appropriate, or more natural, to worship God than on the deck of an ocean steamer, for then do we see how completely we are in his power, and those who have never trusted him before it seems must trust him there.

The first Sabbath services were conducted in the morning by Rev. Mr. Witherspoon, of University of Virginia. After reading that beautiful 104th Psalm, and all joining in singing "Rock of Ages," he discoursed on the reasonableness of being a Christian; then all sang "Nearer, my God, to thee." When we heard those voices of different nationalities, and from nearly every state in the Union, joining in those beautiful hymns, we understood the meaning of the "communion of saints." The sermon on last Sabbath was not less interesting—given by Rev. Mr. Barrows. Text: "Come unto me all ye that are weary and heavy laden, and I will give you rest." We were sorry and disgusted to see *teachers* forming little religious "rings," the Methodist Episcopals in one group, the Presbyterians in another, Episcopalians in another, etc. Only thirteen preachers aboard—five Presbyterian, four Methodist Episcopal, two Congregational, one Baptist, one Episcopalian.

Here we do not look at the clock for the time, but listen for the bells: One bell, one-half o'clock; two bells, one o'clock; three bells, half-past one; four bells, two o'clock; five bells, half-past two; six bells, three o'clock; seven bells, half-past three; eight bells, four o'clock; then commence at one bell again.

The first few days out the sea was very calm, and when we touched the Gulf Stream the atmosphere was warm, the water a beautiful green, quite different from the dark blue of the ocean. About the fourth day there came up a stiff gale, and then the ship was "rolled to larboard, rolled to starboard." At night we would go to our berths thinking of what Grace Greenwood thought when trying to sleep in Sacramento during the earthquake, "Rock me to sleep, mother," only we thought father, instead of mother. We heard of one "bloated aristocrat" who was rolled out of his berth, but when we saw his robust form, we were surprised that he could stay in in the calmest night, and did not blame old ocean. Life at sea is an exceedingly lazy life. Some came on board with "stern determination flashing in their eagle eyes," and carrying huge portfolios, books, fancy-work, and we saw one lady with sewing the second day; but before the third day was ended this enterprising woman, like all the rest, had subsided, as far as work was concerned, and had gone to sucking lemons. There are two things—the ocean, and a sunset on the ocean—that we will not attempt to describe, feeling sure that if we did it would be a failure. There is something too grand about them to express. It must be seen to be appreciated, and then we think it will never leave one's memory.

We landed off Moville, July 1st, after making the shortest trip ever made by the Anchor Line. There we met Mr. Cook, junior, who had his arrangements all made for the day, and took us in a tug to Londonderry, eighteen miles, a nice place of twenty thousand inhabitants, where we took the train for Portrush, thirty miles, passing through Colraine, an old place, but nothing of particular interest to be seen. The railway carriages are very different from our cars, and we think pleasanter, being smaller and more secluded. They do not have conductors here on the cars, but *guards*, and no boys go through the trains selling pea-nuts, prize packages, etc. Portrush is the stopping-place for visitors to the Giant's Causeway, and there are many things of interest there besides the causeway. After a nice lunch, and a short speech from our "chief cook," we all went in jaunting-cars to the causeway, a distance of about eight miles, passing the *Castle of Dunluce*, about two miles from Portrush, which is considered one of the most interesting castles in the kingdom. We had a very intelligent driver, a native of the "Emerald Isle," who, when we wound him up at the start, went on talking the rest of the day, telling us all he knew, and, as we afterward found, some things he did not know. At the causeway our company was divided into several smaller parties, with a guide for each. One of the most noticeable things at the causeway is the "Giant's Organ," a great colonnade of pillars reaching to a height of one hundred and twenty feet. Farther east another variety is presented, the "Chimney Tops," three pillars, the tallest of which is forty-five feet. They stand upon an isolated rock some distance from the cliff. It is said that these chimney tops were cannonaded from one of the ships of the Spanish Armada. It was in the night, and the crew mistook them for the "chimneys" of Dunluce Castle. We sat in the "Lady's Wishing Chair," and wished the wish that is to forever after make us happy. One of the singularities of the immense number of columns is that there is but *one* of three sides. More numerous are those of five sides, but the most have six sides, a few with as many as seven, eight, or nine sides, but none of ten.

The road from Portrush to the causeway lies along the beach, and is a very beautiful drive. At Portrush we saw Dr. Clarke's monument. All enjoyed the day very much, and we think came back with higher ideas of Ireland than we had ever had before. The people crowded the depots, with smiling faces, and kind words of welcome, and at Portrush the band came out and played us several tunes, such as "Yankee Doodle," "Our Country," "Star Spangled Banner," etc. We reached the Victoria at twelve o'clock P. M., tired but happy, for we had seen far more than we had expected to see. Two things that are scarce in Ireland are school-houses and cemeteries. Our driver said they had to kill a man to *start* a cemetery at Portrush. Three hearty cheers for Old Ireland and Scotland, we say.

CHAPTER V.

Rev. C. W. Cushing, President of Auburndale College, Massachusetts, writes the following to the *Boston Traveller:*

June 21, 1 p.m., 1873.

Cook's Educational Tour.—We are all afloat. The party consists of one hundred and sixty-five, and quite a majority are ladies. Two of the number have failed to come to time. All seem very happy as yet, for old Neptune is asleep. We are hoping no one will awaken him at present. Cook, Son & Jenkins have done every thing in their power to get us off in good shape. They certainly know their business. Our goodly steamer Victoria is every inch a queen. I will tell you more of her when I know more. I send by mail a printed list of the names of the party. A more select-looking company could not easily be found. I send you this line by the pilot, from off Sandy Hook. More anon if—sailors know what.

Mayence, Germany, July 15, 1873.

Since reaching Scotland we have been traveling over enchanted fields, wandering through the silent halls of palaces and castles which belonged to other days and other epochs of history, and roaming amid delectable mountains. But I want to break the thread of our itinerary just here, long enough to give you a brief sketch of two Sabbaths—one in Scotland, and the other in Germany.

After spending one day in Glasgow, we went, on July 4th, to Stirling Castle—of which I cannot tell you now—crossing the battle-fields of Bannockburn and Stirling Bridge, through Loch Katrine, Loch Lomond, and the Trossachs, to Edinburgh. Here we spent our first Sabbath on shore. In the morning our whole party went, by special invitation, to the old Tron Church, to listen to a sermon from the eminent Dr. McGregor. He is a man scarcely more than forty years of age, of medium size, quite deformed when seen out of the pulpit, of very dark complexion, with curly hair nearly black, and a full black beard. His face is very marked, especially his eye and forehead. He has a rich Scotch voice, with their marked inflections, brogue, and broad vowel sounds. His text was from Matthew iv. 1, 2, etc., and his theme the temptation of Christ. The sermon was a very striking one, full of richest thought and suggestions, and delivered with an enthusiasm and fervor which kindled his whole audience into rapture. I am sure the sermon will not soon be forgotten by any who heard it. A few fitting words were addressed directly to the American visitors at the conclusion of the sermon. During the day I managed to hear two other sermons—one from the venerable Dr. Alexander, and the other from Dr. Scott, and the most of a sermon from the Rev. Dr. Wallace, the reformer in the Established Church. All these sermons, as you would expect, were very rich treats. But what I want especially to speak of is the marked features of a Sabbath in Scotland. In the first place, no horse-cars (or tram-ways, so they call them) are running, and there is scarcely any driving, and very little walking on the streets, except by those who are going to church, and it really seems as though this embraced everybody.

After service in the evening, I walked out with an Edinburgh gentleman through the lower parts of the city, and found every thing quiet and orderly. I saw one small place where beer was sold standing open, but nobody was buying. In the churches there was no spare room—all were filled. But the earnest attention of the audience was what impressed me most. I looked about the house for listless ones. Surely, I said, some of these boys and girls will be gazing about. But I did not find such, though I have no doubt that such may have been in the audience. So far as I could see, old men and women, young men and maidens, and even the children, had their eyes fixed intently upon the preacher, while the expression upon their faces indicated a deep interest in what was said.

It was really delightful and cheering to spend a Sabbath under such circumstances. There is none of that looseness about the observance of the day which is seen in our own country, even in Puritanic New England. I do not suppose that everybody went to church, or that every one who remained at home regarded the day as it ought to be; but there was certainly a much more general regard of it than I have been accustomed to see; and an indication of a prevailing religious sentiment, a high-toned faith in the Bible and Sabbath, which was refreshing to a Christian. I am inclined to think that Edinburgh has a reputation for such Sabbaths; for an Englishman asked me on our way up if we were to spend a Sabbath there. I told him we expected to. "Well," said he, "you will find it the dullest place you were ever in. There is nothing going on on Sunday." "Indeed," said I, "don't they have religious services?" "O yes," said he, "plenty of that; but there is nothing else going on."

Our next Sabbath found us at Cologne, a remarkably quiet and orderly little city, but under entirely different religious influences. The first thing that impressed me as I stepped upon the street was the fact that the stores were all open, and the markets in full blast. A little later in the day multitudes began to gather in the beer and wine-gardens. Crossing the Rhine to the old town of Cologne, we encountered a long procession of men, women, boys, and girls, led by Catholic priests and a large number of novitiates, in full regalia, parading the streets with bands of music in honor of St. Michael. The streets, for miles, were strewed with the branches of trees and with flowers, while in nearly every window along the whole line of the procession were images and burning candles. A large number of the men carried immense candles, burning, while over the heads of the more venerable priests were borne large golden canopies. All along the line children and adults were either singing or counting their beads aloud. In the old cathedral—by far the grandest which we have seen yet—services were held half-hourly, though comparatively few were in attendance, excepting at children's service, at 2 o'clock.

A little away from the cathedral the museum and other public buildings were all open, and were crowded. At 11 o'clock we attended the English Chapel services, where seventy-five persons were present.

In the afternoon, just in front of our hotel, there was a grand swimming match, which was announced by the firing of cannon. All day the river was filled with the boats of pleasure-parties. At 3 o'clock P.M. the government band came into the garden of our hotel, and began a grand concert, which was kept up, with occasional intermissions, until 10 o'clock at night. At half-past seven our party held a short prayer-meeting in one of the dining-rooms, amid the playing of the band and the drinking of wine and beer just outside. Coming from our prayer-meeting, our landlord announced that they were going to close up the entertainment with a few fireworks. So just on the veranda of our hotel, fronting on the Rhine, we had for an hour a magnificent display of fireworks, as the closing ceremony of our first Sabbath under the German *régimé*.

Let those who would introduce the German type of Sabbath into America, ponder.

CHAPTER VI.

[I copy from the Edinburgh *Daily Review* the following, omitting the speeches of Mr. Thinex, who presided. Dr. Donaldson made an address, the concluding paragraph of which I copy.]

The American Educational Party in Edinburgh.— On Saturday morning we announced the arrival in Edinburgh of the large party of Americans who are presently making a short excursion into the Old World, under the guidance of the veteran manager of tours, Mr. John Cook. Twenty-seven years ago Mr. Cook first appeared among the citizens of the Scotch metropolis with a party of five hundred English tourists, who were bent on exploring our historically interesting, and naturally beautiful, country. Since then his field of operations has gradually extended until it now embraces the whole world. The chief theater of his tours is, however, the European Continent, over which he yearly guides hundreds and thousands—among the luxuriant vineyards of France and Italy, the fertile plains of Holland, the romantic towns of Germany, the gorgeous scenery of the Rhine, and the almost inaccessible valleys of Switzerland. The party at present under his charge, numbering one hundred and fifty, consists principally of teachers—ladies and gentlemen, collected from twenty-seven different States of America—together with several professors and gentlemen of the press. About fifty of them are acting on the present occasion as correspondents of newspapers, so that doubtless the impressions which they receive of the places which they visit during their sojourn in Europe will be widely disseminated amongst the myriad inhabitants of the United States. Before starting, the party was divided into four sections, each of whose programme of operations differs slightly from that of the others. One of the sections only reached Scotland on Saturday with the steamer Canada, of the Anchor Line, and will join the main body of excursionists at London during the week.

At eight o'clock the lecture hall of the Industrial Museum was crowded by an audience of Edinburgh citizens, congregated to welcome the members of the Educational Party from America. The members of the excursion committee occupied seats on the platform, and the remainder of the Americans were accommodated immediately in front.

Dr. Donaldson then gave a brief account of the early education of Sir Walter Scott, at the High School of Edinburgh, and the progress that he made, as illustrative of the pleasing and interesting nature of a teacher's duties. The great object they ought to have in view was to look after the interest of the average boy. There was no doubt that they exercised a mighty power in the molding of nations; and if they spread sweetness through the boys, if their class-rooms were filled with gentle thoughts and gentle ways, if the bitterness of judgment were removed, if they tried to do justice to every nationality in dealing with the history of nations, to bring out the good points, to show that the evil points were in most part shadows which grew around the central figure when it came into the sunlight, then, depend upon it, wars would cease, they would see nation joining hand with nation, and should bring forth that happy time mentioned by the poet Burns, when men shall be

brothers over the whole world. (Applause.) He
begged in the name of the whole of the teachers
of Scotland to express how heartily they welcomed
their brethren from America, how they were delighted to see those who labored in the same great
work, and how earnestly they hoped that the present visit should be an enjoyable and profitable one,
which should soon be repeated. (Applause.)

Rev. T. D. Witherspoon (Virginia University),
who was received with enthusiastic cheers, said he
expressed the feelings of every member of their
American party when he gave expression to their
profound thanks for the manifestation which they
had received that evening of the kindly feeling and
generous hospitality of the citizens of Edinburgh.
This was not the first welcome which they had received to Old Scotland. The chairman had spoken
of the lines of steamers which connect the United
Kingdom and America, and from the moment that
they left New York city and entered the steamer
that was to bring them to Europe, they felt that
Scotland had already put forth her hand not only
to welcome them, but had reached forth her hand
to take them and bear them to her own country. The
vessel in which they came was built on the banks
of the Clyde—(applause)—and if only a sufficient
number of similar vessels so stout and good should
be built there, and if only such commanders could
be found in Scotland as Captain Robert E. Munroe,
and if only such conductors and guides as Messrs.
Cook & Sons could be provided for them, he safely
believed it would be only a short time until the
people of Scotland and America would be so well
connected with each other that they would scarcely
know that there was any difference between them.
(Applause.) Nor was it only the feelings of cordiality which they met with on the vessel, but when
looking over the list of officers they read the names

of Munroe, Laird, Knox, Harrison, Stockdale, and others—all of them names that were connected with historic epochs in Scotland—they felt peculiar security in resting upon the hardihood, faith, and integrity of the Scottish people. On the first day of their sail from America there appeared in the midst of them a warm, generous-hearted Scotchman, who bore another name—a historic name, celebrated not only in Scotland, but renowned across the water—the name of Cunningham. (Applause.) They had hoped to have had him with them that evening, but he had been prevented from coming. He gave them both his hands, and represented to them that they should find a hearty welcome when they came to Scotland. Let him say that they had found it, that they had not been disappointed, but had received everywhere evidences of kindly feeling. He spoke in the name of the whole American party when he declared that they felt the very deepest interest in all that concerned the ancient and historical renown of this country. There were many of them in the party who could not only quote those beautiful words from Scott which were quoted by the chairman that evening, but who could take them up where he left them off—

> Land of our sires; what traitor's hand
> Shall e'er untie the filial band
> That binds us to thy native strand?

(Applause.) The blood of Scotland was in their veins, and though it had been watered by ten generations in America, and though they were proud of being connected with the rise and progress of American institutions, yet all that was connected with the ancient and historical fame of Scotland, and that was connected with its present prosperity and progress, was dear to their hearts. (Applause.) And as they wandered to-day through this beautiful city—majestically beautiful beyond all that they had conceived—as they had visited the Castle and visited the Palace, and all the institutions of the city, they had felt a just and honest pride themselves in all that they had beheld. (Applause.) Yet, farther, let him say that if in America the spirit of devotion to right and truth had been manifested, its fires had been kindled in great measure by memories of the grand and historical struggles for right and liberty which make the history of Scotland. (Applause.) In visiting the field of Bannockburn and the town of Stirling, and other places of interest, they felt that they were theirs as well as ours. (Applause.) He would not occupy the time, however—(applause, and cries of "Go on!")—but would leave to his friend, Rev. Professor Cushing, who was to follow him, the task of replying to the address which had been delivered by the learned doctor who had just spoken. He concluded, remarking that if Mr. Cook brought one hundred and twenty Scottish men and women to America, they would receive in return as hearty a welcome as they had received in Scotland. (Loud applause.)

Professor Charles Cushing said he thought he knew why he was in Scotland, but he really did not know why he was standing just where he did. He had learned when a little boy to love Scotland, and he was only realizing, all too briefly, the dreams of his boyhood, for he was born in Caledonia—in the New World, up in the State of Vermont. (Laughter.) He had to leave it when a little boy, and thought if he was a man he should certainly visit the original Caledonia. When he became older, and put away boyish things somewhat—he did not know whether it was because he was born in Caledonia, or not—but he found the one who was to stand by his side—his dear wife—had a good deal of Scottish blood in her veins, and a good deal of Scottish bloom in her face, and he rejoiced now to be here in Scotland. During the last two or three days he had been wandering with this party of teachers over the beautiful and historical fields, and lakes, and cities of Scotland, and had stood upon the sites where noble men had stood, and wandered down by lakes where had been pointed out the haunts of Roderick Dhu and Rob Roy, and had stood where Burns, and Scott, and John Knox, and Erskine, and those noble men stood. He had felt sometimes as if he almost heard voices behind him saying, "Put off thy shoes from thy feet, for the place where thou standest is holy ground." The impression had been left upon his mind that they were a very young people in America; they had no history. They had entered old castles here, and asked the guides—perhaps they ought to have been ashamed of their ignorance of history—when they were erected, and they had been told it was not known. (Laughter.) He had been told that more than once. They were now in a land where there were castles and temples standing so old that it made them feel that they were very young, and that they ought to feel that they knew very little, and he was glad to be here in Scotland, where there had been so many famous men—and women too—and where they might catch a little inspiration from that old history, and be reïmpressed with the feelings which they had so often felt, and he was sure as teachers they should go home again and toil —for the teacher's life was a life of toil; some of them did not know it, but it was—with a great deal more enthusiasm and a great deal more courage. About half of their number were practical teachers. (Applause.) He was glad to say that the majority of them were ladies. (Renewed applause.) Almost all of them were subordinate teachers. The professors and presidents of their colleges had been in Scotland, and been through Europe, and could take time for it;

but the subordinate teachers had to run away during a summer vacation, when the boys and girls had gone home for a few weeks. They had come to catch a little inspiration from these old historic fields, and now they were glad to be here. They regretted exceedingly that they could not meet directly with the teachers of Scotland in their places of work, and see how they worked. They were trying in America, in the States, as well as they could to do a little. They were trying to do much, and they hoped they were doing a little, to educate the people as they ought to be educated. (Applause.) They had not the men and women—especially the men—of fame which they had in Scotland. They had no such reputation, but they were working in their own way, in common places amongst the people. Of course, they were Republicans (applause), and the only security of the Republic was integrity and intelligence in every individual man and woman. (Hear, hear.) Every boy was to be a prince of the realm; he was ultimately to stand in a place where he would have as much voice to decide the destinies of the Government as any other man. It mattered not what his character was, what his attainments were. And so they felt that their life depended upon the thorough education of the masses of the people. It was for that reason, he supposed, that the efforts in America had been attracted so specially to the education of the people everywhere. In their public schools they were gathering in, so far as they could, and educating the boys and girls; and just now there was an effort being made to give to their girls and young women a more thorough education than they ever had. Some of the best colleges and universities had thrown open their doors, and though that might not be the best education for girls—he doubted very much if it was after they were fifteen years of age—still they were throwing the doors open for the ex-

periment of allowing the girls to stand side by side
with boys and young men to determine what they
could do. There was no question what they should
do; the only question was, what was the best way
to have it done, and the best circumstances under
which it should be done. A very large majority of
the teachers in their common, and often higher,
schools, excepting colleges, were ladies. (Applause.)
But he heard it said every now and again that women
could not teach so well as men. He always met
that charge by remarking that there was no reason
why they should be expected to do so, for no nation
had ever given women any thing like the same opportunities of making preparation to teach as had
been given to men. (Applause.) He should not
expect women to teach Latin and Greek, when men
received six or eight years of thorough drill, and
women only got perhaps one or two years for the
study of Latin, if they ever study Greek at all. In
America a great deal was said about educating
women for the best positions, and they were striv-
ing to balance the whole, and to give not only to
children of every class and condition opportunities
for common education, but to give to every class
alike, and to both sexes, equal opportunities for education; and they felt that when they shall have done
this, that they shall have done what no other nation, not even Scotland, has done for the elevation
of the race. (Applause.) On behalf of the teachers
present he thanked the meeting for the cordial welcome they had received, not as Americans, but as
teachers. Teachers only knew how to sympathize
with one another. When they sat down to talk
they understood each other's trials and each other's
toils; and he only regretted that their limited time
prevented them from seeing the teachers of Scotland conducting their classes, and making such men
as they had been accustomed to make in Scotland.

If they could get but an idea in the day or two they were here, they should be more than compensated for any toil and inconvenience they had experienced since they had left the shores of their own country. (Applause.)

While the professor was speaking the Lord Provost entered the lecture-hall, and was received with loud cheering. At the conclusion of the learned professor's address,

The Lord Provost said that it was with extreme regret that he had been unable to be present at the commencement of the proceedings, owing to his having been engaged on a public duty which took him to the country. He had written to say such might be the case; but if it had not been for the proverbial lateness of the trains on a certain railway, he should have been there in time. He congratulated upon their arrival in this old country the distinguished party who had come over from the United States. Our American cousins were objects of peculiar interest, and at the same time we might say we loved them as our sons and daughters. (Applause.) When he thought of what that country, so great and yet in embryo, might become, compared with ourselves at the end of a very short period, when many of the young people present would be still living—that it would contain two hundred millions of people, whilst this country would remain in about the same ratio as at present—he thought they would agree with him in congratulating themselves in being waited upon by a deputation of that people who were to spread our name and fame, and our language and customs, and our religion, over that vast continent. (Applause.) If, in the future, any jealousy should be excited on the part of the one nation toward the other, when that time came, he thought that country, which was so great and so powerful, would look back to and respect the country to which it owed its name and existence, and which, though comparatively small and feeble, was the land to which it owed its origin, and from which it derived its greatness. He congratulated the members of the American party, in the name of the citizens of Edinburgh, upon their arrival here; and begged to offer them a most cordial welcome, and to say how proud we were of the visit they had paid us, and how happy we were in having the honor of their presence. (Applause.) Nothing we could do to show them how hearty we were in joining with them in one common cause for the advancement of religion should be wanting, or in giving them a cordial welcome both in public and in private. (Applause.)

Mr. John Cook said that since he had previously visited Edinburgh he had encompassed the world, and he now supplemented his previous work by bringing a party of Americans on a tour to the principal places on the continent of Europe. There were on the platform three generations of Cooks—(laughter)—and when the first passed away, he hoped the second and third would still carry on the work he had commenced among the mountains and lakes, and the islands of the west of Scotland. He felt proud to have been the means of bringing together that body of American citizens to receive the welcome of the citizens of Edinburgh—(applause)—and he begged to propose that a hearty vote of thanks be accorded to the Lord Provost, who had kindly come forward, though at a late moment, and to Mr. Thomas Knox, for the kind interest they had taken in the meeting. (Cheers.)

[Editorial from the *Review*.]

Our American Visitors.—Our American visitors must not complain that we have taken up part of their brief opportunity for sight-seeing in Edinburgh by interviewing them in the lecture-hall of the

Science and Art Museum. We could not let them pass from our city without taking some friendly notice of them. There was no time between our hearing of them and their arrival to organize such a reception as we would like to have given them; and that being so, they will, we hope, take it as a compliment that we introduced them in this old country to the ceremony of an interview and exchange of speeches. That is peculiarly an American institution, and as such it was the expedient which appeared to be most suitable for giving them a welcome, and making them feel themselves at home. Our Yankee cousins, moreover, are all born orators; it is easier for any one of them to make a speech than to let it alone, so we did not apprehend that in giving some of them an opportunity to "orate" we were inflicting upon them the annoyance which the more taciturn Briton sometimes feels under that ordeal. Most heartily will the whole community of Edinburgh indorse all the words of welcome addressed to our visitors on Saturday-night by the Lord Provost, and other citizens. The parent has no jealousy of the increasing strength and intelligence of the child, and we may be permitted to look upon the great body of American citizens as bone of our bone, and flesh of our flesh. If they should "rive the bonnet" of their father, John Bull and Brither Sandy will look on with complacency. In all human probability they must increase while we—comparatively at least—decrease. Every right-hearted Briton will care less for that than for the channel in which the future might and influence of the great American Republic is to be directed. They got a good start in the world. The old Puritan stock of England is the tap-root from which American life has grown; and how much the United States owes to that providential arrangement it would not be easy to estimate. The citizens of the

States have had the farther benefit of large infusions of Scotch and Irish blood from generation to generation; and that makes not a bad cross with the original stock of the Pilgrim Fathers—we speak, of course, of north country Irishmen; the native Irish element is of doubtful advantage. It was pleasant to hear from Mr. Witherspoon, and Professor Cushing, on Saturday-night, that their countrymen had not forgotten their descent, and that they find a trip to this country very much like a visit to the old folks at home. That is one of the reasons for which we welcome our American brethren. They have the same hereditary interest in our history, our literature, our struggles for civil and religious freedom that we have ourselves; and the quickening of this community of sentiment and sympathy is a precious outcome of American visits to our shores. We have no doubt one and all of Mr. Cook's excursion party will return to their countrymen with the assurance that the heart of the old country beats in unison with theirs, in desiring and working for the progress of civilization, enlightenment, liberty, and Christianity all the world over. And we could hardly have conceived of a company of American tourists whose friendly feeling toward us is of more consequence. More than half of the one hundred and fifty are practical teachers; others are journalists, and almost all are among the educators of their country. Their direct influence extends over hundreds of thousands of their compatriots, and their indirect influence it would be impossible to compute. Most glad we shall be if—as we believe to be the case—they are able to report that they have found the people of Scotland, and of Britain, not jealous, but proud of the greatness of the United States, and desirous of showing their respect and attachment to the utmost. The more they know of us we are sure they will be the more convinced that they have our heartiest wishes for their welfare and prosperity. That is not always the opinion the rising generation of America receive about us from their school histories, but even they—to the extent of the influence of the teachers of Mr. Cook's party—will, we believe, learn to judge us more charitably, and not to visit the sins of the fathers upon the repentant children. But if, as we believe, our American friends have something to learn from us, and about us, we have certainly something to learn from them. "Scrape a Russian," said Napoleon I., "and you will find a Tartar." Scrape a Yankee, we may add, and you will find an Englishman or a Scotchman. When we listen, not to the anti-British diatribes of a section of the American press, but to the honest opinion of intelligent and candid American citizens, we always find, as we found in the speeches of Professor Cushing and Mr. Witherspoon, that they have a warm corner in their hearts for the land of their fathers. We venture to say that our visitors of the last three days know more about the history and traditions of Scotland than not a few educated people among ourselves; and that they glow with enthusiasm in presence of scenes, and in memory of associations which have too little power over the masses of our own population. We may learn from them to prize more highly, and improve more zealously, the noble heritage patriotic Scotchmen in Church and State have left us. And we may learn from them, too, that when the time comes—as probably it will—when there shall be another and greater struggle than the world has yet seen between the champions of freedom and the abettors of despotism, in both kinds, civil and religious, Britain, which must be in the thick of it, will not look in vain for the powerful aid of the United States of America.

CHAPTER VII.

A trip from London to Antwerp—A look about the ancient city.

ANTWERP, Belgium, July 10, 1873.

WE left London at 4 P.M. yesterday for this place. Having been there five days sight-seeing, we felt relieved to get away.

We took the Great Eastern Railway to Harwich, about eighty miles. This country is not of the kind from Liverpool to London. That was densely settled, this but sparsely. It is a fine country for hay and small grain, and every part of it sown down, with scarcely a tree, only along the hedge-rows; but the houses are scattering compared with other parts of England. Some farm-houses scattered along the way were all that we saw, except a few towns of but little importance.

The ship on which we came over was an inferior one, with but little accommodation. There was scarcely room for us, even on and under the table, to sleep. The channel was smooth, and we slept awhile comfortably. Soon in the morning we enter the river Scheldt, on which this city is situated. It is several miles wide for some distance. As we ascend, it becomes narrow, until it resembles the Mississippi. For some distance it looks very much like the coast above New Orleans. Instead of the sugar-cane they have the rushes growing luxuriantly. As we approach the city we see a large fort, with many cannon pointed out toward the river, looking very warlike. The number of soldiers we see over the city indicates that they keep prepared for defense.

The custom-house officers come aboard and examine our baggage, which has been very much reduced since we left London, as we are only allowed fifty pounds on the Continent. This farce over, we fill up inside, and cover over outside, the omnibuses waiting for us. A brush and a wash, and, with conductor and guide, we are off to see the great cathedral, of magnificent architecture, near by our Hotel de Europe. This is one of the oldest and largest churches in the world. It was commenced early in the year 1400. It is said that one of its towers is the highest and most delicately-finished in the world. The clock and bells together chime sweet music every half hour, and every hour play a fine piece of music, heard, I suppose, all over the city. From here we went to the museum, one of the finest collections of paintings in Europe. It is especially rich in the works of Rubens, Vandyke, and other Flemish artists. There were several of the crucifixion, very impressive. It was very extensive, containing several large rooms filled with paintings. We then went to see the silk manufactory. It is woven in the old-fashioned "fly-shuttle" loom by hand. No machinery whatever is used in its manufacture. The ladies examined the goods, and thought them very cheap; but when the duty of sixty per cent. and the difference in money is added, it makes the cost nearly as much as in the United States. We return to the hotel to dine at 5 o'clock. Nine courses are run through in an hour and a half, and yet not a very hearty meal at that—for every thing a separate plate, except, I believe, for potatoes, which were about the size of common marbles. Captain D. and myself took their only street railway, to see the suburbs of this Belgian city. Having a few coppers left, we paid our way out to a fine park, small but tasty, fitted up for beer-drinking, music, etc. On our return we hand the conductor some English silver. He shakes his head and passes on. The car is filled with ladies, chattering like a flock of black-birds, and by us as little understood. The conductor returns after awhile, and we try to get him to take our fare in silver. One of the ladies says to us: "He says you must go away," and out we got to walk to the hotel, if we could find it. We had not proceeded far before we saw people going into a large church, and we enter the finest we ever saw. Indeed, I have never seen any building finished so gorgeously—gilding, glittering walls, ceilings, columns, altars, with such an amount of decoration as I never saw any thing to compare with before. A minister was perched up in the air, near the center, preaching away, as I suppose, very eloquently, but it was all Dutch to me. Yet I was intensely interested. His manner was so earnest, his zeal so fervent, and the vast crowd so deeply in sympathy with him, that we were captivated with what we heard and saw all around us. All at once he stopped, and the audience arose to their feet; many of them rushed to the altar in the far end, prostrating themselves before it, while the two large organs in the other end of the church, and the choir, discoursed such music as never fell upon our ears before. A grand concert, it seemed, was given, and we staid till it was over. During this time the audience knelt in their chairs, with their heads and arms resting on a board on the top of them. I, too, knelt in one for a time to see how it was done, and to practice what to me was a new form of worship. The priests were dressed in long black robes, down to the floor. We have seen quite a number of such on the streets, but have not learned as yet what church they are. This worship was the grandest affair I ever saw, and when I learn what it was I may tell you.

How to find our way to the hotel is now the question. We start off in the direction. The narrow, crooked streets and tall houses soon destroy our idea of locality; but we go on, as we think, in the direction. We make inquiries; they shake their heads, and laugh. We laugh too, but still feel very different from what they do. I thought then they certainly could understand Hotel de Europe, and so I asked, pointing my finger, and they understood it, and pointed theirs, and, after making these experiments, we found our way to the hotel at 10 o'clock, enjoying our walk very much. And thus ends our first day on the Continent.

Sights and impressions in Belgium and Germany—Experience in Brussels and Cologne—Habits and occupation of the people—The great Cathedral and other objects of interest.

COLOGNE, Prussia, July 12, 1873.

I wrote you hurriedly at Antwerp, giving an account of my first day on the Continent, without having time to look over it. I mounted the top of an omnibus, with several others, that we might have a better view. In an open place, between a quarter and a half mile long by some sixty to eighty yards wide, was the vegetable market. It was almost literally filled with women selling and buying vegetables. They were a motley crowd, such as I had never seen before. We were all interested in this our last sight-seeing in Antwerp.

We take the carriages, as they call the cars here, much on the English style, with from four to eight persons locked up together. The distance to Brussels is only twenty-eight miles through a low, flat, rich country in a high state of cultivation. Arriving at the capital, each party is soon off to see the sights. Having met with some young men who came over in the Canada with us, who had been there several days, and proffered their services, we availed ourselves of them several hours. We pass along through the Arcade, filled with all sorts of things to sell, to Cook's office, where we procure aid in our work of exploration.

The Cathedral, City Hall, Palace of the Duke, Museum, boulevards, halls of justice, etc., etc., are the principal places to see. We go from one to the other as fast as we are able to examine them; but a description of them is out of the question now. We ascend the tower, from the top of which there is a fine view of the whole city, with its massive buildings, and boulevards encircling it. The king's palace is a very large building, but nothing like Buckingham, in London. The park, too, is on a much smaller scale. The Hotel de Ville (the townhall) and Grand Place are magnificent. The Place des Martyrs, where there is a monument containing the remains of the patriots killed during the revolution of September, 1830, is full of melancholy interest. The statue of Leopold I., on the Column du Congres, is very fine. In the Museum we saw the skeleton of a whale over sixty feet long, and between its ribs from nine to ten feet, making room for several persons to be domiciled.

Brussels is not only the capital of Belgium, but the most important city in the kingdom. It is nearly in the center of one of the richest and most highly cultivated countries in Europe. The people here are much more refined than those at Antwerp, judging from their appearance. The city is partly situated on a little river called the Seine, a tributary of the Scheldt. Its origin is not known. Its name is mentioned as far back as 706, and was a town of considerable importance in the tenth century. The

French language and manners have been predominant since the fifteenth century.

Manufactures.—There are extensive manufactories of cloths, carpets, silks, and lace. We visited the latter, and were surprised at the costliness of it. It is made by hand. One piece we observed contained five hundred threads used in the netting. Those who make it get from thirty to forty cents per day for their labor. The city contains one hundred and forty lace manufactories and seventy retail lace-merchants. We are now where he who shook Europe as an earthquake, dethroning kings and making princes, moved with such unparalleled success. Antwerp was his principal sea-port, through which he received supplies, and upon which he expended so much money, improving its harbor.

Belgium was incorporated with France for twenty years. On the 1st of February, 1814, the allied troops arrived in their turn, and Belgium was given to Prince William of Orange; Nassau to the new King of the Netherlands. The battle of Waterloo, twelve miles from Brussels, gained by Wellington and Blucher over the French army, put an end to the reign of Napoleon, and established for a time the union of Belgium with Holland. But the intrigues of the Southern Princes against the Dutch Government produced the revolution which broke out on the 24th and 25th of August in Brussels, and to which Belgium owes its nationality. The National Congress voted the most liberal constitution of the Continent of Europe, and on the 21st of July, 1831, Prince Leopold was inaugurated First King of the Belgians. In July, 1856, the twenty-fifth anniversary of the event was celebrated throughout Belgium with the greatest solemnity. Leopold died on the 10th of December, 1865, and his son and successor, Leopold II., took the oath of office and was inaugurated the 17th of December, in the same year. The kingdom has a population of over five millions; Brussels, one hundred and seventy-one thousand three hundred and seventy-seven on the first of January, 1870. The court, the militia, and a portion of the middle classes use the French language. I find our professors of French are not able to learn much from the people. Some very amusing incidents have occurred with us, showing that "book French" does not pass here. The present king, Leopold II., was born in Brussels, in 1835, and is a nephew of Louis Philippe, King of the French. He was married to Princess Maria Henrietta, of Austria, in 1853. Thus he and his wife are of "royal blood," and have a nice little fertile kingdom of Belgians, with an army of forty thousand, and eight thousand eight hundred horses.

Street Scenes.—By the way, they have the largest horses, and they haul the heaviest loads, I ever saw anywhere. Their wagon wheels are very low, but very heavy, with tires about one inch thick, and they carry with one horse what we do with four. Their hacks, 'buses, and other vehicles, have only one horse. Smaller ones are hauled by men and dogs geared up, which are as true to pull as any thing I ever saw. The women work in the fields, sweep the streets, and do almost any thing, even to work side by side with a big dog, pulling a cartload. All these people drink beer; many of them, the higher classes, wine, in the open air. On the streets, and almost everywhere, you see tables set, where during the day, but mostly in the evenings, thousands of them congregate to drink and chat, men, women, boys, and girls, all together, as happy as they want to be, seemingly. I have not seen a man intoxicated in the least since I have been over on this side of the ocean.

We left Brussels this morning, satisfied that we had seen all that was worth staying to see. We go on the morning train for this place, about one hundred and sixty miles. The country for some fifty miles is rich and well cultivated; generally level. In the vicinity of Liege it is more broken, and beautifully picturesque. Here are large iron manufactories; then for some distance farming on a more extensive scale, with larger fields, but still sown down in small patches of every size. There are but few hedges now to be seen. As we approach Cologne, as far as the eye can see there seems to be vast fields of grain nearly ready for harvesting. We arrive at 4 P.M., dine at 5:30, and soon are off to see the great Cathedral, which, when completed, will be the grandest Gothic church in the world. But when that will be no one can tell, as it was begun in 1248. The towers are yet unfinished, but are to be five hundred feet high. The interior is four hundred and forty-eight feet long, and one hundred and forty-nine feet broad; the south portal two hundred and thirty-four feet high. I am tired looking at cathedrals, yet they are the places to which we are told to go to see the wonders of Europe.

Sunday in Cologne.—I heard the sweet sound of music in a church near us, and arose to go again; found an audience on their knees; and as I am on my way to Rome to do as "Rome does," I knelt on the chair and took a view of what was before me—"Christ Blessing the Children."

Breakfast over, we go to church again at the grand Cathedral, to see the worship and hear the music. Then to the Church of St. Ursula, of the twelfth century, which is reputed to hold the bones of the eleven thousand virgins martyred by the Huns. These remains are worked in the walls in a species of sepulchral Mosaic, and exhibited at every available part of the church. We looked upon them with sadness—first at their sacrifice, if it be so, and then at the folly of preserving such relics in a church. But churches, music, paintings, wine and beer, seem to be the all-absorbing things here. We go through the narrow, winding streets to the English church, in a room about twenty-two feet square; seventy-six persons present, half of them our party; service one hour; then a sermon one-quarter, and we are out again with the crowd in the streets; the stores open; business going on as on other days. As we have dinner at 5:30 P.M., we go to the museum of paintings with the crowd. Some of these were very fine—more modern than any we had seen.

I judge there must be a large military force here, from the number and kind of uniforms we see everywhere; guns are firing and soldiers marching, looking quite warlike; they are a fine-looking body of men. We are now on the far-famed Rhine. One very wide iron bridge, and one pontoon bridge, supported by some forty boats, span the river. The mountains around, seen from our (Belleview) hotel, covered with fields and mansions, look sublimely beautiful; but the smoke from the chimneys of the manufactories show that the Sabbath-day is desecrated by this people; yet the church-going bells are continually sounding, calling those who are disposed to worship every hour. We, too, have had our worship in the reading-room of the hotel.

And with this I close my first Sabbath on the Continent. We go up the Rhine early in the morning.

Cologne and the Rhine.—This city is in a semicircle of about seven miles in circumference, of which the Rhine is the cord. The length of the inner line is about two miles. A native settlement of great antiquity by the Romans, into the Colonia. The Cathedral was founded in 1322. On the 24th of August, 1349, the houses of the Jews resident at Cologne were set on fire, and the greater part of these unfortunates, with their families, perished in the flames. Not for this act of cruelty, but on account of its rebellious conduct toward the archbishops, Cologne remained under the ban of the Church and the empire till 1377. The Reformation produced fresh disturbances, and in 1685 more than fourteen hundred families were forced to quit the town. The French took possession of it in 1794. Three years later it was incorporated into the French republic, and at the peace of 1814 it was made over to Prussia. The Cathedral is the great lion of the place. It is the largest Gothic church in the world. The ground on which it stands was once a Roman fortress. It is thirty-three feet above the Rhine. The first cathedral was commenced in 748; was completed in eighty-nine years, and dedicated to the Apostle St. Peter. It was destroyed by fire in 1248. The edifice is four hundred and forty feet long by one hundred and fifty wide. It has one hundred and two columns, five and a-half feet in diameter, stained-glass windows, forty-eight feet in length by sixteen feet wide. In the church are many remarkable monuments, and some very fine paintings. It is intended that the towers shall attain an elevation of five hundred and twenty-five, but when they will be finished none can tell. They are still working on it. One of the most imposing edifices is the Church of the Apostles. The artillery barracks occupy a building that was once a monastery, and the ecclesiastical seminary is in the ancient College of the Jesuits. The residence of the first and second commandants, the main guard of the city, is said to date back to the Romans. The upper portion was erected in 1262, is one hundred feet high, and is a military prison. We saw more soldiers there than we had seen anywhere, indeed a large proportion of the men were in uniform. The bridge of boats across the Rhine is one hundred and twenty-five feet long, and is a great thoroughfare between the two portions of the city. The

5*

iron railway bridge is also much frequented by pedestrians. Cologne is a place of great commercial activity. There are about two hundred wholesale and commission houses, and about seven hundred retail houses, exclusive of wine, grain, and wool dealers, and the book and print sellers. It has a number of manufactories in the city and surrounding country. Previous to its being incorporated with the Prussian territories it had only about forty thousand inhabitants; now it has over one hundred thousand, besides the little town opposite with five thousand, encompassed with fortifications. From here to Mayence is perhaps the most intensely interesting scenery, with the most thrilling history of any in the world. I shall never forget the day we spent on the steamer Emperor of Germany, going up the Rhine one hundred and twenty miles, stopping at many places. Some of these I propose to notice.

Bonn is twenty miles distant. There was a town here before the Christian era; both town and fortress were demolished by the Germans about the middle of the fourth century. Ten buildings are devoted to public worship—eight to the Catholic, one to the Protestant, and one to the Jews. The most remarkable of these is the Cathedral, which is said to owe its origin to a Church founded A.D. 316, by St. Helena. It has a bronze statue of St. Helena, cast in Italy, in the seventeenth century. The present edifice dates from the twelfth century. It has four towers, a temple of Mars having been near it. The most remarkable building here is the *University*, one thousand two hundred and eighty feet in length (about a quarter of a mile), with three hundred lecture-rooms and halls, with a library of one hundred thousand volumes. In an old house with pointed gable, on the Rhine street, Beethoven was born, 1776, and passed the years of his youth there. He died in 1827.

Siegberg is a town of two thousand inhabitants. Here lived the king whose daughter married Arminias, who conquered the Romans. Here is a large lunatic asylum, two hundred feet high, and in a romantic, healthy place.

Godesberg is a lovely place in summer, with pleasure-grounds. Here was a Roman watch-tower; near the tower is a chapel of the seventeenth century. A short distance above is a monument erected in honor of those who fell at the passage of the Rhine, in 1814, and is one of the most celebrated in Europe. There are mountains some twelve hundred to thirteen hundred feet high, with romantic scenery, and an old castle, once a place of much interest.

Remagen has three thousand inhabitants. The market frontier is composed of relics of antiquity. Then comes Erpel, with twelve hundred. Then on to Linz, with two thousand seven hundred. Here are slate factories, iron-works, and other manufactories. The place is very ancient. Sinzig, with two thousand, is one of the most ancient places on the Rhine, having been a Roman stronghold. The father of Charlemagne created several documents that are still extant at this place. A monastic nunnery was erected, and a chapel by the Empress Helena. An ancient church here is built in the form of a cross.

According to the altarpiece it was here that Constantine beheld the cross in the heavens; of this nothing is certainly known. A curiosity is exhibited here of a Christian mummy, to which the name of Vogt has been given. In former years it used to be carried about in the carnival procession, decked out in tawdry finery. The French carried it to Paris, when it was returned in 1815. All along the banks are towns, villages, and old castles on the mountains, in glowing grandeur, demonstrating that this country has been the most important strategic point in Europe for many ages. There Julius Cesar commanded his legions, and here Napoleon I. moved with such alacrity as to astonish and bewilder his enemies, as well as conquer them.

Andreneah is a town of three thousand five hundred inhabitants. This place is very ancient, even fifty or sixty years before Christ. Seven fairs are held here annually. Fine yards abound here, extending at times from the water's edge to the summits of the mountains.

Lake of Laach, the crater of an extinct volcano, the termination of whose activity is supposed to be four thousand years ago. The lava-pits are upward of two hundred feet deep, and the thickness varies from three hundred to four hundred feet deep. The lake has twelve hundred and thirty-five acres, and is two hundred and eighteen feet deep. Here was an old castle and monastery. A fine church has been restored by the King of Prussia.

Newied has six thousand two hundred inhabitants, including all professions. The town is divided into twenty-five blocks, five streets lengthwise, with four cross streets. The palace in which the prince resides was completed in 1722, and connects with the castle garden, in which is the residence of the celebrated Brazilian traveler, Prince Maximilian, and of his brother, Prince Charles, and here also are the meeting-houses of American preachers, and a synagogue.

Coblence owes its origin to a Roman fort. It retained its sovereignty for over eight hundred years. The French emigrants made it their head-quarters in 1791. The town was occupied by the Republican troops, and was soon after incorporated in the French territories, in the beginning of 1814, and by the Congress of Vienna made over to Prussia, together with the Rhine Province. At that time the population was seven hundred; it now numbers two thousand eight hundred, exclusive of five thousand soldiers distributed among the various fortifications. There are eight Catholic churches, one Protestant, and one synagogue. The Electoral Palace was built between 1778 and 1781. It is five hundred and twenty-five feet in length, and three stories high; that portion of the edifice which projects in a horse-shoe form, has a longitudinal diameter of three hundred and eighty-five feet. The apartments recently fitted up for the reception of royalty are of handsome proportions, and delightfully situated toward the Rhine.

St. Goar, with a population of one thousand seven hundred, owes its name to him who settled here in 575 to inculcate the doctrines of Christianity. The cell once inhabited by the holy man became a church of pilgrimage, out of the ruins of which the present Protestant church arose in 1469. In it there are several monuments.

Oberwesel contains three thousand three hundred inhabitants. The ancient town wall was three thousand four hundred and seventy-five feet in length. The rotund battlements, gates, and turrets, present a very picturesque subject. An extensive castle is still in existence, which belongs to Prince Albert of Prussia.

Caub, with two thousand inhabitants, at the foot of a steep hill, on a rocky projection of which is situated a castle. The town took its rise in the eighth century. In 1805 this castle was in a good state of preservation, but Napoleon, in his passage over the Rhine, having been saluted by cannon-balls from its battlements, gave orders for its immediate demolition.

Just above, at Bacharack, is a small ancient town of one thousand five hundred souls. Here is a castle now owned by the Queen of Prussia. Its walls are fourteen feet thick. During the thirty years' war it was taken eight times. Here also is a Protestant church which formerly belonged to the Knight Templars. It was built in the tenth century, and is in a very remarkable style. There are many other places of interest, with castles away up on the mountains, some of them having been there over two thousand years. Take this country altogether, it is the most romantic, the most sublime and magnificent, there is in the world. It possesses more historic interest than any other. The most powerful nations of the world have here met in mortal combat for its possession. For thousands of years it has been the scene of the most fearful conflicts, while the waters of this classic river have been crimsoned with the blood of thousands who live in the annals of history, and whose names have been handed down to posterity as the world's conquerors.

No one who visits Europe should fail to see the Rhine. They will be amply compensated for the time and money expended viewing these time-honored places, where the world's heroes have performed deeds of valor along the banks of this most interesting of all the rivers of Europe.

From Cologne to Munich—The Rhine and its marvelous beauties—How railroads are run in Germany—The people and their habits—A day in Mayence—Guttenberg's statue—Munich and its attractions, etc., etc.

Munich, Bavaria, July 15, 1873.

My last was written from Cologne, where we spent the Sabbath. It is the capital of the province, and the first walled city we have seen. It is in the form of a crescent, about seven miles around it. It was a Roman colony, and takes its name from that fact. During the middle ages, and for a long period, it was one of the most populous cities in Europe.

Monday morning, after visiting the barracks and seeing the soldiers parade—among them Bismarck's regiment of cavalry—we cross on the pontoon bridge, and take the finest boat on the river, called the Emperor of Germany, for Mayence, some one hundred and twenty miles above, at the head of steam navigation. I have heard much of the scenery of the Rhine, but it far exceeded my most sanguine expectations. For about twenty miles, to Bonn, the land is low, with some fine buildings seen in the distance; but after we pass that place, the mountains on either side, rising higher as we ascend, present the beautifully grand, not excelled, perhaps, in the world. For a while we were inclined to think the scenery of the Hudson equally grand, but soon every one acknowledged there was no comparison. There is an amphitheater of undulating heights, with imposing piles of old citadels, some of them dating back before the Christian era, that bewilders the imagination. The bold summits and picturesque outlines, and the luxuriant, vine-clad, terraced hills, utterly defy description—so I shall not attempt it. Just to think of some of these old forts, which have been here since the days of Julius Cesar, and the countless millions who have lived, fought, and died along these banks, and see the numerous old castles, "grand, gloomy, and peculiar," upon the summits of those mountains overlooking the Rhine, and then think of Napoleon's rapid marches across this stream, affords food for thought more impressive than any I have ever seen. Some of these old castles have been rebuilt, and are now owned and occupied as summer resorts for royalty. We spent the day on deck, with our guides, glasses, and photographs procured at Cologne, viewing what has been for more than two thousand years one of the most important strategic countries on the globe.

We arrived at Mayence after nightfall; sleep awhile, and as we have but a few hours there, we are off early to see the city, which is lost in a haze of antiquity. It was once a Roman fortress, and is now strongly fortified. The town and fortress were surrendered to the allies on the 14th of May, 1814. Its population is now only forty-four thousand, and a garrison of eight thousand Prussian soldiers.

As usual, the old cathedral is the first object of interest. There is a gloomy grandeur about it. The red sandstone of which it is built is yielding to time's influence, and they are repairing a portion of it. It was founded in the eighth century, and it is said that no church in Germany contains so many monuments and epitaphs as this.

But I am now out with these, and turn away from them to one of far more interest to me than any that I have ever seen. It is the monument to Guttenberg, the inventor of that art by which my hasty scribbling, while my company is reposing in the arms of Morpheus, can be deciphered by you, perhaps, Mr. Printer, and given to the readers of the *Avalanche* some of these mornings. Yes, here he was born, here he was brought up—the house still stands near the hotel—and here he invented "the art preservative of all arts." I felt a profound veneration for the man as I gazed upon the statue, and transcribed the following inscription from his monument: "An art which neither the Greeks nor the Romans understood, the genius of a German found out; and whatsoever the ancients knew, and the moderns know, is not for himself, but for all mankind." On one side of the monument is a printing-press, and the discoverer reading the proof; on the other this: "The citizens of Mayence erected this monument to Guttenberg by money collected throughout Europe. Erected in 1837."

We visited the vegetable market, which, as usual,

is attended only by women, out in the open air, and some other places; but soon we are off for Munich, at 10 o'clock.

The country is variegated for the two hundred and seventy-nine miles we travel to-day, all in a fine state of cultivation. Here we see orchards, vineyards, old castles, modern fortifications, rifle-pits, etc.—all looks warlike. The women seem to do the work, the men the fighting. Along the Danube the land is very fertile.

My sheet is full, and I will suspend until I can see something of this capital before I conclude.

Wednesday.—We slept a few hours in a regular German bed, taking off the feather-bed used as a covering. We have a fine view of a park and monuments from our windows.

Having a few moments, I wish to say a few words about the railroads of this country. I have seen none of wider gauge than four feet; that seems to be the width of all. They run about fifteen to twenty-five miles per hour, and make but few stops. Their carriages are English style, for six or eight persons. Every mile there is a telegraph office, and a man always on duty. As the train passes he raises his hand to his hat to let it be known that all is right ahead.

Sights in Munich.—At 7 o'clock A.M., soon after breakfast, we went out, with a guide, to see all we could in one day. First, to the collection of statuary from various countries, ancient and modern, embracing many men who have distinguished themselves by their works in history. A mere mention of their names would be tedious. The most magnificent buildings have been erected for them, finished off in the most exquisite modern style of architecture, and decorations of the most gorgeous character.

We then go to the public galleries of paintings.

In the first room we find a large painting of Maximilian Emmanuel I.; Maximilian, King of Bavaria; Theodor, and others. "The Crucifixion," "Taking Down from the Cross," etc., in several pictures, were very impressive. "The Apostles," as it is supposed they looked, are painted in the most life-like manner. "John's Revelations," in the Isle of Patmos, with the river and tree of life, and the hanging fruits, were very fine. The "Last Judgment" was terrific. There were some fifteen hundred, in perhaps twenty or more rooms, selected from the finest paintings in the world, collected here. This being the capital of Bavaria, King Louis I. has made a thousand costly improvements, and it now rivals Paris and Rome as a repository of art.

The next place we visit is the Royal Palace. It is open for visitors from 11 to 12 o'clock; but our party, being from America, were permitted to go after the crowd had gone, and look through all the apartments, ancient as well as modern. The king being absent, we went into his private as well as his public State apartments. The great Splendor Throne room, with its noble historic bronze statues, fine pictures and frescoes, is said to be one of the finest collections in the world. In the ancient portion were many things that have had their day, and live only in the history of the past. There is the bed of Charles VII., which bed cost over three hundred thousand dollars, currency. The tapestry took forty persons fifteen years to make it. The ball-room is one hundred and ten feet long by seventy-three broad, and is lighted by about a thousand candles. Such splendor dazzles the populace, and makes them venerate royalty. Napoleon spent one day here, when he suffered himself to acknowledge the power of the Pope. He would not sleep on that fine bed, but slept on his own camp-bed in the palace. There are the portraits of thirty-six of the most beautiful women of Bavaria here. This is the first time we have ever seen inside of royalty, and I must confess that when the people have been brought up to it, there is something fascinating about it to them.

These people take great pride in their bronze statue manufactory. After having seen so many of them, we felt like seeing them made, and, after spending considerable time at the palace, we took carriages and went to see them. The model of Washington, that stands in Washington Square, New York, was the first that attracted our attention. There were quite a number of American models—Benton, Peabody, and others whom we honor. They say the largest one ever made is the statue of "Bavaria," sixty-six feet high. A lion of like proportions stands by her side. A bird has its nest in his mouth. Some three or four of us went up inside the statue. Others were there, and seven of us could stand in the neck. I felt like the author of a guide-book, advising others to keep out of it. Munich is the best-built city we have seen on the Continent. The streets in the new part are wide, and straight, with many public buildings, and grounds tastefully laid off, and finely improved. It has a population of over two hundred thousand, and, though it has a king, is a part of the German Empire.

The people are intelligent, refined, and (as all Germans are) fond of music. While I write a band of one hundred instruments is playing not far away. I think they have about ten thousand soldiers here. They are seen wherever you go—finely uniformed, well equipped for their profession of arms. There is a beautiful little river running through the city, the Aar, affording immense water-power. We leave in the morning for Vienna, where we hope to meet friends from our Bluff City.

From Munich to Vienna—Notes by the wayside—The Austrian Capital and the Exposition—Sights and improvements—Condition of the people of Europe—Something for Americans to think about—Some of the features of the great Exposition—Sights and sight-seers.

VIENNA, Austria, July 19, 1873.

We left Munich Thursday morning for this place. The country through which we passed was more diversified than any we have seen in Europe. For some fifty miles it was level, covered with a luxuriant crop of grass and grain, with vegetables. The people live in villages, and some of them must go miles to their work; one church usually in a village, all of olden-time appearance. At the railroad-stations there are buildings of more modern style. We pass over, or rather through, a mountainous region. Some of them very high; green vegetation all over them, while on the northern sides the snow, glistening in the sunshine, presented a beautiful picture for the artist, and might have inspired the spirit of poetry in our youthful days.

Wayside Notes.—We pass through some timbered country, and then emerge again into fields of grain as far as we can see, ripe to the harvest. We see men at work in the fields to-day. The women with their broad sun-bonnets are there too, in great numbers, at work. A rich scene occurred at a town where we passed from Bavaria into Austria. Our conductor thought he had made arrangements to go through, near three hundred miles, without change of cars. We stopped for dinner on the line (remember every one must take care of their own baggage in the cars, holding, some three, others six persons). They have, as usual, every thing in the car. About the time they got fairly at gobbling down a hasty lunch, it was announced we must change cars. A rush was made for them by a party of fifty of our company about half of them women;

just at that time the train rolls off. It was amusing to see the effect produced: believing all would come out right, I enjoyed it hugely. After awhile the train returned, and all the baggage safe, and we are off on Austrian cars.

In Vienna.—We got here about 11 P.M., found conveyances waiting for us, and soon we are going at a rapid speed, some miles, it seemed, to our magnificent Hotel de France.

Early in the morning we are off for the Exposition, by street-car. It is some two and a-half to three miles, through very wide streets some distance —the boulevards—then across the river, and in a magnificent park, of about one thousand acres, we find the World's Fair. There is no use in attempting to describe it. This you have doubtless seen by others who had time that I have not. Just imagine the finest stores with their finest things; the most extensive manufactories with their most costly fabrics, and the machinery running by which they are made, actually at work in the building; the most valuable, as well as the most useful metals; the finest sculpture and paintings from Italy and other nations. In a word, the richest, rarest, and the most remarkable productions in material and manufactured goods that the nations of earth could produce are here on exhibition. Volumes might be filled with descriptions of them.

The buildings are the largest of the kind that have ever been built. They exceed by far all previous ones at London and Paris. Having visited the Crystal Palace the last day I spent in London, I should judge these buildings contain several times the space that does. That is mainly of glass, this is mostly of iron. This is one very long building, with a central dome. The main gallery, or the nave, is intersected in the middle in two equal parts by the rotunda, which is the greatest circumference that has ever been covered without pillars. We went up on that and had a splendid view of the city and the surroundings. I stepped it, and found its circumference over a quarter of a mile. In the distance can be seen the battle-ground of Wagram, where Napoleon fought one of his greatest battles. The charge of McDonald, with some sixteen thousand men, by which he lost all but one thousand, is one of the most remarkable in the history of this wonderful man. From this point we have a bird's-eye view of the nations of earth, as their houses are arranged around the building. I am tired of ancient warlike things. What is the present condition of this people is a more important and practical question than to recount their deeds of valor, or look at the monuments intended to perpetuate their memory. I think they are a more intellectual people than any we have seen since we left England, but morally I think they are deeply degraded. The first thing that I saw as I looked out of my window on Sabbath-morning was men turning a windlass to elevate the brick upon a large building near at hand. The next was eight women making up mortar, some conveying it up in tubs for the masons, or rather emptying it in something to be carried up, and thus they have toiled on, desecrating the Sabbath, which seems to be only a holiday at every place we have been in Europe. No legal Sabbath is recognized anywhere that we have seen. They may have a religion, but I think it is mainly of imposing forms, and to us unmeaning ceremonials, while the practical duties of morality and religion are ignored by the masses of the people of all classes.

From all I can learn we have but few emigrants from Austria to the United States. I think the laboring classes know but little of America, nor do I think their rulers intend that they shall learn much, only to toil on to keep up royalty and superstition.

The introduction of railroads, and the number of American travelers, will, I think, have a tendency to turn the attention of this people to the New World, about which, I think, they now hear but little.

The women have a hard time of it all over this country. They labor hard in the cities, and do most of the work in the country. One reason, no doubt, is that so many men are required to keep their regular armies.

This is the first Sabbath that we have not attended religious service several times. We knew of no place where any worship would be held that we could understand, so we made a virtue of necessity, and have made it a day of rest, which we all very much needed, as we have had a laborious week since we left Cologne. The last two days, for twelve consecutive hours each, we have been going through and around the Exposition, and we were tired down, and worn out with it.

To-morrow morning, at five o'clock, we start for Venice, to travel all day and night, to see the water city. As our traveling there will be along the streets, in gondolas, we anticipate some repose. I will say just here, that whoever comes to Europe expecting a pleasure trip will be disappointed. It is a hard task to perform, which I expected, but we have fine health, and are able to eat all they give us at the hotels, and more too. There has been quite a falling off, from our four or five meals a day on the ship, down to two, and they but small affairs at best. Labor is very cheap here, so they can afford to keep waiters for near two hours to hand around, in some ten or twelve courses, what a hungry man could eat in as many minutes; but after all we may learn an important lesson—to eat slowly. I believe most of these people live at the restaurants and beer-gardens. Men and women spend their time there promiscuously, and seem to enjoy themselves hugely, socially, around the thousands of tables we see all over the city. The water here is not considered healthy, and we have to drink beer, too, in self-defense.

Happy America.—I think we will all appreciate and love our own land much better than we have done after this tour in Europe. I have now scribbled my thoughts just as they came up, without the slightest regard to manner or matter. If there is any thing that will interest your readers you can give it to them, only give it in broken doses. As it is near dinner-time, 6:30 P.M., and my sheet is full, I will close for the present.

VIENNA, July 20, 1873.

The Austrian Capital.—Vienna is the capital city, and residence of the Austrian Emperor. It is situated in a wide valley, surrounded by hills, on the southern arm of the Danube. The small River "Wien" runs through it, which has fifteen bridges, and Danube Canal has eight, connecting the city.

Vienna has improved faster in the last few years than any city in Europe. In 1857, with its nine districts, it only numbered fifty-six thousand; in 1864 there were five hundred and sixty thousand six hundred. This rapid increase has been owing to the fact that previously it had been kept within the fortifications. In 1858 these limits were removed, and now the population is nine hundred and one thousand three hundred and eighty. It is the best-built city we have visited in Europe. The new portion has wide streets, and extensive boulevards, but in the old part the streets are like all others we have seen, narrow and crooked. The buildings are very large, nearly all stone, or stuccoed like it, presenting a beautiful white appearance. The suburbs have been fortified with the still-existing wall of

1704. The French occupied it twice for a short time, in 1806 and 1809. The celebrated Congress of 1814 and 1815 was held here. The year 1848 brought along with it the insurrection, and ended with the occupying of the city in October.

The present emperor, Francis Joseph, has done much for the city. He has taken a deep interest in the Exposition. He gave his private gardens to be used for the houses of the nations, on the outskirts, and his eight fountains and lakes add much to the beauty of the surroundings. We had the pleasure of seeing him yesterday without the trappings of royalty. He is a tall, spare-built man, keen eye, quick movements physically, and, I "guess," mentally; well dressed, in a kind of loose sacque coat, with sword, cap, and spurs. Though taller, he reminded me in his appearance and movements of A. T. Stewart, of New York. We did not seek to enter his palace, but we looked around it and saw inside, but it does not begin to compare with the King of Bavaria's Palace. Notwithstanding the rapid increase in the population of this city, and the vast improvement in the new portion of it, making it one of the handsomest cities of Europe, it is far less powerful as a capital and political center than it was before the commencement of those late revolutions which have freed Italy and concentrated Northern Germany. They have about twelve thousand soldiers in the city. It must, however, be regarded as among the most noted cities, having been founded by the Romans, and afterward the Capital of the Eastern Province of Charlemagne, seat of the Court of Hungary in 1484, and soon after, to this time, the Capital of Austria. The present emperor has expended a vast amount of money upon it to make it the rival of Paris. It has a circumference of some sixteen miles, including the new portion. Its imperial library is said to contain four hundred thousand volumes, from twenty thousand to thirty thousand manuscripts, and over three hundred thousand engravings. They boast of St. Stephen's Cathedral, of the twelfth century, with a splendid spire, only second in height to that of Strasburg. We visited St. Peter's Church, modeled after St. Peter's of Rome, in which we expect to worship next Sabbath. Here we saw the representation of Peter and the cock which crowed when he denied his Master. There are here laid away two skeletons, one of them a pope, in the most gorgeous array of glittering diamonds I ever saw. What folly to keep such relics as these in their churches! The Burg, or Imperial Palace of Austria, is an irregular building, dating and remodeled from the thirteenth century.

We saw the house in which the wife of Napoleon lived whom he married after the divorce of Josephine. This place seemed to have been an unfortunate one for the French Emperor. Here is where his son, the Duke of Reichstadt, died, in this church he is buried, and the city in which the Congress was held that terminated his eventful career.

The imperial arsenal contains extensive barracks, and a very large collection of arms, ancient and modern, in Europe. We went round to see the different nations, living as they do in their countries, and at work making the things they have on exhibition. This was very interesting, to see the Egyptians, Chinese, Japanese, Siamese, Portuguese, Russians, Grecians, Turks, Persians, and how many others I can't tell, as they are seen in their own lands. This was to me intensely interesting. But I must go back into the Exposition building, entering as we do at the west end. The side gallery on the right belongs to the United States, as well as the open court abutting upon it. This was originally ceded to England, but she generously ceded it to us. I am sorry to say we are so poorly represented. I presume our people inferred it would not pay to come so far to exhibit what they had to show, and they declined coming. The sewing-machine men are well represented here. I observed one bale of fine cotton from Memphis, by Messrs. J. W. Jefferson & Co. There was also cotton from other Southern States.

A quarter of the first side gallery belongs to England, the rest to South America. You are now in the third main gallery, or nave, which, with the second and third transverse galleries, and open courts lying between, belongs to England. These are well filled with the products of old England, of which her people may well be proud, in many respects.

Next comes France, which extends in the nave from the third transverse gallery to well-nigh the sixth. She has three covered courts between the third and sixth, and the open court between the third and fourth transverse galleries on the south. Here is a grand display, surpassing all others, I think, in some respects.

The fifth gallery on the south belongs to Switzerland, as well as the court touching upon it.

The sixth transverse gallery belongs to Italy, as well as the open court on the south side.

Belgium comes next, occupying the portion of the nave between the sixth and seventh transverse galleries. The space in the nave is occupied by Holland and Sweden.

You have now reached the central part of the building, surrounding the rotunda. It forms a square, and four galleries all around. Two galleries are here allotted to Germany, as she occupies the center of Europe. Next comes Austria, which has the eastern gallery of the central square, and the next three transepts, with the eight courts lying between them, of which seven are covered. Hungary has the next transverse gallery, with the space in the nave intersecting it. Russia has the eleventh and twelfth galleries; Greece the thirteenth. The southern portion is divided between Tunis, Morocco, and Egypt, while the nave and half of the northern portion belong to Turkey, Persia, Central Asia, and Roumania. The last gallery, forming the eastern *façade* and entrance, is shared by Turkey in the south, China, Japan, and Siam, in the north. The same geographical arrangement has likewise been adopted in the machinery-hall. The other countries that could not be accommodated in the hall have two buildings allotted to them, on the right and left of the hall. Denmark, Sweden, Norway, and Prussia, have each one hall; Germany, Austria, and France have each two, Hungary one.

Take it altogether, it no doubt far exceeds any thing that has ever been. The buildings, covering one hundred and seventy acres of ground, and the vast amount and variety of things on exhibition, come up to, and far exceed, the expectations of those who have visited it, but it has been, financially, a terrible failure. It has not attracted the world's attention as was expected. Millions of money have been expended that will prove a loss to the projectors, and those associated with them. The policy pursued at first has kept thousands away, and shortened the visits of those who came. Extortion is realized everywhere, in and out of the Exposition. The result is that not one-half of the people have been here that were expected, had a different policy been pursued. The machinery part of the Exposition is all that could be desired. There you see, as nowhere else you can, how hundreds of things are made, all in a few hours. My eight pages are filled, and I have scarcely began to tell of this world's fair at Vienna.

CHAPTER VIII.

Letters from Rev. T. W. Hooper, of Lynchburg, Virginia, written for the *News*.

MUNICH, July 29, 1873.

I WROTE you last at Lucerne. While I was writing, quite a number of our excursionists had gone up the Rhigi to see the sun set and rise. Some fortunately returned that evening, having made the ascent on that famous railroad where the cars are moved by a central rail and cogs. They were delighted with their experience; but those who staid all night were inclosed in a thunder-storm before night, and the next morning came down as wet and woe-begone a looking set of sight-seers as I ever met with. The view from the mountain, on a clear day (which comes once a month), is said to be magnificent; but I had climbed too many mountains in my day to pay seven francs for a ride to the top of one that does not compare with the Peaks, or Salt Pond, for variety or extent.

I should like to have gone down the lake of four Cantons, to see the Chapel of William Tell; but there has been some question of late as to whether this whole story of Tell and the apple is not a myth from the poetic brain of Schiller, and as they do not stop the boat long enough to see the bow and arrow, I contented myself with a splendid bath in the classic waters of the lake, and a sound sleep to the rippling music of its rushing outlet, which here forms the river Bouss.

That night, too, we had a pleasant chat and comparison of notes with Dr. Witherspoon, who was on his way, *via* St. Bernard, Mt. Blanc, and Chamounix, to Geneva, where he expected to rejoin his "Section," on their return from Italy, where they are scorching at this time. I never saw any one improve as he has done since he heard that he was not elected professor at the University of Virginia, and can now accept the charge of the Tabb-street Church, in Petersburg. I am sorry for the University, but glad for him and for the Cockade City.

The next morning, about 11 o'clock, we took the cars, and, after a pleasant ride of two hours, found ourselves at the quaint old town of Zurich. In olden days this was famous as the home of Zwingle, the compeer of Luther and of Calvin; and it was interesting to see the old cathedral, where he fought so gallantly the pretensions and follies of a bloated and beastly hierarchy, until it tottered and fell before the solid blows of Scripture and of logic. The town is now famous for the educational interests, which make it a kind of literary center for Switzerland, and also for its manufactories of machinery and of silk. We saw some samples of silk at sixty cents and one dollar per yard; but there was such a diversity of opinion among "the marms" as to its quality, that I would not indulge. I did, however, take a splendid boat-ride on the lake, with J. T. and another young man as oarsmen, while I handled the ropes and steered. That night, too, we had some fine music in a beer-garden on the lake, from about thirty performers, with all kinds of instruments. The admission fee was twenty cents, and the music superior to one of our first-class concerts.

The next morning we took the cars again, and in two or three hours reached Schaffhausen, and put up at the magnificent Switserhoff, on a lofty eminence overlooking the famous Falls of the Rhine, and in full view of the Black Forest. I walked that evening near its dark shadows, while the roar of the adjacent cataract sounded like distant thunder—until I got the blues, and was deathly homesick.

The next morning we left this miniature Niagara, with all its sylvan beauties of park and flowers, and its grand old castle on the hill, railroad-bridge of stone, and small antiquated town in the distance, and at 12 o'clock we reached Bomanshorn, where we took the steamer on Lake Constance, and marched at once to our dinner-table, where we eat most heartily of our Frenchy viands on deck, and watched the spires of Constance, where the Catholics held, in the dark days of their power, that remarkable Council which deposed three Popes, and elected another, and burned John Huss, who had more religion than all the Council put together. Talk about Servetus and Calvin! Well, I am not on a sermon, and will only say, if you want to be confirmed in Protestantism, just come over here; revive the struggles of the great Reformers, and look upon the miserable mummery and degraded ignorance of those who are still tortured with this spiritual rack, that lacerates and murders the soul.

That night we reached Munich in safety, after a long, hot ride on the cars, from Lindeau, and were pleasantly quartered at the Belle Vue Hotel. As to Sunday, the less said about that in a secular paper the better. I can only say I hope I shall never be compelled to spend such another.

Monday we visited the most remarkable paintings in existence. They are the choicest originals of Raphael, Rubens, Titian, and Vandyke. I had no conception what sermons could be preached from canvas. "The Perdition of Lost Souls," and "The Last Judgment," are two of the masterpieces of Rubens, and are the strongest appeals to religious passion that ever entered the brain of an artist.

There were hundreds there, which would demand hours of study, and give months of exquisite pleasure; but these two struck my fancy and riveted my gaze, as no other paintings have ever done, before or since. I should like to visit them again; but time is precious with us, and we scarcely had time to see through the Glyptoths, and look at the statues, ancient and modern, when the closing hour arrived.

We then strolled around to the palaces, old and new; admired the bronze statues in the streets; saw the house of Mozart, etc., etc., and that evening we took a ride, first to the Statue of Bavaria. This is the largest bronze cast in the world, and is composed of cannon captured in their various wars. It is sixty-nine feet high above the pedestal, and is in the form of a colossal woman, in the head of which six of our party sat down without crowding. "How is that for high?" was the spontaneous exclamation of more than one beholder. We then took a drive through the city to the English Garden, which seems to be a kind of royal park, with fine old trees, and about the center of it is "Iser rolling rapidly." But we rolled more rapidly than Iser on our return; for a sudden storm had struck us, driving the sand into our eyes, and nearly upsetting our carriage, and we just had time to reach the hotel, when a fearful thunder-storm, with torrents of rain, came crashing and pouring all around us.

We leave here for Vienna, where I will write again.

VIENNA, July 31, 1873.

I thought we had seen some noisy places in the course of our travels, but this certainly "removes the dilapidated linen from the diminutive tree," as they used to say when I was a boy. I went to bed at 9 o'clock last-night, thoroughly jaded, and was aroused half a dozen times by the racket of wheels below me. I supposed at first it was the breaking up of some entertainment; but if so, they must have kept some of them going all night. We are most delightfully located, in a splendidly-furnished room on the fourth floor of the Hotel de France, and from my window I have been looking down upon the street called Maria Theresa. I have seen the oddest mixture of sights that were ever accumulated in the same space. I saw them relieving the guard with a whole brigade of infantry, with blue pants and white coats. They marched in perfect order, and, having no guns, they kept time with the arms as well as feet, the right arm swinging time with the left foot. I have also seen lots of women pulling their little wagons to market—a woman on one side the pole and a dog on the other, and no child's play for either. In Glasgow I saw three horses hitched abreast to their omnibuses, which will carry as many on the outside as within—the center horse in shafts. Here, in Munich, I see one horse hitched to a wagon with a pole instead of shafts. In Scotland I also noticed that the plows are made of iron, in all their parts—handles, beam, and moldboard—but here they are made of wood, pointed with iron, and are hitched on to a two-wheeled vehicle. But, everywhere on the Continent, the men seem to do the talking, and the women do the work. Sometimes, in cutting hay, a woman will lead the row. They wear very short blue cotton dresses, of scant pattern; but little girls are bundled up with dresses that nearly touch the ground. We found them in the midst of the wheat-harvest in Bavaria and Austria, and the crop is a splendid one; but I have neither seen a "reaper" nor an old-fashioned cradle. They prepare the bands before leaving the house, and one of our hands will bind as much as three of theirs, while one of McCormick's reapers would in one day cut down all that grows on a dozen of their farms. But still the people manage to live, and look as brown and hardy as pine-knots. If they would just get an education and speak English, I would like to talk to some of them; but I will not degrade my mother-tongue by learning their Dutch lingo.

Vienna is a beautiful city, and comes nearer to Paris in the way of boulvards and buildings than any city we have seen. From the number and magnificence of its churches, it would seem that piety ought to be prevalent; but I am afraid the whole virtue of the place might be compressed into Buzzard's Roost, and still leave Brother H. a congregation at Sandy Hook that needed the gospel. But priests are plentiful, and so is money—such as they use, for it takes one hundred kreutzers to make fifty cents—and some people expect to get prayed to heaven in Latin for a small amount of money. Yesterday we spent at the Exposition, and, as one of the party said, "it is no slouch of a show." Indeed, it is one of the grandest exhibitions that was ever seen, and I might as well attempt to paint a Lynchburg sunset as to try to picture it. I suppose you could easily put all our churches in the central dome, with the Court-house on top, and then crowd around them all the goods sold in our goodly city for the last five years, and there would still be room for the ancient Market-house, Green's oyster saloon, Fort Snacks, and Mr. Phat-man as salesman. In some of the little transepts to the side I saw carpets enough to make Bridge street smooth enough for a carriage to run on, and in others silks enough to keep all of Guggenheimer's clerks busy measuring for a whole week, even without talking. In others I saw sole-leather enough to stock Seabury's and De Witt's until their great-grandchildren are as old as Mr. Washington was when George cut the apple-tree. In others there was perfumery enough to scent the Market street, and make it smell like Latham's drug store, and in others glass-ware enough to stock Kinnier's and Boyd's, if they were to extend their stores beyond the Watering Branch.

In the mechanical department I saw machines from all parts of the world, and for every conceivable purpose. I think there must be locomotives enough on hand to stock the great A., M. & O. R. R., or that other road that passes through—with a name too long for this paper to hold. There are also water-wheels, printing-presses, pumps, spinning and weaving-machines—all at work, and producing a clatter equal to a big break at Friend's warehouse, with an organ and monkey attachment on the outside, at dinner-time.

As to the crowds that assemble there—just put the Tower of Babel and Pentecost together, and you may form some conception of the confusion of tongue, and of nationalities, too, that is collected in that wonderful place. "All the world and his wife," say some, are to be found there; but I did not *find* them. I looked for the agent of the "Occidental," and "Lone Jack," and "Old Sledge;" but while the tobacco is all there, looking as bright and as yellow as it does at home, there was no agent to be found, and so I shall have to put up with the stumps of old cigars cut up into smoking-tobacco. I might smoke cigars, for they are remarkably cheap and good; but I want a meerschaum pipe, and want to color it on the way back home, and I want to color it with nothing less than Lynchburg smoking-tobacco; for, say what you will, we can beat the world on that, as this Exposition will decide.

I have had many things to remind me of home; but these brands of tobacco seemed to bring back the dear old city more strikingly than any thing else. I had parted from Tanner on going out, and as soon as I met him, he excitedly asked: "Did you see the Lone Jack?" "Yes," said I, "and the Occidental." Another word, say "Highlander," and we would both of us have burst into tears, as those Norfolk refugees did during the war in Liberty. They met unexpectedly at court, and began to talk about home. One mentioned "soft crabs," and the other "oysters," one "hog-fish," and the other "spots;" and so they went on, until the memories of the good old epicurean days were too much for them, and they sat and wept in silent sorrow over the "joys they had tasted." Jack and I only escaped a similar fate by dropping the subject.

I have gotten to be a real "Old Mortality" since I came to this Old World, and to-day I went to visit the graves of Maria Theresa, Joseph, and others, who have given name to and made the history of Austria. The fact is, that with the exception of Queen Victoria, the great of these famous countries are in the dust, and you must go to the tomb if you would derive that inspiration which travel is expected to impart. We find here no Napoleon nor Wellington, no Frederick nor Ludwig, to occupy the places made vacant by the death of those whose names are so familiar to us in America. "Peace hath her victories," etc.; but when we come all the way to Europe to see strange things, we are not interested so much in these peaceful scenes, but want to look upon the emblems of valor and the trophies of victory that have made history readable, and heroes familiar to our memories. It may be one more evidence of the depravity of human nature, but it is none the less true, that we look with more pleasure upon a battle-field than upon a harvest—with more interest upon some old castle, where thousands have been slain, than upon a modern palace or chateau, where a noble family now live in peace and plenty.

We are all the time looking for celebrities, and,

like the Floyd man who would n't eat buckwheat-cakes in Christiansburg because he had "enough of them victuals at home," so we will not deign to look upon the most beautiful valleys, or most towering mountain, because we have all that in America, and came here to see something that we do n't have there.

By the way, I have been disappointed in these rivers. "The beautiful blue Danube" is as muddy as "Blackwater," only the mud is whitish, and "Iser rolling rapidly" will not compare with James River at Balcony Falls, while "New River" has more romantic scenery than the Tweed, and York River is more beautiful than the Thames.

But I must close. Several Englishmen have been imprisoned for making slighting and invidious comparisons, and somebody might get hold of this and report me.

MAYENCE, August 4, 1873.

"Westward the star of Empire takes its way," and I am happy to say that this is the star by which my course is directed. Yes, "We're on our journey home;" "Home Again," "Home, Sweet Home," and every other song that has "home" in it, has been ringing in my ears with a merry chime ever since I left Vienna. Seeing sights in a foreign land is pleasant to read about, and a pleasant pastime for a season, but a man gets tired of it, and it certainly would take a first-class sensation to disturb my equanimity after all that I have seen. Miles of pictures, and whole acres of statues, together with innumerable cemeteries and vaults where earth's greatest heroes are "resting in royalty," as Dr. Armistead used to say about Dives, are enough to be compressed into one or two months, in the way of art. And as to nature, we have seen "Loughs," in Ireland, "Lochs," in Scotland, and "Lacs," in Switzerland, which have inspired such men as Moore, and Scott, and Byron, and Rousseau, and Schiller, and the mountains we have climbed are associated with the names of Cromwell and Richard, Hannibal and Cesar, Charlemagne and Bonaparte.

As to palaces, we have walked in the gilded hall where roamed such characters as Mary Queen of Scots, Douglas, Richard, and Elizabeth. We have seen the beds of the First and Third Napoleon, as well as those of Queen Mary and Maria Theresa; have trod on Mosaic pavement, and walked through marble halls that once echoed with whispers of intrigue that have set all Europe on fire with the torch of war, or that have echoed the footsteps of the dancing nobility, where each beau was a hero, and each belle a heroine that was worthy a volume to portray their charms, or to commemorate their deeds of glory.

I read that page of bombast to the Doctor, who had just waked up, and his only remark was: "Halloo, I didn't know we had done all that," and as you may have some other readers who can't appreciate such a style, I will get down from my stilts, and as I am approaching the land of Froissart, give you the styles of his "chronicles."

I wrote you last from Vienna. That day we went out to Schonbrunn Palace, memorable as the summer-residence of Austrian emperors. It is a quaint old palace, that reminded me of the old "armory" in Richmond, only indefinitely extended, and with wings to the front at each end of the main building. But it is of a whitish-yellow color, and it is too flat and squatty for good architecture. We could not gain admittance, however, to the palace, and contented ourselves with a walk through its beautiful gardens and parks, associated as they were, in my mind, at least, with "Joseph II. and his court," by Muhlbach: the whole scene was alive with memories of Theresa, and their numerous offspring, so many of whom she would like to have buried in their childhood, could she have foreseen the years of sorrow and agony to which her ambitious intrigues were consigning them. Here, too, God put an end to that poor prince for whom Napoleon sacrificed his honor and his love for Josephine. Yes, it was in that very house that the poor fellow died, in the bed that his father had occupied before him, and he is now buried in the same vault with Francis, Joseph, Maria, etc., whose names, a capuchin monk, with the garb of the grave and the face of a Bacchus, repeated in Dutch, while we read them in Latin upon the coffins.

We strolled on through the grounds where trees are trimmed so smoothly that they look like a brick wall overgrown with ivy, climbed through a tangled pathway, instead of the sunny walk around the fountain of Neptune to the "glariat." This is a beautiful specimen of architecture, and a fine place for an emperor, or a poor preacher, to air himself, and enjoy the picturesque scenery which God has furnished in profusion for the poor and the rich alike. We sat there in its cool shade, and pleasant breeze, dreaming of the past, and thought we could see "Ichabod" written under the names of Maria and Joseph, while a voice from Solomon seemed to whisper in the breeze: "Vanity of vanities, all is vanity."

But leaving these monuments of departed glory we descended to the right of the main avenue, when, just as the guide-book says, we came to an old Roman ruin, unmistakably ancient, and with the figures of the "fasces," and other emblems that mark it as genuine. We first took a drink at its crystal (?) fountain, which the Doctor thought might proceed from a bathing-house we had just passed, and where we thought of taking a bath in memory of Francis and Theresa, and then we sat down and dreamed of Cesar and his cohorts, and what a pity it was that poor little Marie Antoinette had not fallen in that pool where that tadpole is wriggling, instead of waiting until she was old enough to amuse herself building the little Trianon at Versailles, and then amuse the volatile French by losing her head on the guillotine at the spot now marked by the "Place de Concord."

I was thus musing upon the past, having put a few remnants of brick and marble in my pocket, for a young friend who is fond of such things, when I heard the Doctor pecking away at an arch of the old ruin, and had scarcely had time to warn him against the profanation when a female employee darted out from behind the wall, and put out in a run toward the palace. We both concluded that we had seen enough of that ruin, and as the sun was still warm, we preferred the aforesaid shade by-path, the crookeder the better. Then we concluded we had rocks and marble enough without these we had just collected, and threw them away in the bushes, and after much winding about, and not much leisure, we walked out boldly into the avenue, through the lines of the sentinels, and never breathed freely until we had taken a street-car and mixed up with the crowd at the Exposition. Catch me gathering mementoes from old ruins hereafter! Not that the woman meant to report us, or that we were arrested and imprisoned, but all that rushed through our minds, with a probable war between the United States and Austria to deliver two of its loyal citizens from some damp and dismal dungeon, where they had been imprisoned for stealing rocks from a Roman ruin. For my part they may crumble away to the dust, with the old chaps who erected them, or with those who once enjoyed them, and after that scare, if I secure any relics I will buy them from the priests in the sanctuary, and thus know that they are genuine. But I must close now, as it is most time for breakfast, and we leave for a ride down the Rhine on a steamer to Cologne. This will be a most delightful change, after six hundred miles on the cars, from Vienna to this place, which we made in two nights, spending the intervening day at Munich.

We heard on yesterday that Mr. Spurgeon is to preach for our especial benefit next Sunday evening at the Tabernacle, in London. A real gospel-sermon will be to me now as "honey from the rock," or "Horeb to Israel."

BRUSSELS, August 7, 1873.

I wrote you last from Mayence, from which point we took the steamer down the Rhine to Cologne. It was a splendid journey of six hours, over the finest scenery of the Rhine district, and is the only portion, I believe, that is covered by the famous engravings called "Panorama of the Rhine." In some places the hills on shore are almost bare of verdure, but generally they are green with grapevines, which are so closely trimmed, that trained as they are to a single stick, they look at a distance like a corn-field when the corn is just in silk. But along each bank, and at a distance of from half a mile to two miles, were the old Roman castles that make this country so famous to tourists, and that add historic interest to the scene. Around these cling the legends of childhood, and some of them still bear the marks of recent wars of Napoleon and his successors.

Arriving at Cologne about 6 P.M., we crossed the river on a pontoon bridge to the beautiful Hotel

Belle Vue, which contains a splendid view of the city opposite, as well as of the Rhine, and has a beautiful garden in the rear adorned with flowers, shade-trees, and tables where beer-drinkers and wine-bibbers spend their evenings. We soon found that there was a "fete-day" on hand, and pushed our way through the crowd to a place where "Donnybrook Fair" must have been assembled, and where the whole of Cologne, without the "eau de," had collected to witness it. For about half a mile, on each side of a narrow street, were cake and beer stalls, and I am sure they had gingerbread enough to supply all our Sunday-schools with picnics for the next ten years. Then we came to side-shows, theaters, Punch and Judy, riding-rings, monstrosities, jugglers, circuses, etc., until at last we had worked our way down to the main show, which was a "shooting-match" at targets. We watched them for some time, and saw some of the finest rifle-shooting that I have seen since the days of squirrel hunting in Bedford. That night I had to close my windows to shut out the discordant sounds of a Dutch concert, which may have been kept up all night for what I know, at a neighboring beer-garden. The next morning we were aroused pretty early by the rattling of carts and carriages, and as we do not breakfast before eight or nine o'clock, we concluded to "do" Cologne before that time.

We have acquired such a facility in that line that an ordinary city of fifty thousand inhabitants will require half a day—larger ones in proportion. Crossing the pontoon bridge, we purchased a bottle of the genuine cologne from the manufacturers, and thus armed proceeded to march bomb-proof amid the ten thousand historic scents of this dirty place. But it may have been due to the fact that I came from Lynchburg, and hence was not peculiarly struck with the filth, and had I not seen Paris and London, might have regarded this as a model of neatness and sweet smells.

We went through the magnificent Cathedral at early mass, listened awhile to tolerably good music, while we eyed the architecture and paintings, and then went on down to the Church of St. Ursula. This church was intended to commemorate the chastity of Ursula and her virgins—eleven thousand—who, instead of marrying, as the Bible commands, went into a convent. Not satisfied here, as no woman is, they went off on a long tramp to Rome to see what the chances were for a happy marriage among the priests. They found them a jolly set of fellows, but more inclined to wine than to marriage. So after this hopeless attempt at matrimony, like our schoolmarms, they determined to go back "to him and try their luck in the old country again." But while they were sorrowfully wending their way, downcast and melancholy, a lot of free-lovers from the North came upon them, and they had a big fight, in which, they say, all the women got killed, and now their skulls and bones are stuck around the walls of this church in a kind of iron net-work. We went in and gazed upon the bones, while the little children sang most beautiful chants to the music of a splendid organ, and the image of the chaste "old maid," St. Ursula, looked down complacently upon them, and a venerable priest drank the wine at the altar instead of giving it to their parents.

Well, we left St. Ursula without even a bow of recognition for fear of mistake, and wended our way across the splendid railroad bridge, which is guarded at each end by a fine-looking old gentleman in bronze riding General Washington's horse, as it appears on the monument in Richmond, only the head is turned the wrong way, which may be due to seasickness while crossing the Atlantic.

I am not joking about that horse. We did not go to the bronze foundry in Munich, where we might have seen all their models, but it is evident that he has a model of a horse which he mounts with Washington, Leopold, Napoleon, or whatever hero may be needed, and as horses do not differ as much as men, the world is none the wiser for this "trick in trade."

That morning we took the train at 11:40 for this place, to which we had a fine journey through a splendid section, where men, women, children, and dogs, were all engaged in gathering in the harvest. Belgium, so far, is the finest agricultural region we have passed through on the Continent, and there seems to be a better system of agriculture, as well as larger farms and finer houses. The people all speak French, which sounds more familiar to us than German, and the money is decidedly more easily calculated. It takes one hundred centimes to make a franc, and a franc is worth twenty cents. So, in this way, a man who is at all acquainted with Pike "can easily compute the cost of lace," etc.

Yesterday we went around by the Cathedral, Palace, Royal Park, etc., to the Zoölogical Gardens. Here we spent two or three hours most pleasantly in watching the animals, birds, fish, and plants, for it is a general combination of all in one inclosure, about half a mile square. We saw all kinds of dogs, from a bench-leg fice to a St. Bernard; animals from a guinea-pig to an elephant; birds from a wren to the North American eagle. There was a splendid collection of birds of the most gorgeous colors, enough to keep all the gravel-shooters in Lynchburg busy during a whole vacation. Here, too, we saw one of Mark Twain's pilgrims, a kind of crane, who has a curious fancy for standing on one of his spindling legs, which is about the size of a drum-stick, and about two feet long. We also saw a splendid specimen of the ostrich, whose tails were gone, and as many old hares from India as would stock a pine-forest in Amherst.

After passing through this and the aquarium, which is formed out of an artificial grotto, and where we tried to stir up a crocodile which was either asleep, or like M. T.'s mummy—"dead" —we strolled on down the boulevards, which are wide, shady streets, built on the foundation of the old walls, into the old city. Here we first went into a lace factory, where they employ two thousand five hundred women. They showed us the whole process, which is very simple to look at, but rather tedious to practice with a cambric needle by the life-time. We made some small purchases, commensurate with our funds, which are "growing small by degrees, and beautifully less." I could have spent a whole year's salary and put the result of it in the pocket-book out of which the money was taken to pay for it, or in my pocket-book just as it is at present.

We then went on down to look at the local monument, called the Menachin Fountain, said to be copied from nature, and commemorative of the finding of a little prince who strolled away from home and got lost, as many other small boys have done before and since.

We might spend weeks here looking at pictures, and specimens of ancient armor, etc., or we might go to the battle-field of Waterloo, which is twelve miles off, but I have seen paintings enough to last me, and I lived on a battle-field too long to have any special curiosity about that. Some of our party have gone, however, and some yesterday went into ecstasies over the ball-room where the ball was held the night before the battle, and on which was written, "There was a sound of revelry by night." But after they returned to the guide-books they found that that particular ball-room was torn down several years ago, and so all their enthusiasm was wasted. Well, we leave here in the morning for Antwerp, whence we sail at 4 P.M. for London, where I trust I shall be able to write to you again.

CHAPTER IX.

Letters from the Rev. A. B. Whipple, President of Lansingburgh College, New York.

MUNICH, July 15, 1873.

MY last letter closed, I think, with the word London, a place known as a large city. Arriving there at 9 P.M., and leaving the next day at 3 P.M., left us only eighteen hours to eat, sleep, and see what we could. Some three of us went in the morning to see the Zoölogical Gardens, containing a large part of all the animals described in our natural histories. They are all in ample grounds, or rooms, well adapted to their nature. A bird-house, for instance, containing mostly *Columbæ*, or birds of the dove species, was about one hundred and seventy feet long, forty wide, and in the center fifty feet high, all woven together, with meshes about an inch square, or rather, diamond-shaped. Within were trees of different kinds, climbing ivy, and many beautiful flowers; and flying or resting among these were the many-colored birds of the class above-mentioned, and a few other smaller ones of different kinds, that would live in harmony. Probably the place where my young friends would linger longest would be the monkey-house—nearly as large as the other, and, like it, made of stouter wire, while outside was a brick wall, and over all a slated roof. Here, in the wire house, were all varieties of monkeys—not all in one section; for, like men, some are for quarreling, and some are for peace. One could stand there for hours, had he the time, to see their various ways of spending their strength. All the apparatus of a good gymnasium was theirs, and such agility as they manifested was truly amusing—swinging by hands, or feet, or tail; jumping from a swing to bars; amusing themselves on ladders, poles, and in rings; chasing one another up and around their wire-sided home; their fights—apparent or real fights—their laughing chatter—all with their serious, sober faces —is truly amusing. There were elephants and rhinoceros, giraffes and hippopotami, seals and other amphibians, and so on and so on, till our whole day was spent. We have several days in London when we return.

By 8 o'clock we were crossing the German Ocean. "Rocked in the cradle of the deep," we slept, and in the morning were steaming up the Scheldt, for the old Dutch city of Antwerp. The sail up the river is not particularly interesting; for the country is very flat, the river banked on both sides with levees, over which we could not see, save here and there the tops of a few trees and the spires of some churches. Narrower grows the river, and by 11 o'clock we make fast to the pier, and go off the gangway-plank to see and to be seen.

We spend the rest of the day in sight-seeing. I shall only try to tell something of the Cathedral of Notre Dame, wonderful not only for its architectural beauty, but especially for its many and magnificent paintings by the celebrated painter, Rubens. "The Ascent of the Cross," "The Descent from the Cross," "The Crucifixion," "The Assumption of the Virgin," "The Holy Mother," and many more, on large canvas, so that, though sixty or one hundred feet above us, they look life-like in size and color. Here we found many artists, with easels, busily engaged copying these works of the great master. One we saw, who has done nothing else but copy these paintings for the last thirty-five years, always finding ready purchasers. To appreciate, one must see them. One thing which may be interesting in this matter is this: The holy mother, in face, is the portrait of his second wife, while in another painting the faces of some of the saints are his first wife and relations, and some of the angels his own children; and in nearly all his paintings the portrait of himself appears. From what I have seen of his paintings, I think I shall know Rubens's masterpieces when I see them. Many other paintings adorned the walls, but his are the glory of Notre Dame.

We then visited the silk works. All silk is woven by hand, in old-fashioned looms; and we were told that it is so woven everywhere in the world.

Next day found us in Brussels. Cathedrals seem to be the chief places to visit in this country; so we march to that of St. Gudule—not so noted for its paintings as for some of its architectural work, carvings in wood, and sculptured stone. Selecting one thing, let me mention the pulpit of carved oak. Its base represents Adam and Eve just after eating the forbidden fruit, with bowed heads and sorrowful faces, and Eve with the fruit still in her hand. On their shoulders is the pulpit, and under their feet and around them is the serpent, in many folds about and above the pulpit; above is a canopy, and on the top of this, in horizontal position, with open mouth and forked tongue, is the head of the serpent, and above the serpent, with heel upon his head, stands the Son of man, crowned with radiant glory. This altogether forms the frame-work, and around and ornamenting the whole are carved trees and branches, on and among which are various animals in various attitudes, yet all with ears turned in the direction of the pulpit, as if to hear the fearful doom pronounced on all the world for this first sin. Even a poor monkey, with some of the forbidden fruit in his hand, imitating Eve, no doubt, is faithfully represented, suggesting, perhaps, his fall in common with our race. As a specimen of carved work, it, in design and finish, surpasses any thing I have yet seen. I climbed to the top of a monument, some two hundred steps, where could be seen the whole city as a map, and away northward the battle-field of Waterloo. I visited the Royal Palace, Town Hall, parks, and Museum, which are all well filled with works of art—painting or sculpture. Here, too, I found my way into the lace-factories, and saw the slow process of making all forms of lace "with needle and thread." To see five hundred pins and as many threads, with little handles, stuck here and there, and pulled this way and that, all in a space not so large as your hand, was at least amusing, and somewhat instructive; for, by inquiring, I learned that eighteen months are spent on a good lace kerchief by women working twelve and fourteen hours per day, for twenty cents, and, when done, worth about one hundred dollars—enough to keep an ordinary nose clean.

Next day we arrived at Cologne—so-called from a Roman "Colonia." Here, too, cathedrals gather all the wealth and art of the city. Amid much sameness of purpose, an endless variety of means is made apparent. The Cathedral is the one most noteworthy—one of the most stupendous specimens of Gothic architecture in the world, dizzying to the mind in size and details. It was begun in 1248, and they hope to finish it in a few years—the two towers remaining unfinished. Each tower will be five hundred feet high, and this is the length of the building. It has one hundred and sixty-nine cloisters, five hundred and seventy-six windows—many of them very large—and five hundred turrets, or small towers. It is magnificent without as well as within. It has a chapel, "Three Kings of Cologne"—the three wise men of the east—behind the high altar; and the wealth of a nation seems lavished on a case said to contain their bones. It is also in paintings, but so like others that I will not discuss them. You must know that it was Sunday, here a holiday, though every church is open. A procession of five hundred children were marching along the streets, strewn with oak-leaves and evergreens; houses were adorned with flags, and lights were burning before images in niches and windows. I believe the day was St. Michael's, and all was in honor of him. Following along, we went into different churches, all beautiful, and rich with medieval art. We paused longest in Ursula, where we saw the bones of eleven thousand virgins, or little girls, who had been on a pilgrimage to Rome with St. Ursula, an English lady; on their return they were murdered by the Huns, and here, in various forms, carved, ornamented, and colored, are kept these relics of the past for the curious tourist to see, and devout Catholics to worship. To see eleven thousand skeletons, each bone separated from its fellow, and piled up like so many bundles of faggots, is what an anatomist would call going back to "first principles." We found also an English chapel, where we attended service, and heard a good story on the sin of worshiping. It being a holiday, all places of art exhibition and amusement were open, and all stores and street venders seemed to be doing a very thriving business. The many oddities of dress, and other things, I reserve for a letter by itself. Our hotel is on the banks of the Rhine, with several terraces, each shaded, and seated like beer-gardens, as they are, where all day Sunday and Sunday-night, thousands gather to eat, drink, hear the band of music, and finally go home after a fine display of fireworks. Such has been a Sunday in Cologne.

VIENNA, July 19, 1873.

MY DEAR READERS:—We left Cologne, the city of smells, Monday-morning, by rail for Bonn, where we tarried for an hour, running through the famous University, one thousand two hundred and eighty feet long, with three hundred lecture-rooms and halls, and a library of one hundred thousand volumes. In the classical recitation-room, covering nearly one side of the wall, was a painting by Raphael, representing the great scholars of the past—Homer, Plato, Eschylus, Euripides, Socrates, Demosthenes, among the Greeks; Virgil, Cicero, Cesar, Horace, of the Latin race; and of more modern men, Dante, Shakspeare, and others; all with some symbol whereby a reader of their works would know them. Along the library were busts of the honored great, among which the deformed Æsop was worthy of notice. Here, too, we saw some of the nondescript compositions of Beethoven, and not far thence we entered the house where he was said to have been burned; plucking a rose-leaf from the garden, we placed it between the leaves of our note-book to bring home, or, more likely, lose on the way. For the sake of seeing this place we had taken cars and so gained the time. Now our steamboat, the Emperor of Germany, came along, and we went on board to spend the day in steaming up the Rhine. Below Bonn there is not much that is worthy of notice. Above, the beauty and the grandeur begin. For awhile I try to persuade myself that the Hudson is equal in beauty, in palisades, in mountain scenery, but I am compelled to give the first prize to the Rhine. Most of the way the rough, bold mounts, crowd down to the river on both sides, and, up the sides, where it would seem there is nothing but rocks, industrious hands have made terraces, and planted grape-vines nearly to the summit. One needs to see them to understand the phrase, "The vine-clad hills." On many of the bold and projecting cliffs stands the remains of castles built far back in the small centuries. Much of their history is the history of the nation, now proud of their ruins. Under them, on the river's bank, are small villages, surrounded by the old walls within which the old castles stood. No doubt they were thus placed to be under the protection of the castles, or to flee into them in time of need; for a castle is not simply a large house, or a tower, but quite a village of itself, surrounding and occupying many acres of ground, protected sometimes by walls fourteen feet in thickness, with massive buildings within to contain vast supplies, for large numbers and for a long time. Under the safe-keeping of such defenses, in old feudal times, gathered the sparse population, and in steaming up the Rhine we read past history. So numerous now are little villages along the river that we are seldom out of sight of one. The mountain scenery, and the cultivation up their steep sides of the grape, gives constant exercise for eye and imagination. Where horses and cattle cannot get to plow, women can, and we thus learn that woman-power is here highly prized, and highly used; and all along this valley they are far above the men in the culture which makes Rhine wine so acceptable to their loving husbands. We turn from such pleasant reveries, and fix our eyes on Coblence—Confluenza—situated at the confluence of the Moselle and Rhine; a large, walled city, back, and above it, one of the castles like others, only a living, or occupied one, named Fort Kaiser Alexander, while nearly opposite is Ehrenbreistein castle and fort, deemed the strongest in all the German States.

We pass Schönburg—a place frequented by Luther, and easily recalled by the readers of the

"Schönburg Cotta Family." Amid ever-changing delights for the eye, we stop a few moments at "Bingen, fair Bingen on the Rhine."

On and on into the darkness, until we enter Mayence, a city founded thirteen years before the Christian era began, and capital of the Grand Duchy of Hessia. The imposing pile of the Cathedral, founded in the eighth century, the isolated groups of churches, the commanding aspect of the citadel, and the far-stretching girdle of massive fortifications, address themselves at once to the eye and to the imagination. Tired as I am of describing churches, I will here say, it is said no cathedral in Germany has as many monuments and epitaphs as this. What pleased me far more was to find a monument in the public square of, or to the memory of Johann zum Geusfleick, of Guttenburg, the inventor of the art of printing, in 1450. His statue is of bronze, after a model by Thorwalsden, and cast in Paris. He is represented with some types—a b c—in his hand, each separate, and therefore movable. On the pedestal sides are different representations; one setting type, one a boy printing with a screw press, and another himself, in the act of reading the proofsheet, and another an inscription in Latin, as follows: "An art which neither the Greeks nor Romans understood the genius of a German has found out. Now, whatever the ancients knew, and the moderns know, it is not for himself, but for all mankind." The citizens of Mayence erected this monument to Guttenburg, by money collected throughout Europe, in 1837.

From Mayence to Munich, so far the finest German city. We visit the Glyptothek, a large building filled with statuary, mostly Grecian and Roman, every thing in the highest style of art. To any one having read the mythologies of these nations a sight of all the ideal gods and goddesses is well worth the time spent in looking at them, but no verbal description will make one to fully appreciate them. We cross the street to another like building filled with fine oil-paintings of modern times. Here one can revel in all the beauties of color and imagination, so blended as to charm the beholder. A little walk and we enter another art-gallery, containing one thousand four hundred and twenty-two paintings. We look at some of the finest in each room, and pass on satisfied, and satiated with manifestations of this pictorial art. At 11 o'clock we enter the palace of the king, and spend two hours in wandering through royal halls, and rooms, and gazing at huge historic paintings adorning the halls and ceilings of most of the rooms.

In the royal dancing-hall the paintings represent various styles of dancing and of dress; and as to the latter, more of the person than of the dress appears. In one, or rather two rooms, are thirty-five oil-portraits of the handsomest women said to have lived in Munich. They are very fine, but we could equal them at home had we equal artists. Lola Montez was one among them formerly, but so much has been said to her disgrace that, despite the beauty of her face, her picture has been removed to another place.

The throne-room was the grandest in style and finish. On each side a row of kings, beginning with the first and ending with Charles XII., King of Sweden, all of bronze, of more than life-like size, and clothed in the style of the different ages in which they lived—a kind of running history of itself. At the end of the room was the throne, raised several steps above the floor of the hall. The talk of the Yankee schoolmasters has been heard in royal halls, and gliding out into the free air we sought and entered the bronze manufactory where are made most of the bronze statuary of the world.

Saw many models of American works—Washington, Clay, Benton, Mason, Governor Andrews of Massachusetts—in process of molding and casting; also a soldiers' monument for Worcester, and one for Cincinnati, and many of the kings, and queens, and soldiers, and artists, and scholars with which many cities of the world are adorned. It is a wonderful establishment. Here was made the largest bronze monument in the world—the Bavarian statue. It represents a human sixty-five feet in altitude, and every way well proportioned, the hand six feet, and the nose twenty-three inches; yet, standing so high on its pedestal that at a not great distance it seems of natural size. Though hollow, it required seventy-eight tons of brass in its construction, made of cannon taken in wars, mostly from the Turks. It cost ninety-seven thousand dollars, and was ten years in making. In the hollow head nine or ten persons can find room, and out through her curls can crawl up on to the outside of her ample head. Her hair hangs in curls down her back. One hand rests on a huge lion by her side, while in the other was grasped the royal scepter. Altogether it was well worthy of the nation, the artist, the design—and the carriage-ride to see it. Thence to the establishment where are made the beautiful stained-glass windows which adorn and beautify the windows of so many churches in this and other lands. Here we saw some of the finest paintings yet seen, and done in glass. Having a little time to spare, we rode around the city of two hundred thousand inhabitants, listened a few moments to a concert of one hundred brass instruments, in a beer-garden, and weary, seek our beds, preparatory to an all-day ride along the base of the Bavarian Alps, and the Tyrolese Alps, snow-covered, till at 11 o'clock P.M., tired and hungry, we enter this city of nine hundred thousand inhabitants—Vienna.

The Vienna Exposition—Description of the building—Scenes and incidents—The population of Vienna, etc., etc.

VENICE, July 22, 1873.

Since my last communication Vienna has entertained us for three days, and we have done what we could to see and learn. In 1855 Vienna had some 70,000 population; in 1865 it had 500,000, and to-day has over 900,000—a growth more rapid than any other known city, Chicago not excepted. A reason for it is found, in part, in the enterprise of the emperor, who caused the old city-walls to be demolished, and thus let the city spread; and partly to the fact that it is the resident city of the nobility—some nine hundred of them living here, and spending their wealth in efforts to outdo one another. Buildings are being constructed everywhere in great numbers, of good size and solidity, made mostly of brick, and stuccoed outside and inside, so as to resemble stone-work. It is the best-built city in Europe—widest streets, best paved, and kept cleanest. To ride through its magnificent parks and boulevards gives one a very favorable impression. Its military, horse and foot, attract attention, and one begins to feel that he is under a government not like that at home. The nobility in their grand mansions, or rolling through parks in gay equipages, spacious hotels and highly-draped servants, are not all. Among and under them is the teeming population of the laboring class—men, women, and children. Here we see women at work mixing mortar and carrying it up ladders in hods, like men, sweeping streets, drawing away filth, often with dogs to help them; for here even dogs are harnessed, and compelled to earn their living. In short, in the markets, in the streets, and in the fields, women seem to be the working-class. So in trade—in stores and shops the women act as if they were as good as the men, not even omitting beer and tobacco. All this we

7*

cannot fail to see as we pass through the city to the great attraction of the place at present—the World's Fair, or Exposition.

Each country presents its peculiar and best products, and each seems to excel the other in some one thing—America in sewing-machines and mowing-machines; England in iron-works and weaving-machinery; France in silk and tasteful fabrics; Italy and Greece in statuary; Germany in oil-paintings and lager-beer; Austria for the finest display of the largest number and variety of useful and ornamental things; Egypt, China, and Japan, of course, had their noted peculiarities in luxurious abundance. Please fancy the finest fabrics you have ever seen from these countries; then imagine them arranged under the most favorable circumstances for exhibition; then add the greatest skill in their complete and unique arrangement, and even then you will fail to fancy it as it is. Take, for instance, one article—thread, in spools of all sizes and colors, in balls, in skeins; then fancy them arranged in columns, turrets, windows, domes, painting, sculpture—in short, a complete cathedral, well proportioned and thirty feet high, and you may fancy how one company show their thread.

The buildings are situated on the east side of the city, inclosing one thousand acres, a part of which is made up of royal gardens. The building is shaped like the frame of a fish. The dimensions are almost three thousand feet in length, with sixteen transepts or thirty-two side-sections, like the ribs of a fish, so made that light enough may be had in the main building and transepts, and in many instances the spaces between the transepts have been filled with additional buildings, till the whole single structure covers one hundred and seventy acres of ground. We enter at the west end, and enter at once rooms marked North America, and in the other transept South

America; for the arrangement of nations is eastward in order, beginning with America, North and South, two sections, then England five, Spain and Portugal one, France seven, Switzerland two, Italy three, Belgium two, Austria twenty-two, Russia three, Egypt one, China two, Turkey two, Japan two. All this shows the comparative space in the main building occupied by different nations, and some in parts by nations not named in the above list. Again, see samples of silk piled one above another in such a way as to represent the side of a room tapestried with animals, and trees, and flowers. Or see a huge shaft, like Bunker Hill monument, with medallions and inscriptions on its pedestal, white as marble; go up and read: "*In memoriam* of Mr. B——, manufacturer of wax, porcelain, and spermacetti." Of all ingenious devices to attract attention and challenge notice, the most noteworthy of each nation can be found here. Do not think every thing is within the main building. There is a machine-shop of nearly the same length, in which, by steam-power, is used a great variety of machinery, doing very wonderful work. I saw a complicated machine making tapestry, or figured lace. It was a kind of loom, yet without any shuttle; farther I cannot describe it. Wood-work, iron-work, clay-work, leather-work, wool-work, cotton-work, silk-work, paper-work—nearly every thing but shoddy-work. Besides the main building, called the Palace of Industry, and the machine-hall just mentioned, there are a few others I might mention by name if you were willing to read through a list of names to the number of two hundred and eighty-eight, including many large houses filled with fine arts, many illustrating the war-weapons of different nations, large musical-instrument establishments, Swiss toy-shops, model school-houses and dwellings of many parts of the earth, agricultural halls, metal industries, model stables, not to omit restaurants of and for all nations. Should I enumerate them all, without a more complete description, the story would be as tedious as the one, "And another ant came and took a grain of corn."

In the center of the Palace of Industry is a grand dome of twice the area of that of St. Peter's church at Rome. It is three hundred and forty-six feet in diameter, and seventy-five feet to the top of the pedestal and base of the dome, with a circular walk within, from which we look down on the grandest display in the building. So far, we go up in an elevator; then, in a winding way, half round and up the dome, on the outside, for five hundred feet we walk, looking down upon all the surroundings of this World's Fair. Then, in a smaller circle by one-half, we walk around the outside and see the whole city, as a map, below us. North of us flows the Danube, with its turbid waters, through a level country teeming with a busy population. A little to the north-east of us we see the famous battle-field of Wagram, where Napoleon, by the charge of McDonald, sacrificed fifteen thousand men to gain his point. At different points around the dome were placed telescopes, through which we aid the eye in a circle of twenty miles radius, and behold the pride and pomp of Austria. Still higher above us rises the dome, till, some three hundred feet from the ground, it is crowned with a most magnificent golden crown of Austria, reflecting every way the burning rays of the rising, midday, or setting sun. While underneath afterward, and within the Industrial Palace, we saw Francis Joseph II., the Emperor to whom for the present the crown belongs.

Having seen the Fair, we took a little run among the churches—all remarkable for something, and each differing from the rest. I will mention only two or three. St. Peter's, built like the one in Rome, is very old, and contains an immense amount of genius, in the shape of architecture, sculpture, and painting. The wealth of many rich men has been lavished on the adornment of the church—one of the ways by which the rich lessen the pains of purgatory. Many of the columns were covered with carved vines, among the branches of which were numerous little naked angels, or cupids, in every variety of attitude, with distended cheeks, as if blowing the praises of some one, once white and beautiful, no doubt, but now dark and dirty with age and dust. By the way, in parenthesis, this is true of much of the ancient statuary. Age has colored them dark and gloomy, and time has gnawed them with her teeth, till they are not what fancy painted them. Within this church, in a crypt, lies the son of Napoleon, and in an urn the heart of Maria Theresa; and underneath an altar was a skeleton arrayed in gorgeous apparel, with glittering tiara, eye-sockets with jewels, bony fingers with flashing rings, patela bright with diamonds, feet in finely-worked slippers. I was told it was the skeleton of one of the popes. Under another altar was another in like memorial habiliments. Never have I seen such a mocking contrast of death in life. The Cathedral of St. Stephen was, or is, worthy of note for several particulars. In it are the letters A. E. I. O. U., the motto of Fredrick; they are the initial letters of Latin words meaning, "Austria must rule the world." Let Latin scholars guess the words. In its crypt is the burial-place of royalty. For the last two hundred years only their *bowels* are buried here, their *bodies* in the Church of the Capuchins, and their *hearts* in the Church of the Augustines. Who would not be a king?

CHAPTER X.

Letter from Vienna, by the Rev. Charles W. Cushing.

OUR party (Cook's Educational Party) reached Vienna on the evening of July 17, *via* Munich. Thus far every step of our journey has been delightful beyond description, so that it really seemed that from the time we stepped on board the grand steamship Victoria, at New York, a good Providence had been preparing the way for us; and now, though we have heard rumors of cholera in Vienna, we are prepared to go forward without fear, for we found that the rumors, though not entirely without foundation, had greatly exaggerated the facts. It is sufficient to say, that without unusual precautions, excepting not to drink their miserable water, our party were never in better health than in Vienna.

Thus far we have found no city in Europe which is laid out on a scale of such magnificence and grandeur as Vienna. The present emperor, while doing a good work abroad, is also doing nobly for his people at home. The magnificence, however, is not due to the influence of the emperor alone; for there is no other city in Europe which has so many resident nobility as Vienna. Not less than two hundred families of princes, counts, and barons live here. The city has a large number of parks, aside from the Royal Park (where the Exposition is held), which embraces one thousand acres, while many of the streets, which run entirely through and around the city, are laid out on a scale which would astound American economists.

Many of the churches at Vienna, some of which are very old, have peculiar histories linked with them. The Maximilian, or Votive Church, not yet completed, is one of the most beautiful. Though not large, it is almost an exact copy of the Cathedral at Cologne. Its foundation was laid by the ill-fated Maximilian, of Mexican fame, who was a brother of the present Emperor of Austria. In 1853 there was an attempt made upon the life of the Emperor Francis Joseph, and this church, it is said, was projected by Maximilian as a thank-offering for the escape of the emperor from the hand of the assassin. It is hard to reconcile such religious consecration with the facts connected with the private lives of many of these men.

In the Church of St. Augustine is the famous monument of the Archduchess Maria Christina, the masterpiece of the great Venetian sculptor, Canova. In Loretto Chapel, in this church, are the silver urns which contain the hearts of the imperial family who have died within the last two hundred years, such as Maria Theresa, Napoleon II., etc. The bodies of all these imperials are buried in the Church of the Capuchins. Maximilian is also entombed here. The old Church of St. Stephen's, which is exactly in the center of the old city, was begun early in the twelfth century, and is the largest and most important church of the city, though it contains nothing of special interest excepting the bodies of the Austrian Emperors who died prior to the last two hundred years.

But these are things whose special features of interest are with the past. What makes Vienna an object of world-wide interest to-day, is her great International Exposition. Beyond question, this is much the largest and finest the world has ever seen, and without doubt the largest it will see for a long time to come; for it is such a stupendous failure, financially, that no nation will venture to undertake another on so grand a scale for many years. The *Exposition* is here on a scale of grandeur which is bewildering, not to say overwhelming; but the *people* are not here. The admission is amazingly cheap (only twenty-five cents on ordinary days), and yet there is no crowd. Strangers are not in the city, only in small numbers.

It is not possible to give those who read about it any thing like a just conception of its magnitude, still a few statements, which must be for the most part repetitions of what has been said by others, may start thought in the right direction.

The grounds on which the Exposition is located, and much of which is occupied in one way or another, embrace one thousand acres, all inclosed. The buildings containing the articles for exposition, cover about one hundred and seventy acres, and most of them are filled in every part to repletion. The main building is about three-fifths of a mile in length, with deep transepts on either side, as closely as they can stand together. When we first arrived at the Exposition, a friend and myself determined that we would first walk through the aisles of the main building, and its transepts, as quickly as we could, without stopping to examine any thing, merely to get an impression of its magnitude. By walking fast we were able to accomplish this in a day and a-half, and the hardest day and a-half of work I ever did. Now, when you remember that on both sides of these aisles, displayed in the most fantastic manner, the best and the richest productions of nearly every nation upon earth are arrayed, you may begin to get some conception of this Exposition. But it must not be forgotten that this is only one building—that the machinery fills another building of the same length as this—and that the department of fine arts occupies still another building, which is immense in size. Besides these, there are nearly two hundred buildings more, many of which are devoted to the exposition of useful and curious things from the different nations of the earth.

The American department, with one or two exceptions, makes the poorest display, and for two reasons: We show *very* little that is ornamental, and we exhibit very little machinery. In regard to the first, we are a practical, utilitarian people, devoting comparatively little time or money to ornament. So we have not much to show in this line. We might have made a good display of machinery, but the Austrian government would give us no protection in the matter of our patents, and our machinists and manufacturers would not send their machines here when they knew that their patents would be stolen and appropriated. But laying this aside, an American can't help feeling that, judged by the exhibition here, we must be grossly misjudged. Still, the great disgrace comes from the mismanagement of our department.

Whatever may be said of Mr. Van Buren, there can be no doubt that his appointment was an unfortunate one. From all I can gather from those who have been on the ground from the first, I conclude that Mr. Van Buren was not guilty of complicity, but that, though an able man in many directions, he had not the talent for organizing the machinery here, and setting it at work. The subordinates were, without doubt, in many instances, men who cared very little for our national display or reputation, providing they could make money out of the operation. Mr. Van Buren had not the ability to control them, and so was led into many schemes for which he was not personally, though he was officially, responsible. Besides this, our Commissioners have been changing so often that there has been no well-defined plan of action, and hence no system. Taken away from the other nations, we have a good display; beside them, it is very meager. The want of system has put us at disadvantage in every way. It is only a week ago I was told by one of the department that boxes were found containing collections of our periodicals, and some other things, in one corner of the grounds, having been in the rain so long that every thing was spoiled. I suppose that every thing is being done now that can be, but it is too late to redeem ourselves this time.

It is really marvelous to see the world brought together in an exposition of this kind. To study it is to get enlarged ideas of the race, and to feel that the nations upon which we are accustomed to look down, are not so far beneath us as we have been wont to think; and that in many things they can teach us important lessons which we ought not to fail to learn. We are a great people, but we are a small part of the world. We have made much progress in many directions, but we have much more to learn, and the teachers are at hand.

CHAPTER XI.

Letter from Miss Hattie Stanard, of Des Moines, Iowa.

NEW YORK, August 27, 1873.

EDITOR OF SCHOOL JOURNAL:—Our party arrived in Munich, Munchen, Saturday-evening, and after having our supper, all started for the gardens, of which that city contains many, and where we heard some very fine music; but we could not understand how those intelligent people could find pleasure in coming there night after night, with their whole families, and, from the oldest to the boy or girl five years old, each with a glass of beer, pass the evening that we enjoy so much at *home*.

Sabbath-day some of our party broke by visiting a picture-gallery that would not be open any other day while we were there, but the more pious ones visited cathedrals, monuments, etc. The finest of all at Munich are the art collections, and first among these are the Glyptothek gallery of sculpture, and the Pinacothek, the gallery of paintings. In the latter we saw fine paintings from the Italian, Dutch, French, German, and Spanish schools, and one hall devoted entirely to Rubens. In order to appreciate them, one needs to study each of the fifteen hundred. Among those we noticed more particularly, in the short time we had to spend there, were Van Eyck's "Adoration of the Magi," Rembrandt's "Descent from the Cross," Rubens's "Last Judgment,"

Vander Werf's "Ecce Homo," and Murillo's "Beggar-boys eating melons and grapes."

The finest church in Munich is Basilica of St. Boniface, built by King Louis, to commemorate the twenty-fifth anniversary of his marriage. The interior is elegant, with its sixty-four beautiful columns of gray marble, making a nave and four aisles. The walls are magnificently frescoed, and the paintings show the progress of Christianity in Germany.

Some of the streets of Munich are broad and handsome, and in the square we saw some fine statues, especially one in Karolinenpeatz, about one hundred feet high, made of captured cannon, in memory of the Bavarians who fell in the army of Bonaparte in the Russian campaign; also the bronze statue of Bavaria, outside of the city, representing a female with a sword in her right hand, and the wreath of victory in her left. On one side is the lion of Bavaria. It is sixty feet high, and stands upon a pedestal thirty feet high. With all the pleasing sights we saw in Munich, we saw one that was not pleasant—women carrying the hod up a ladder to the top of a three-story building. We thought then, O Munich! you have done well with the arts, but why not have elevated your women a little? And we come to America feeling that American women hold an enviable position to the women of any country we have visited.

At Munich Mr. Cook, who had been with us since we arrived in Glasgow, and who had been a kind father to us all, and done much to make each day pleasant, not only with his knowledge of the country, the railways, steamers, etc., but with his ever cheerful face and pleasant words, left us to the tender (?) mercies of a German conductor, who if he had had control of his temper in any reasonable degree would have been quite passable. However, we soon learned to not address him unless we expected our nervous system to be shattered beyond recovery for at least twenty-four hours.

Our next stopping-place was Vienna (Wien), and as we rode through the streets we were reminded many times of Paris by some of the buildings, the display of goods in the shop windows, etc.

The next three days were spent at the Exposition, and when they were ended we felt almost as though we had seen the whole world together; especially when we were in the Japanese department, and saw the Japanese women and men at work, it seemed quite like being in their own country. The only real good glass of lemonade we had while we were in Europe we got at the American restaurant, on the Exposition grounds. It was hot and dusty in Vienna, and notwithstanding there was much of interest we had not seen, we were rather glad when we took the night express train for Mayence, a very old town, founded by the Romans; and in the walls of the citadel is a monument erected by the Roman legion in honor of Drusus, their commander-in-chief. Mayence is the strongest fortress in the German Confederation. There we saw a novelty, in the way of a bridge of boats, two thousand two hundred and twenty feet in length, made of fifty boats.

And now we are going down the Rhine. Some one has very appropriately named this a "river of romance," for who could ride on one of those nice little steamers, amid the beautiful scenery, hearing on all sides of him legends of castle and tower, without feeling romantically inclined? However, we heard of no serious cases in our party, and we think no rash act was done.

We pass the old castle of Johannisburg, three hundred and forty feet above the river, surrounded by the vineyards from whence comes the celebrated Jo-hannis-bagger—as it is called—wine, called the finest wines of the Rhine. And then we come to "Bingen on the Rhine." Nothing of particular interest here, excepting that it was the home of the soldier about whom the beautiful poem was written; so after saying the poem, and feeling sorry for the other, "not a sister," we turned our attention to the Mouse Tower, where Bishop Hatto's bones were picked. And then we are passing great vineyards, and as we go round a little bend in the river we see the fine old castle of Rheinstein, two hundred and fifty feet above the river, and many other castles too numerous to mention here. As we look far down the river we see a train of cars coming, and we can scarcely realize that they are not a part of the natural picture, and that the rocks were not placed there with tunnels already in them purposely for the cars to run through, but the shriek of the locomotive brings us back from romance to the practical. Far up above the river we see two castles called the "hostile brothers." The legend of these is of two brothers loving the same lady, which was the cause of the castles' hostility. Then Hildegarde, the lady, retired to a convent at the foot of the hill and the brothers were reconciled, and ever after lived in one castle.

Stolzenfels was the most beautifully rebuilt castle we saw, though smaller than many.

As we passed Fortress Ehrenbreitstein (Gibraltar of Germany), we saw the pyramid Byron speaks of in his Childe Harold.

> Beneath its base are hero's ashes hid,
> Our enemy's—but let not that forbid
> Honor to Marceau!

Here is where the "Blue Moselle" comes into the Rhine, or rather flows along by the side of it, for the Moselle does not mingle with the dark waters of the Rhine for some distance.

We pass the Castles of Drachenfels (Dragon's Rock) and Rolandseck, and in the distance see the seven mountains, while just by us is the island of Nonnenworth, with its convent.

So we go on, not stopping our sight-seeing even to eat, for the saloon and *dinner-hour* are so conveniently arranged that we can eat and at the same time see all of interest that we are passing on either side. At 5 o'clock in the afternoon we land at Cologne, and our ride on the Rhine is ended. Cologne is not a nice looking place, neither is it a pleasantly scented place, as its name would imply; on the contrary, the perfume of its long, narrow, winding, dirty streets, is exceedingly disagreeable.

A beautiful stone bridge, and a bridge of boats, connects Cologne and the beautiful little town of Dentz on the opposite side of the river. The great Cathedral here is an imposing Gothic building, commenced six hundred years ago, and as far as we could learn, it seems probable that it will never be finished, although they keep busily working on it. The interior is four hundred and thirty feet long, and one hundred and forty in width; the transept is two hundred and thirty feet in length, and the choir one hundred and forty feet high; the part used for service has an area of seventy thousand square feet. Every thing about it is elegant.

The most amusing thing we saw was the Church of St. Ursula, where our guide told us were the bones of *eleven thousand virgins!* who were murdered on that spot on their return from a pilgrimage to Rome. We looked very sober about it, and of course believed it all, for could we not see for ourselves the bones, which were four feet deep and two feet thick in the walls of the church, sticking out through the little iron grates, and the skulls hanging all around the church, and the huge boxes of bones? To be sure many of them looked like chicken bones, and other kinds we were familiar with, but then they were not, O no! it could never have been, and we thought what a great scarcity of virgins there must have been after that. Then our guide took us into the Golden Chamber. We had to pay more to go in there, it was worth more, and I think he would have liked to have had us present certificates of good moral character before we went in. There we saw a thorn from the Saviour's crown, one of the very pots used in making the wine at the marriage of Cana, a box of teeth once used by the eleven thousand virgins, and other things too wonderful to mention.

Every one bought cologne water at Cologne, and although hardly any two of the party purchased at the same place, yet each was positive that he had his from the "original Jean Antoine Marie Farina." Now we must say good-bye to Rhineland, for we are off to Brussels (Bruxelles)—Paris in miniature.

We reached Brussels late in the afternoon, and after having our suppers, went to a palace garden in the upper part of the city, where we heard a fine instrumental concert, admission eight cents. Of course we had to go shopping. Who ever came away from Brussels without going shopping, even though he bought nothing? And as we went through the lace-stores, of which there are so many, and the manufactories, we thought—

Here are tissues fit for angels, wrought with wreath, and point,
    and star,
In most curious devices. Never saw I aught so rare—
Where found you these frail webs, woven of the lightest summer air?

We visited the great square of Brussels, where "the sound of revelry by night" was heard and noted; Hotel de Ville, a fine old Gothic structure, its central tower three hundred and sixty-four feet high. In front are two statues, of Count Egmont and Horn, the Duke of Alva's victims, who perished there.

We were interested in the dog-teams drawing milk-carts, and loads of vegetables, to market, driven by old women with queer head-dresses and wooden slippers. There is a fine museum of paintings in Brussels, and a gallery well worth visiting of very original pictures, formerly owned by an artist named Wiertz, who is now dead. Before going there prepare yourself to be continually surprised, and in the most unexpected ways.

Our stay at Antwerp (Anners) was short—only time for a visit to Rubens's two paintings, the "Elevation and Descent from the Cross." They are kept veiled in the cathedral. By paying two and a half francs (fifty cents) the veil was lifted and we could see them.

In the Church of St. Jacques we visited the tomb of Rubens. In the Place Verte is a fine statue of the artist.

The next morning we congratulated ourselves that we had crossed the English Channel twice without being sea-sick. We were soon back in London.

After a call at 98 Fleet street, the office of Cook & Son, where we found letters from home, and got the latest news from over the ocean, we went to Westminster Abbey. Saw the monuments to England's greatest, best, and some of her worst, men. One can spend much time at the Abbey with interest. On Sunday morning we heard Spurgeon, and in the evening went to St. Paul's Cathedral.

"It is," as some one has said, "in the sculptured marble you may, in Westminster Abbey, St. Paul's, and the old cathedrals of the country, read England's history again, and seem to approach nearer, and have a more realizing sense of her great men and their deeds, than from the pages of the printed volume." After this short visit to the Old World, we feel not at all satisfied, and are ready now for a *long* visit to the same places, and to many we have not seen. Mr. Cook came with us to Glasgow and saw us off on the "Italia." We were sorry to part with him, for we not only respected him and had confidence in him, but really liked him very much.

The passage home was rough and "up hill," not nearly so pleasant as going over, and all were glad to see the spires of New York.

CHAPTER XII.

"Beautiful Venice"—An *Avalanche* correspondent in the city of the sea—From Austria to Italy—Highly romantic scenery—Sights and impressions in Venice.

VENICE, July 22, 1873.

THOUGH I wrote you two long letters from Vienna, a day or two since, I want to say something of our route to this "water city" before I go out to see it. We have just landed here out of the gondolas, after a travel of about twenty-four hours over a very interesting country by rail. The country for some two hours from Vienna is level, between ledges of mountains seen far away. It has a fine crop of wheat ready for harvest, and being gathered, mostly by women, with reap-hooks. We then come to fields of corn, the first we have seen; it is small, but looks well. Then comes the pine, in rows, of different sizes, in plats like their wheat and corn. After these are past we strike in the highest mountains, and by winding round and round ascend them to a dizzy height. It was estimated that we traveled five miles circuitously to advance one in the proper direction. After running to every point of the compass, we gain the heights, to behold the most romantic scenery I ever witnessed. The valleys below us, with fine little farms, "well tilled," nice little houses, perhaps well filled, and for aught I know, pretty little wives, "well willed." The serpentine road below almost as white as the snow-clad mountains above, upon which stand old castles, built in other ages for defense—still grand in their ruins—presented a scene it has never been my fortune to witness before. It is the most remarkable structure in Europe. It was built by the Austrian government. The first twenty-five miles cost $7,500,000. It is carried along the face of the precipices by fifteen tunnels—one of them is four thousand five hundred and eighteen feet through, two thousand two hundred and ninety-four feet above the level of the sea. The mountains are seven thousand seven hundred feet high, and on some of the peaks there are churches. These people seem to be religious. All along you see crucifixes at or near their houses. We all think this was the most interesting day of travel we ever had in any country.

About nine o'clock we leave Austria, and enter Italian cars, and about two o'clock we have to collect our baggage for examination. This farce over, we roll on, but did not discover the sky to look more beautiful, as some say, but at daylight we saw one of the loveliest countries we have ever seen. It is level, and almost literally occupied by fruit-trees and vines, with vegetables between. When the sun arose there was a mellow yellow light, different from what we had seen before. It was lovely indeed to behold. We arrive at Venice, or rather to the water, where a large number of boats are waiting for us. In a few moments we are aboard, four in a craft, and off to the Hotel Victoria. This was a novel sight to us all. To see these long, narrow craft, raised up at both ends, nearly half of it out of the water, fitted up like a carriage, gliding through the water by the boatman's oar, which he manages as dexterously as a fish his fins, was exciting. Ten of these novel craft soon run up a narrow street, as they call them here, and land us safely, when in a few minutes I am writing this.

Breakfast over, our conductor announces that at nine he will have a guide for us to go to see the sights in this, in some respects, the most remarkable city in Europe, or anywhere else. We go until five o'clock P.M., and I return to my hasty scrawl to tell you something of what we have seen among the shows.

Seeing the Sights.—We first go to the palace of the king, a large old building. His dominion now is a small one compared with those who once occupied it. They claim a republic, and have as much as they are prepared for improving.

Venice is literally crammed with objects of interest, principally historical. A city of such antiquity, and once the mistress of half the power of Europe, must be of the deepest interest to all who reflect upon it. The next place we visit is the Church of St. Mark, near by. It is very old, having been begun in 900, and not finished until 1600. It is of Saracenic architecture, with Gothic additions, with the celebrated bronze horses of Constantinople over the doors, and the richest pictures within. These horses are the ones which Constantine carried from Rome to Constantinople. Manni Zeno brought them here in 1205. They were taken to Paris by Napoleon 1797, but restored to Venice in 1815. A great dome rises in the center, and four smaller ones around the arms of the cruciform structure. A multitude of pillars and white domes clustered into a long pyramid of colored light, seems partly of gold, opal, and mother-of-pearl. Angels, and signs of heaven, and the labors of men are seen around. Underfoot and overhead a combined succession of crowded imagery, one picture passing another—faces beautiful and terrible, mixed together. Dragons and serpents, ravening beasts and graceful birds drink from running fountains—the passions and pleasures of life symbolized together, and the mystery of its redemption carved on every place. Such things may have been useful in their day, but I think that day is forever gone among intelligent people. Yet this is the place where they say that St. Mark is buried, and their church is named for that apostle. A funeral is going on of a man who has been dead long, long ago, but gave a large sum to have his funeral celebrated three days every year, and this is the last one this year. They sung and played finely, I suppose, but, so far as worshiping God is concerned, it was mockery.

We go out to look at the clock-tower, and see the hours struck by two bronze figures on a bell. The Ducal Palace is the great work of Venice. The Giant's Causeway forms the main entrance, and the grand council-room the largest, which is one hundred and seventy-four feet, by thirty-five high. Many other rooms are filled with paintings and statuary, some of which would not be on exhibition in our country. At one place they say eight hundred faces are painted on the largest painting in Europe.

On the Gondolas Again.—At one o'clock we take ten gondolas at the hotel door, and away we go through the streets, the oarsmen jabbering away like blackbirds, and to us with no more meaning. They seemed to be proud of their calling. We go to see another very fine and costly church of more modern date. It would seem that all had been done that could be in the way of glittering decoration, statuary, and paintings, as usual in the churches, to make the grandest display possible.

In this there are seven chapels, built by seven noble families, I suppose to perpetuate their name. I will attempt no description of this monumental folly. The architecture is more modern, and all its equipments have only been finished a hundred years—this they call new. We go to see the glass manufactory. This, however, is more of the gaudy trinkets than for service. We pass the American Consul's residence, on the main canal, which is some eighty or one hundred yards wide. The city is built on a cluster of islands in a lagoon, which is separated from the Adriatic by a long, narrow sand bank, divided by several inlets, which are the entrance for ships. This canal winds through the city in a kind of double curve, nearly in the shape of an S. It is a marine Broadway, on which may be seen hundreds, if not thousands, of boats, doing the same work that is done in our thoroughfares by hacks, drays, and 'buses. There are one hundred and forty-six smaller canals, or streets, forming a net-work all through the city; yet one can walk from one to the other with a guide, by means of arched bridges to let the boats pass under.

The canal, however, is the great highway, and the gondola is the vehicle used for traveling. The great place of resort is St. Mark's Square. I walked down in the evening, and there were thousands of persons there. The area is five hundred and seventy-six feet, by from one hundred and eighty-five to two hundred and sixty-nine in breadth, and extends to the harbor, where ships and other boats come, and where a fine view is had of the harbor, and the Adriatic Sea. This is a great place of resort by the citizens and travelers in the evening. We visited another old church of the monks, who showed us through it, but I need not repeat. We had a fine sail with our fleet out in the harbor some distance, the gondola-men singing several songs, the boats all abreast. I failed to mention our visit to the famous prisons, and the terrible Bridge of Sighs, with which your readers are familiar. It is approached by long, narrow, dark passages, to the execution block upon which thousands of heads have been severed. The Venetian guide explained and commented on these things to some extent. My sheet is full; the first day in Venice is closed, and I will terminate my scrawl and renew after the morrow's tour.

Venice—The art galleries and the Royal Palace—Characteristics of the Italians—Among the gondoliers, etc.

VENICE, Italy, July 24, 1873.

Soon after I mailed my letter to you this morning we started out with our guide to see the Gallery of Fine Arts. We go by to see the place where Luther preached before the Reformation, about which I need say nothing, except that another reformation is very much needed all over this country. We go to this gallery, said to be one of the finest in Europe. Volumes might be filled in describing and giving the history of them. I will mention some of them, which impressed me more forcibly than others—one of the "Creation," "Queen Esther's visit to Solomon;" the "Four Evangelists," one Matthew with the eagle, another with the ox, John with a child, the other one is St. Luke. A very large painting, representing the "Ascension of Mary," with those below and the angels above to receive her is very fine. This is regarded as the best of the artist's, three of which were shown near each other; the first painted when he was fourteen, next at forty-five, and the last at ninety-nine years, having died before it was finished. Then there was the "Coronation of Mary"—fine. "Death on the Pale Horse" was very solemn; the "Conversion of Ten Thousand Venetians to the Christian (Catholic) Religion," by Palmer; "St. Mark working a Miracle;" "The Woman taken in Adultery;" "First Miracle of Christ—turning the water into wine at the marriage at Cana of Galilee;" "His Washing the Disciple's Feet," and "His Transfiguration;" "Solomon's Judgment about the two Mothers claiming the child;" "The Supper after the Resurrection;" "Resurrection of Lazarus;" "Rich Man and Lazarus;" "Christ in the House of the Pharisee," and in "St. Luke's House;" "His Ascending," and the "Taking Down from the Cross," are all very impressive paintings. "The Destruction of the Temple," "John the Baptist," "Bonaparte," "Hercules," and hundreds of others. After spending some time in these galleries we started to see the interior of the king's palace; on the way we go to see "Shylock's" place, a building four hundred feet by seventy-two, where the law was read to the people; a stone pillar in which was cut the shape and size of the smallest fish that was to be caught or sold, also the size of the oyster; *Post* newspaper, bank, and first church, built in 421. The bond-broker here gave the original name "Shylock," where all sorts of trickery was carried on. His descendants are here still, while his posterity have scattered all over the world. It was well worth visiting, not only for its history, but from what is seen at present.

The king's palace is a grand old establishment, large enough to contain a town of considerable size. We are taken through the largest and most important rooms, and told what they were for, but have not time, nor would you have the patience to read it. There are twenty-nine finely furnished rooms on a side, nine hundred rooms in the building. Victor Emmanuel visits this palace once or twice a year, his residence now being at Rome. His audience-room, reception-room, and the ball-room are the largest.

This was built when monarchy was the power that men worshiped. Now that power is on the wane, and the buildings are to a great extent vacant, though furnished in the most gorgeous and costly style. We were shown some very important works of art, which Napoleon took to France, but after his reign the Congress of Vienna had them returned. This people have what their ancestors looked on with reverence, but their glory has departed. Their living king has a large likeness hanging in his room, but he is gone to the center of his power, Rome. I have procured some photographs of him and others, with stereoscopic views of the palace, St. Mark's Church, and other places and things in this unique city, whose glory has. departed. It is now only about the size it was four hundred years ago, some one hundred and thirty thousand, or one hundred and forty thousand, pent up in their water-bound homes. We return to the hotel to rest an hour, and are off in gondolas to see other things of interest. We walked each morning on our routes. We pass out the streets into the harbor, our guide, with our United States flag, leading the way round to see their arsenal. In this they have preserved well the arms with which they fought in the past ages of their history; also, the models of their boats they used at the same time. Their cannon-balls were stone, some eighteen inches in diameter, shot out of leather guns (cannon they call them). Their fighting galley was a queer craft about A.D. 1500. One of these ships was one hundred and twenty feet long, by twenty-one wide, twenty-four high, built in 1571, and carried four hundred and sixty-eight men. They have hundreds of weapons of olden times, and some of them show superior skill. They have guns showing precisely the principle of Colt's revolver. Also, breech-loading cannon, and revolving barrels, shooting twenty times. The regular Damascus sword is here shown, used just before powder was invented. There was a model of a gondola built of gold in 1500; it is the same size and form as they have them now. This was built for their king. The guide said that Napoleon stole the gold of which it was made.

Their law requires all their boats to be black, with a representation of a sea-horse at the bow, all just alike, and numbered. They also carry printed rates of fare in them. Cheap traveling. They showed us the sword with which they beheaded criminals, and the model of a ship the British burned before it was finished. They have preserved the armors worn in the past ages, and many other things in which they seem to glory as worthy of veneration, as well as preservation. As we went into the arsenal a crowd of boys commenced revolving on the stone pavement. Some pennies were thrown, to see them scamper after them, as the pigeons at St. Mark's Square for corn. One little fellow had his shirt off, or had none, and some of our party gave him some money. As we returned they all had their shirts off, and followed us some distance, swimming alongside to get money. These people I think are a superior race to many we have seen, but are indolent. They stay in their houses in the daytime, and crowd St. Mark's Square in the evening. There seems to be no business doing, only a little huckstering. How they live I know not. No business seems to be doing anywhere, save the selling of some things in the shops.

We row across the harbor, some two miles, over to a neck of land, one-fourth of a mile, and see the Adriatic rolling its waves up on the beach. We gather some shells to remind us of our pleasant voyage, which gives us a fine view of the suburbs of Venice (islands). They built the city on seventy-two islands, so as to be protected from their enemies, by whom they were surrounded.

They are a gay, and, apparently, a happy people, who are fond of luxurious ease, if such a term can be applied to them. It is very obvious that they have greatly retrograded from what their ancestors were. In the darkness which succeeded the fall of Rome, Italy was the first country to burst the trammels in which the world had been so long buried. Political freedom first arose amidst the contests of the popes with the German emperors. And in the republics of Italy the human mind was developed to an extent which Rome never equaled. Europe is indebted to Italy of the middle ages for its first lessons of political wisdom, literature, and arts. We must ever regard with admiration and respect a people who have done so much in the great cause of human amelioration. Theirs is the most brilliant history on record.

The worst thing that Louis Napoleon did, I think, was, while allowing some liberty in France, he kept a standing army in Italy to keep this people in subjection to the papal dominion. And it is a most remarkable fact that just as their Council declared the pope's infallibility, a war was declared by which that power was destroyed, not only here, but in France. The Protestant rises upon the fall of papacy. I see I must not moralize—no time for that.

Our fleet returns to Venice. The "Stars and Stripes," sung over by the gondola-men and Americans, are complimented everywhere we go. Dine at 6 o'clock, and go out again to St. Mark's Square to see the assembled thousands in their nightly amusements.

My sheet is full. We are to be off on the morrow to Florence, and thence to Rome, to spend the Sabbath, and four days, in the most important city of Europe.

From Venice to Florence—Observations by the wayside—The ruins and beauties of Italy.

FLORENCE, Italy, July 25, 1873.

After I mailed my letter to you yesterday at Venice, I went up on the tower on St. Mark's Square, where I had a fine view of the city, with the harbor, and Adriatic Sea. The city occupies all the space there is, except what the canals and streets use. The houses are built on piles, driven down, which after a time become petrified, forming a very substantial basis for these old buildings. The country from here to Bologna is the most delightful. There are trees planted in perfect street-rows, about fifty yards apart, and the trees ten or twelve; on these the vines grow and hang from one to the other, forming a continuous grapery. These trees are mulberries, the leaves of which constitute the food for the use of the silk-worms. We saw them gathering them. They make two crops in this country. Their grain is harvested, and they are planting for another crop. I observed ten oxen to a plow. The finest cattle I ever saw are here, all white. There are a great many roads, all as smooth as a floor, and almost as white as snow. The contrast with the wilderness of trees and vines, with their magnificent avenues of Lombardy poplar, combine the beautiful with the grand in a most lovely manner. We see churches, with their little spires pointing to the heavens; old castles, and ruined walls of cities and forts, showing these people to have been warlike in other days. Now they seem to be an industrious and thrifty population. Their rivers are leveed very high, so that they keep the water in the proper channel. They raise a good deal of hemp, which they are now pulling. Indian corn constitutes a part of their crop. We stop a while at Bologna, change cars, and our direction also.

In Florence.—This place is one of the most ancient and important towns in Italy. It was anciently the capital of Romagna. It is situated in a fertile plain, at the base of the Apennines; population about ninety thousand, one hundred and thirty churches, twenty monasteries, and a venerable university with four hundred pupils—in 1200 it had ten thousand. It is now antiquated, as well as the town. Here the celebrated Council of Trent was held in 1547. In 1796 it was annexed to the Republic by Napoleon. In 1815 it again became subject to the States of the Church. In 1831 and 1849 revolutions broke out, and in 1869 the town finally united itself with Italy. The numerous old palaces and venerable churches, surmounted by quaint-looking towers, all bear testimony to the peculiar character of the place. Its glory has departed, never again to return. We soon, after leaving here, pass into a very mountainous region, grand and gloomy. On some of the highest are old churches, which seem almost inaccessible at first, but we discover a serpentine road up to them. The sunset here is lovely beyond description, but it and its influence is gone, and we pass through forty-six tunnels (some of them over a mile long), on to this place at 11 P.M. We had quite an excitement on the train last night. It stopped for five minutes. Miss Conkey and Miss Pegues, both of Oxford, Mississippi, were in our car and got out. Miss Carrington, from Virginia, who was in another, also got out. Not knowing how short the time was, they were both left. Mr. Richardson, under whose care they were traveling, knowing they were not in, pled with the conductor to wait, but he could not. The station-master regulated that, and off goes the train, leaving the ladies. We supposed only the one in our car was left, but after we learned the other, who spoke Italian, was left also, we were relieved. Mr. Richardson was very indignant, saying, "I told him in 'plain English' they were left, but he would not stop." His plain English was not good Dutch to the conductor, as he knew nothing of English. Our conductor got a dispatch from them at the next station, and I expect to meet them at the breakfast-table soon.

While at breakfast Colonel Notoman called to see me to take me out to see the city. He had his accomplished daughter with him, who has been at school several years in Europe, near Paris, and in Rome. She speaks Italian, as well as German, French, and other languages. Rev. Dr. Speer and myself took a seat with them, and spent several hours very pleasantly. We went first to an eminence outside of the city, where we had a fine view of the whole city below. Then to the king's palace, where we saw many things of interest in the way of paintings, statuary, and Mosaic, the finest of that kind I ever saw. There were some tables of Mosaic work that were said to have cost $125,000. Here was the most imaginative statue yet—Cain and Abel, the latter lying down dead. There were many artists copying paintings of the most celebrated artists, as here only are the originals of some of them.

From here we went to the Cathedral. It was the celebration of high-mass, and the music was the most lively I ever heard in a church. There were four chapels in which candles were burning, and in three of them worship was being performed in the most military style I have ever seen. These people are devout and religious, in their way, and, however we may differ, I have a profound respect for their sincerity. The Cathedral is a magnificent old building. The dome is two hundred and ninety-eight feet, with the lantern three hundred and fifty-four. Its length is five hundred and fifty-five feet, and three hundred and forty across the transepts. The choir is underneath the dome. We went home with our friend and spent some hours very pleasantly with him and his family. His wife is a very superior woman, in bad health, but full of mental vigor. Her brother was the American Consul, and resided several years at Venice. I learned more here about Italian matters than any place I have been. Every thing is almost as cheap as labor. His servants receive only from four dollars to six dollars per month. He lives in a palatial residence with nine large rooms, all furnished by the owner in princely style, every thing but his linen, and it costs only forty dollars per month rent, and the use of every thing in the house, and a fine garden and yard. Here I saw the first magnolias, which reminded me of home. I would prefer living here to any place I have seen in Italy. Having once a school-mate who resided here, I learned more about it than other places. They have good water, which we have found scarce in Italy. Mountains all around almost, and the clear little river running through it gives it the appearance of health and comfort. Some of the streets look very much like ours— stores and a passing crowd.

This is market-day with them. We saw the crowd of men, not women, as we have mentioned at other places. Florence has been the capital of Italy since 1864, until the recent war, by which Italy has become comparatively free from popery, and the capital is now, and since 1871, at Rome, where Victor Emmanuel resides. It ranks with Rome, Naples, and Venice as one of the most attractive towns of Italy. Rome was in ancient times the grand center of Italian development — the modern metropolis since the middle ages superseded it as the focus of intellectual activity. The modern Italian language has emanated from Florence. The fine arts have here attained the zenith of their glory. It is situated in a valley on both banks of the Arno, a small stream picturesquely inclosed by the Apennines, about three thousand feet high. The city has undergone great improvements. As early as the fifteenth century it had ninety thousand; now it has about one hundred and fifty thousand.

It was founded by the Romans before the Christian era.

The walls of the city, like Vienna, have been recently almost entirely removed. They were constructed at the same time of their cathedral, between 1285 and 1388. The ancient gates have been spared. A number of broad, new streets have been constructed on the site of the old fortifications. There are six bridges connecting the town. The city possesses eighty-seven churches, and a number of grand old houses and palaces, which bear testimony to its ancient prestige. The hall, which has been fitted up for the Italian Parliament, was the great hall constructed in 1495; but parliament, king, and all have gone to Rome, whither we are bound tonight. So I leave you to look over this hasty scrawl, as it is six o'clock—dinner-time—and though I have dined with my friend, Colonel Notoman, and having to travel till nine o'clock, will need another meal.

The Colonel and his lovely daughter are to take us out again to see Florence at night; so that I shall close abruptly, as the waiter says, "Monsieur, dinner."

The Eternal City—What a Memphian saw in Rome—Scenes on the banks of the Tiber—The great Cathedral—Statuary, paintings, etc.

Rome, July 26, 1873.

After I finished my letter yesterday, my friend, Colonel Notoman, came round for me to ride with him and his daughter again. We took Miss Sylvester, of Boston, with us, and visited the Protestant cemetery, to see the new-made grave of Hiram Powers, who died here recently. We also saw Theodore Parker's grave, who died here in 1860. We went through their fine park, and other places. We leave Florence at 11 P.M. At daylight the same beautiful country of which I spoke is seen until we get within an hour or two of Rome. The trees now are the olive, instead of mulberry, on which the grape-vines run. The people are at work by light. There are more horses and cattle here than any place we have seen. For some distance we pass through a hilly, poor country, until we get near the city, where the hills are covered with vines and fruit.

The Eternal City.—The long-sought city appears, but we see not St. Peter's. It is on the north side of the Tiber. Our hotel is centrally located, near the summit of a hill that overlooks the entire city. A dozen fountains pour out of a stone boat within a few steps of us. Rome, unlike any city we have seen in Europe, has an abundance of excellent cool water flowing from hundreds of fountains, some very large, all over the city. The streets are much wider, and generally straight. We arrive at 9 A.M. Breakfast over we are off, some to one place, some to another; I to picture galleries, statuaries, etc. Dine at five, after which Rev. Dr. Speer, two ladies, and myself, take a carriage to visit the Imperial Gardens, park, and public buildings. St. Peter's, seen in the distance, did not meet my expectations, but when we got there, and went inside, it far surpassed them. As I am going there to church to-morrow, I will say nothing more of it now. We saw a grand funeral procession of men clothed in black, head and face covered, singing. The coffin was covered, and carried on the shoulders of four men. We went to the Church of the Cardinals, and St. Andrews, but did not go in. The Pantheon! We must see the interior. It was near dark, and they were concluding service. There was a gloomy grandeur about it we have never seen before. The streets are crowded now by thousands as we pass several other important public places.

Sunday morning, soon after breakfast, we start

with ten ladies to see several places of interest. The first is the temple of Vesper and Clolenda. These, with the House of Rienzi, in the same vicinity, have been excavated from the ruins of the old city. They show great antiquity, and that even marble must decay or wear away by the teeth of time. We go next to the Protestant burying-ground, near the Porta San Paola, adjoining the Pyramid of Calus Cestinus. There are buried the poets Shelley and Keats. I copied the following from the tomb of Shelley: "Percy Bysche Shelley, *Cor Cordium Natus*, MDCCXCII, *Obit* 8. Nothing of him that doth fade; but doth suffer many changes, into some thing rich and strange."

We pass on through the ruins of the city, now covered with grape-vines and fruit-trees, where once millions lived, to St. Paul's Church, some two miles. This church does not possess the imposing exterior of St. Peter's, but within it is finer, and more modern in its architecture. There are some of the most splendid paintings here we have seen anywhere. "The Crucifixion of St. Peter with his head downward;" the "Ascension of Mary, and the angels above her;" "The Martyrdom of Stephen;" "The Death of Ananias and Sapphira;" "The Transfiguration;" "Moses and Elias Appearing," and "The Apostles Peter, James, and John." All these were very impressive scenes. There was a considerable noise of worship, to which we went, and found three men reading aloud. These constituted all the worshipers we saw. It is too far away to be of much service, only as a magnificent work of art and genius. Much might be said of it, but we hasten on to the Capitol, which occupies the square of Capitoline Hill, the site of the ancient capitol, and contains the palaces, senators, and magistrates of Rome. Here we saw the most ancient sculpture, obtained from the ruins of Rome. Many men renowned in history are seen here—Julius Cesar, Augustus Cesar, and the Popes and Emperors of Rome. Here is where Brutus performed his bloody deed, and this square is where he harangued the populace after the assassination so remarkable in history. This I know, but I do not that St. Peter and St. Paul are both buried under the altar of the churches named after them. They say a part of them is in each church. We go from here to St. Peter's again, and spend two hours in this, the largest church in the world. It stands on a slight acclivity, in the north-west corner of the city. It is built in the form of a Latin cross, the nave being, in length, six hundred and twenty-nine feet; the transept, four hundred and forty-four; the east front is three hundred and ninety-six feet wide, one hundred and sixty high; height of the dome, four hundred and sixty-five feet. In front of the church is a large piazza. It is the place of Nero's Circus, and where they say St. Peter was martyred.

It was one hundred and seventy-six years being built, and required three hundred and fifty years to complete it. Cost over fifty million dollars. I shall attempt no description of it now. There are eight acres of ground covered by it. I observed confessionals all about, and at one place counted seventy persons said to be waiting their turn. The subterranean church contains many tombs of popes, emperors, and kings, including the Stuarts.

There are some of the imposing ceremonies that have been regularly performed here that are now prohibited by Victor Emmanuel. He having taken possession of the city now nearly three years, is showing the people that he is their king, and not the pope. At Christmas, Easter, and on the festival of Sts. Peter and Paul (June 28th), the pope used to celebrate high-mass here in person. "The papal regime, illuminated in the evening by four thousand four hundred lamps, throwing the lines of the architecture into singularly prominent relief, and one and a quarter hours after sunset this illumination was changed by four hundred workmen for a blaze of torch-light. This remarkable spectacle, however, will probably never again be witnessed." This is one of the things prohibited by Victor Emmanuel.

The pope has not come out of the Vatican since the occupation of the city by the Italian troops, on the 20th of September, 1870.

After dinner we have service in the parlor of our hotel, after which I go with a friend up to the Royal Gardens and Park, where a fine view of the city and surroundings is obtained. Here we have a fine Italian sunset. Soon after we return the Waldensean minister calls to see Dr. Speer and myself, and we go with him to his church service, which is much like the Presbyterian service. We return to hear Professor Wood, our archæologist, lecture over an hour on what he is to show us to-morrow of the antiquities of Rome.

July 28, 1873.

Sketch of Rome.—Rome, the capital of the kingdom of Italy, the city of the popes, and once of the Cesars, is on the Tiber, partly on a plain and partly on low hills, with their valleys, about sixteen miles from the mouth of the river. The walls, fifteen miles in circuit, surround the entire city. It is passed by open gates, with large arches turned over them. They are built up with flat brick about one and a half inches thick, with mortar about as thick between them. Stones of all sizes seem to be worked in the wall. The modern city is built to the north of the seven hills which formed the ancient city of Rome. Four of these hills, once the scene of so many exciting events, are now almost entirely deserted, or covered by gardens, vineyards, or broken buildings, or ruins. It is said to be the best watered city in the world. Present population, two hundred and twenty-five thousand. The walls have an average height of fifty feet. There are twelve gates by which to enter it. The Arch of Titus, built on his return from his war against the Jews, continued and dedicated by his son, A.D. 80. It was calculated to hold from eighty thousand to one hundred thousand people, to witness the gladiators' and wild-beast combats. At its inauguration five thousand wild-beasts and ten thousand captives were slain. The early Christians stained it with their blood. By far the greater portion of the area inclosed by the walls inhabited during the Imperial period by two millions, is now uninhabited. The once densely populated streets are now the bleak walls of vineyards. The modern city is divided by the River Tiber, spanned by five bridges.

According to the census of 1867, there were six thousand two hundred and sixty-seven clergymen, four thousand nine hundred and forty-five nuns, four thousand six hundred and fifty Jews, four hundred and fifty-seven Protestants, seven thousand three hundred and sixty soldiers. We have been six hours to-day with Professor Wood explaining ancient Rome. I have taken extensive notes, but shall not give a synopsis of them now. We go out again this afternoon to see several places, among them the prison in which St. Paul was confined for two years before his martyrdom.

This is a wonderful city, the one that has been, and is now being excavated, more so than the one on the surface. We saw one of the modern palaces to-day, only three or four hundred years old, filled with antiquities from the excavations made by Louis Napoleon.

I mentioned in one of my letters from Rome that I had taken memoranda of which I had not time to write. As these letters may be published in a more permanent form, I am inclined to write something more about this most interesting city in the world.

So many objects of interest present themselves to the traveler that he scarcely knows which has the strongest claims to his attention. I will, from my notes, and "Walks in Rome, by Augustus H. Hare," with your permission, give the readers of the *Avalanche* something more relative to this ancient and renowned City of the Cesars.

From my boyhood I have desired to see this great city, which for so many centuries controlled the destinies of the civilized world. My feelings on arriving there were different from any other city we had visited. I could scarcely realize that I was in the "Eternal City," when I found at the railroad station a crowd of hackmen, porters, etc., and carriages awaiting our arrival. I expected to see St. Peter's rising above the horizon in stately grandeur, but it was within the horizon, and was so much less conspicuous from the nature of the ground it occupies on the opposite side of the Tiber. In front rise the Alban hills, the white villas on their sides distinctly visible for more than thirty miles. On the left were the Apennines, and Tivoli was distinctly seen on the summit of its mountain. We had a good hotel, in the best part of the city, to see most of its wonders. A stranger's first lesson to learn in a European city is its geography. Having our own experienced conductor, Mr. Plaggy, and Professor Wood for guide and lecturer, we lost but little time in that study, but proceeded soon after our arrival to see the city, which for ages has been the capital of the Catholic world. Monks have come hither to obtain the foundation of their orders, priests and bishops from distant lands coming here to receive the highest dignity which Christendom could confer. And kings and emperors have come here to ask coronation at the hands of the reigning pontiff; but we came as the "Italian section" of "the Educational party," to learn all we could in the allotted time of this city, which has been daguerreotyped upon our minds from childhood's days. There was one remarkable personage whose visit to Rome is worthy of reference in this connection. It was Martin Luther, a young monk, obscure and fervent, little dreaming that ten years later he would burn the bull of the pope in the public square of Wittenberg. His heart experienced nothing but pious emotions. He addressed to Rome, in salutations, the ancient hymn of the Pilgrims. He cried, "I salute thee, O holy Rome, venerable through the blood and tombs of the martyrs." But after prostrating on the threshold, he raised himself, and he entered into the temple, but he did not find the God he had looked for in the city of the saints and martyrs; it was a city of murderers and prostitutes. The arts which marked this corruption were powerless over the stolid senses, and scandalized the austere spirit of the German monk. He scarcely gave a passing glance at pagan Rome, and, inwardly horrified by all that he saw, he quitted Rome in a frame of mind very different from that which he brought with him. He went there with the devotion of the pilgrims, now he returned in a disposition like that which characterized his future history. This Rome, of which he had been the dupe, and concerning which he had been disabused, should hear from him again. The day would come when amid the many toasts at his table he would cry three times: "I would not have missed going to Rome for a thousand florins, for I should always have been uneasy lest I should have been rendering injustice to the pope."

No such feeling as this existed among our party. We had no salutation to offer his holiness, or prostration on the threshold, but, like anxious inquirers, desiring to see all we could of pagan as well as Christian Rome.

We honor this city for many reasons—her greatness, her beauty, her power, her wealth, her warlike exploits; yet, over and above all these things, on this account, that St. Paul in his life-time wrote to the Romans before he was permitted to visit them. (The fore part of this epistle I read and commented upon the Sabbath we spent in the city). Here he afterward lived and labored for "two whole years in his own hired house, and received all that came unto him, preaching the kingdom of God, and teaching those things which concern the Lord Jesus Christ, with all confidence, no man forbidding him." —See Acts of the Apostles, xxviii. 30, 31.

In the Church of St. Maria they still have a little chapel in which, as hath been handed down from the first ages, St. Luke, the Evangelist, wrote, and painted the effigy of the Virgin. The subterranean church is shown as the actual house in which St. Paul lodged when he was in Rome. I felt much interest in this place because of its associations, and may refer to it before I close these sketches.

The most matured period of St. Paul's Christian life detained him a close prisoner in the imperial city. It was from within the walls of a prison that St. Paul indicted the Epistles to the Ephesians, Philippians, Colossians, and Hebrews. It was here that he converted the slave Onesimus, and wrote the Epistle to Philemon, his master. Of all the disciples now ministering to St. Paul, none has a greater interest than the fugitive slave Onesimus. He belonged to a Christian named Philemon, a member of the Colossian Church, but he had robbed his master and fled from Colosse, and at last found his way to Rome. Here he was converted to Christianity, and had confessed to St. Paul his sins against his master. There is in this crypt a fountain shown as having miraculously sprung up in answer to the prayers of St. Paul, that he might have wherewith to baptize his disciples. The fountain is there at present, and doubtless has been for ages, but as to how it came there, no one knows whether nature or art produced it.

We find him during this Roman imprisonment surrounded by many of his oldest and most valued attendants. Luke, his fellow-traveler, remained with him during his bondage. Timotheus, his beloved son in the faith, ministered to him in Rome, as he had done in Asia, Macedonia, and in Achaia. Tychicus, who had formerly borne him company from Corinth to Ephesus, is now at hand to carry his letters to the shores which they had visited together.

All these associations clustering in and around this city give an intensity of interest to it more than any other in the world.

Capitol statues—Hall of emperors—Hall of illustrious men—Historic prison.

The first object of interest to the traveler on arriving at Rome is the Capitol. To this place we went, with a number of our party, the first morning. From this place we look down upon ancient Rome. Capitoline was the hill of the kings and the republic, as the Palatine was of the empire. Composed of tufa, its sides, now concealed by buildings, or by the accumulated rubbish of ages, were abrupt and precipitous, as are still the sides of the neighboring citadels.

When Romulus had fixed his settlement upon the Palatine he opened an asylum for fugitive slaves upon the then deserted Saturnus, and here, at a sacred oak, he is said to have offered up the spoils of the Calcinenses, and their king, Acron, who had made a war of reprisal upon him for the manner in which he treated their women. Here, also, he vowed to build a temple to Jupiter, where sports should always be offered. But in the meantime the Sabines, under Titus Tatius, besieged and took the hill, having a gate of its fortress opened to them. After the death of Tatius, the Capitoline hill again fell under the government of Romulus and his successor. The Temple of Jupiter occupied a lofty platform, the summit of the rock being leveled to receive it. Its *façade* was decorated with three ranges of columns, and its sides by a single colonnade. It was nearly square, being two hundred Roman feet in length, and one hundred and eighty-five in width. The interior was divided into three cells. The figure of Jupiter occupied that of the center, Minerva was on his right, and Juno on his left.

Close beside this queen of Roman temples stood the Temple of Fides, said to have been founded by Numa, where the senate were assembled at the time of the murder of Tiberius Gracchus, B.C. 133, who fell in front of the Temple of Jupiter, at the foot of the statues of the kings, his blood being the first spilled in Rome in a civil war. Near this, also, was the twin temples of Mars and Venus. Two cliffs are now claimants to be considered as the "Tarpean Rock," but it is most probable that the whole of the hill on this side of the Intermontium was Mons Tarpeia. Thus we see that in this vicinity there are quite a number of interesting objects connected with and forming a part of Roman history. It is natural for sight-seers to visit this locality first, as possessing in some respects peculiar interest in this city of wonders. We passed through the buildings, ascending the stone stairways to behold on each floor many things which caused our minds to recur to the past history of this remarkable people.

Among the Statues.—At the head of the stairs are colossal statues of the twin heroes, Castor and Pollux (brought hither from the Ghetto), commemorating the victory of the Lake Regillus, after which they rode before the army of Rome to announce the joyful news, watered their horses at the Aqua Argentina, and then passed away from the gaze of the multitude.

Next comes the statue of Constantine the Great, and his son, Constantine II. We now find ourselves in the Plazzo del Campideglia, where Brutus harangued the people after the murder of Julius Cesar. The tower of the Capitol contains the bell Viterbo, carried off from the town during the wars of the middle ages, which is never rung except to announce the death of a pope, or the opening of the carnival. Victor Emmanuel, I presume, will stop that, as he has done some other things in connection with his holiness. A gallery in the interior of the Tabularium has been fitted up as a museum of architectural antiquities collected from the neighboring temples. This building is, as it were, the boundary between inhabited Rome and that Rome which is a city in ruins.

The Hall of the Emperors.—In the center is the beautiful sealed statue of Agrippina, grand-daughter of Augustus; round the rooms are ranged eighty-three busts of Roman emperors and their near relatives, forming, perhaps, the most interesting portrait-gallery in the world. Even viewed as works of art, many of them are of the utmost importance. I was much interested in Julius Cesar, Augustus, Tiberius, Agrippa, and Constantine. There also was Nero, and Julian the Apostate, who have such unenviable immortality.

The Hall of Illustrious Men.—Here are Socrates,

Aristides the orator, Seneca, Marcus, Agrippa, Homer, Scipio Africanus, Cato, Miner, Cicero, and many others who live in the history of the past.

On the first and second landings are magnificent reliefs, representing events in the life of Marcus Aurelius Imp., belonging to the arch dedicated to him.

The halls of the conservators consist of eight rooms, the first painted in fresco, from the history of the Roman kings; the second room adorned with subjects from republican history, and statues of modern Roman generals; the third with subjects from the wars, and contains the famous bronze wolf of the Capitol. One of the most interesting relics of the city, forming a part of the decorations of this room, are the five pictures of a dead Christ, with a monk praying. The seventh room contains a history of the Punic wars. The eighth room is a chapel, containing a lovely face of the Madonna, and a child with angels; also the four evangelists.

A Historic Prison.—The north-eastern height, once the site of the most interesting pagan temples, is now occupied by one of the most interesting of Christian churches.

Descending from the Capitoline piazza toward the forum of the staircase on the left of the palace of the senate, close to the foot of this staircase, is a church, very obscure-looking, with some rude frescoes on the exterior. Here are the famous adamantine prisons, excavated from the solid rock under the Capitol. The prisons are entered through the low Church of St. Pietro, in Carcere, hung around with votive offerings and blazing lamps. Here St. Paul is said to have been bound for nine months to a pillar, which is shown to visitors. We know nothing of this. It may or may not be so. Yet this, with many other things, are told here, and seem to be believed by the people.

I could write much more of this deeply interesting locality, but I am admonished to be brief.

Palaces of Augustus, Palatine, Nero—Church of St. Clement.

The Palatine is formed of a trapezium of solid rock, two sides of which were about three hundred yards in length, the others about four hundred. This building was the foundation-stone of the Palace of the Cesars, which in time over-run the white hill, and under Nero two of the neighboring hills besides. These ruins have been ascertained and recognized. It has only been within the last ten or twelve years a few broken, nameless walls were visible above ground.

Napoleon III., in 1861, purchased it for fifty thousand dollars. Up to that time this part of Palatine was a vast kitchen-garden, broken here and there by picturesque groups of trees, and fragments of broken walls. Since 1861 extensive excavations have been carried on, which have resulted in the discovery of the palaces of some of the earlier emperors, and the substructures of several temples.

The Palace of Augustus increased in size until the whole valley was blocked up by it, and the end of its roof became level with the hill-sides. Before the entrance of the palace it was ordained by the senate, B.C. 26, that two bay-trees should be planted in remembrance of the citizens he had preserved, while an oak-wreath was placed above the gate to commemorate his victories. Upon the top of this building, Augustus Vespasian built his palace, A.D. 70, not only using the walls of the older palace as a support for his own, but filling the chambers of the earlier building entirely up with earth, so that they became a solid, massive foundation.

The ruins which we visit are, for the most part, those of the Palace of Vespasian, but from one of its hills we can descend into rooms underneath, excavated from the Palace of Augustus.

The Palace of Palatine is not the palace where the emperors generally lived. They resided at their villas, and came into the city to the Palace of the Cesars for the transaction of public business. They made use of the subterranean passage which ran round the whole building to prevent the annoyance of the crowd until they appeared in public to receive the morning salutation of the people. The name "Basilica" means "king's house." It was the ancient law court. It usually had a portico, was oblong in form, and ended in an apex for ornament. The Christians adopted it for their places of worship because it was the largest type of building then known. Nero, after the example of Augustus, heard criminal causes in the Imperial Palace, whose ruins still crown the Palatine. Here, at one end of the splendid hall, lined with the precious marbles of Egypt, we must imagine Cesar seated in the midst of the assessors. These counsellors, twenty in number, were men of the highest rank and greatest influence. Among them were the two consuls, and representatives of the other great magistrates of Rome. The remainder consisted of senators chosen by lot. Over this distinguished bench of judges presided the representatives of the most powerful monarchy which has ever existed— the absolute ruler of the whole world.

Before the tribunal of the blood-stained Nero St. Paul was brought in fetters, under the custody of his military guard. The prosecutors and their witnesses were called forward to support their accusation. The subject matter for decision was the written depositions forwarded from Judea by Festus; yet the Roman law required the personal presence of the accusers and witnesses whenever they could be obtained. He was accused of disturbing the

Jews in the exercise of their worship, which was secured to them by law; of desecrating their temple, and above all of violating the public peace of the empire by perpetual agitation as the ring-leader of a new and factious sect. The charge was the most serious in the view of a Roman statesman, for the crime alleged was treason against the Commonwealth, and was punishable with death. These accusations were supported by the enemies of the Sanhedrim, and probably by witnesses from Judea, Ephesus, Corinth, and other places of Paul's activity. When the parties on both sides had been heard, and the witnesses all examined, the judgment of the court was taken. Each of the assessors gave his opinion in writing to the emperor, who never discussed the judgment with his assessors; but, after reading their opinion, gave sentence according to his own pleasure, without reference to the judgment of the majority. On this occasion it might have been expected that he would have pronounced the sentence of condemnation against the accused, but the trial resulted in the acquittal of St. Paul. He was pronounced guiltless of the charges brought against him, his fetters were struck off, and he was liberated from his long captivity.

History has few stronger contrasts than when it shows St. Paul preaching under the walls of Nero's palace. Thenceforward there was to be but two religions in the Roman world—the worship of the emperor and the worship of the Saviour. The old superstitions had long been worn out—they had lost all their influence on educated minds.

Over against the altars of Nero the voice of St. Paul was daily heard, and daily woke in groveling souls the consciousness of their divine destiny. Men listened, and knew that if sacrifice was better than ease, humiliation more exalted than pride, to suffer was nobler than to reign. They felt that the only religion that satisfied the needs of men was the religion of the cross, in which he gloried.

The close of the Epistle to the Ephesians is a remarkable example of forcible imagery. Considered simply in itself, the description of the Christian's armor is one of the most striking passages in the sacred volume. But if we view it in connection with the circumstances with which the apostle was surrounded, we find a new and living emphasis in his enumerations of all the parts of the heavenly panoply. All this imagery becomes doubly forcible if we remember that when St. Paul wrote these words he was chained to a soldier, and in the vicinity of the Roman legions. The appearance of the guards was daily familiar to him in his chains. On the other hand, so he tells us in the preceding epistle, the soldier to whom he was chained to-day might have been Nero's body-guard yesterday. The comrade who next relieved him might have been one of the executioners of Octavia, and might have carried her head to Pophala a few weeks before. Such imaginings would naturally pass through the mind while viewing these ruins where we know this eminent apostle to the Gentiles preached, suffered, and died for his religion. While I have my doubts in regard to many things that I heard while in Rome, yet there are some things mentioned in sacred as well as profane history, the truth of which I could not question. This was one of them.

The Church of St. Clement is one of deep interest. It is under the ground, beneath the present church, and below this is the house of Clement, to which recent excavations and discoveries have given an extraordinary interest. The upper church, in spite of modernizations, under Clement XI., in the last century, retains more of the details belonging to primitive ecclesiastical architecture than any other building in Rome. It was consecrated in memory of Clement, the fellow-laborer of St. Paul, and the third Bishop of Rome, upon the site of his family house, where St. Paul dwelt with him. In the primitive church every thing remains in *statu quo*, the court, the portico, the cancelum, paschal candlestick, virgin. This was to me one of the most interesting places I visited in this once "imperial city." I gathered some relics from there with more interest than from any other place I visited in Europe. From the sacristy a staircase leads to the lower church, first discovered in 1857. Here there are several pillars of the rarest marbles in perfect preservation, and a very curious series of frescoes of the eighth and ninth centuries, part of which are still clear, and almost uninjured. These include the crucifixion, with the Virgin and St. John standing by the cross, the earliest example in Rome of this well-known subject. "The Ascension," sometimes called by Romanists the Assumption of the Virgin, because the figure of the Virgin is elevated above the apostles, though she is intent on watching the retreating figure of her divine Son. In this fresco the figure of a pope is introduced, showing that it was painted in his life-time. Quite a number of inscriptions are found on the walls, of much interest to the antiquary, in consequence of its being where St. Paul resided, and where Christians worshiped in the early history of the Church of Rome, to whom St. Paul wrote and preached.

The Forums and the Coliseum.

Following the Corso to its end and turning to the left, we are at once amid the remains of the Forum of Trajan, erected for the emperor on his return from the wars of the Danube. The Forum now presents the appearance of a ruin between the Capitoline and the Quirinal, but is an artificial hollow excavated to facilitate the circulation of life in the city. The earth was formerly as high as the top of the column, which reached one hundred Roman feet, to the level of the Palatine hill.

All over the surface of what was once Rome seems to be the effort of time to bury up the ancient city, so that in eighteen centuries the soil over its grave has grown very deep. This was the fate of Trajan's Forum until some antiquary a few hundred years ago began to hollow it out again, and discovered the whole height of the gigantic column, wreathed round with bas-relief of the old emperor's warlike deeds.

The Temple of Mars stands at the north-east corner of the magnificent Forum of Augustus, surpassing in size the Forum of Julius Cesar, to which it was adjoining. It was of sufficient size to be frequently used for fights of animals. Among its ornaments were statues of Augustus, and of Augustus's triumphal car and the subdued princes, with inscriptions illustrative of the great deeds he had accomplished there.

Returning a short distance, we traverse the site of the Forum of Julius Cesar, upon which eight hundred thousand pounds sterling were expended. The interest of Rome comes to its climax in the Forum. In spite of all that is destroyed and all that is buried, much still remains which a traveler interested in history will find all but inexhaustible and after the lapse of centuries the different sites seem now to be verified with tolerable certainty. The study of the Roman Forum is complicated by a succession of public edifices by which it has been occupied; each period of Roman history having a different set of buildings, and each in a great measure supplanting those which went before. Before leaving the Forum we visited the interesting group of churches in the vicinity, which have sprung up amid its ruins. Almost opposite the Mamertine prisons, surmounted by a handsome dome, is the Church of St. Martina, which contains the original model bequeathed by the sculptor Thorwaldsen, of his Copenhagen statue of Christ in the act of benediction. The subterranean church beneath this building is well worth visiting. The Church of St. Cosmo was founded within the ancient temple, by Pope Felix IV., in 527. The ancient church was divided in half by the vaulting, which now divides the upper and lower churches. To visit this lower church a monk must be summoned, who brings a torch by which it can be seen. It is of great size, and contains a curious well, into which Christian martyrs in the time of Nero are said to have been precipitated. The third and lowest church (the original crypt) is said to have been a place of refuge during the early Christian persecutions. A passage which formerly led from hence to the catacombs of St. Sebastian was walled up twenty years ago by the paternal government because twenty persons were lost in it. Deserving the most minute attention is the grand mosaic of Christ coming in the clouds of sunset. Near the Church of St. Francisca the Via Sacra passes under the Arch of Titus, which even in its restored condition is the most beautiful monument of the kind in Rome. Its Christian interest is unrivaled, from its having been erected by the senate to commemorate the taking of Jerusalem, and from its bas-reliefs of the seven-branched candlestick, and other treasures of the Jewish temple. Standing beneath the Arch of Titus, and amid so many ancient associations, it is difficult to forbear the commonplaces of enthusiasm on which tourists have insisted. Over the half-worn pavement and beneath this arch the Roman armies have trodden in their outward march to fight battles far, far away; returning victorious, with royal captives and inestimable spoil of Roman triumph, that most gorgeous pageant of earthly pride has streamed and flaunted in hundred-fold succession over the flagstones and under this archway—the street which led from the southern gate of Rome to the Capitol, and by which the victorious generals passed in their triumphal processions to the Temple of Jupiter. Between the Arch of Titus and the Coliseum, the ancient pavement of this famous road, composed of polygonal blocks of lava, has been allowed to remain.

The Coliseum was originally called the Flavian Amphitheater. This vast building was begun A.D. 72, upon the site of the reservoir of Nero, by the Emperor Vespasian, who built as far as the third row of arches, the last two rows being finished by Titus after his return from the conquest of Jerusalem. It is said that twelve thousand captive Jews were employed in this work, as the Hebrews in building the pyramids of Egypt, and that the external walls alone cost seventeen million francs. It consists of four stories—the first Doric, the second Ionic, the third and fourth Corinthian. Its circumference is one thousand six hundred and forty-one feet, its length two hundred and eighty-seven, its width two hundred and eighty-two, its height one hundred and fifty-seven. The entrance for the emperor was between two arches facing the Esquiline, where there was no cornice. The arena was surrounded by a wall sufficiently high to protect the spectators from the wild beasts, which were introduced by subterranean passages closed by huge gates from the side. The whole building was said to be capable of containing one hundred thousand persons.

The Emperor Commodus, A.D. 180–182, frequently fought in the Coliseum himself, and killed both gladiators and wild beasts, calling himself Hercules, dressed in a lion's skin, with his hair sprinkled with gold-dust. The gladiatorial contests came to an end A.D. 403. An Oriental monk named Telemachus was so horrified at them that he rushed in the midst of the arena and besought the spectators to remove them. Instead of listening to him, they put him to death.

The first martyrdom here was that of St. Ignatius, said to have been the child especially blessed by our Saviour, the disciple of John, and the companion of Polycarp, who was sent here from Antioch when he was bishop. When brought into the arena he knelt down, and exclaimed: "Romans who are here present know that I have not been brought into this place for any crime, but in order that by this means I may merit the fruition of the glory of God, for love of whom I have been made a prisoner. 'I am as the grain of the field, and must be ground by the teeth of the lions that I may become bread fit for His table.'" The lions were then let loose, and devoured him, except the larger bones, which the Christians collected during the night.

It is related of Ignatius that he grew up in such innocence of heart, and purity of life, that to him it was granted to hear the angels sing; hence when he became Bishop of Antioch he introduced into the service of the Church the practice of singing the praises of God in responses, as he had heard the choir of the angels answering each other.

Soon after the death of Ignatius, one hundred and fifteen Christians were shot down here with arrows. Some of these the wild beasts would not attack, but on their refusing were killed by the friends of the gladiators.

To stand and view these ruins, and let the mind run back to the scenes which have here been enacted, will produce feelings which may be imagined, but not described. So suggestive and distinct are the impressions made upon the mind, that one may easily fancy he sees the whole terrible, bloody scenes spread out before him. Alas, for poor human nature! to seek such amusements as countless thousands did, and with eager faces stare down into the arena to witness such a whirl of strife and blood going on there as no language can describe. Its solitude, its awful beauty, and its utter desolation strike upon the stranger the next moment like a softened sorrow to see it crumbling an inch a year, its walls and arches overgrown with green, its corridors opened to the dogs, the long grass growing in its porches, and young trees spring up on its ragged parapets. All these teach a lesson worthy of being engraven upon the tablet of every heart, of the vanity of the glory of earth's great and powerful nations.

The spot where the Christian martyrs suffered is now marked by a tall cross, devoutly kissed by the faithful, and all round the arena of the Coliseum are small chapels, or stations used in the Via Crusis, which is observed here at 4 P.M. every Friday, when a confraternity clothed in gray, with only the eyes visible, is followed by a crowd of worshipers, who chant and pray at each station in turn, after which a Capuchin monk preaches from a pulpit on the left of the arena. The pulpit of the Coliseum was used for the stormy sermons of Gavazzi, who called the people to arms from thence in the revolution of March, 1848. Never can one forget the magnificent Coliseum. I passed it often, and always felt inspired with the grandest conceptions I ever had of man's work whenever I beheld it.

The Eternal City—The Catacombs—St. Agnes.

As we rode out the Appian Way, one afternoon, to visit the catacombs, which have to be visited with a guide, on our route we passed the place where a remarkable story is told of St. Peter. After the burning of Rome, Nero threw upon the Christians the accusation of having fired the city. This was the origin of the first persecution, in which many perished by terrible and hitherto unheard of deaths. The Christian converts besought Peter not to expose his life. As he fled along the Appian Way, about two miles from the gates, he was met by a vision of our Saviour, traveling toward the city. Struck with amazement, he exclaimed, "Lord, whither goest thou?" to which the Saviour, looking upon him with a mild sadness, replied, "I go to Rome to be crucified a second time," and vanished. Peter taking this as a sign that he was to submit himself to the sufferings prepared for him, immediately returned back to the city. Where the roads divide is the Church of Domine, containing a copy of the celebrated footprint left here by our Saviour. We did not stop to see the copy which is kept here where the meeting occurred, but we saw what they assert to be the original at St. Sebastian. It is some twelve or fifteen feet high, and has to be seen with a taper. Some of our company were incredulous enough to say they saw the marks of the chisel even on this original footprint on the stone. We lighted our tapers, and following our guide, we wound down and around for a considerable distance among the bones of the ancient dead. Gloomy, indeed, are these catacombs. One visit to them is all any one ever need desire to be satisfied. The temperature is mild, and some of the vaults were almost dry, and the air seems to be pure. We did not go far, but I believe all of us were perfectly satisfied when we came out. Their extent is enormous, not as to the amount of superficial soil which they underlie, for they rarely, if ever, pass beyond the third mile-stone from the city, but the actual length of their galleries, for these are often excavated on various levels, three, four, or five feet, one above the other; they cross and recross one another so, that in the whole there are not less than three hundred and fifty miles of them. If stretched out in one continual line, they would extend the whole length of Italy. The galleries are from two to four feet in width, and vary in height according to the nature of the rock in which they are dug. The walls on both sides are pierced with horizontal niches, like shelves in a book-case, or berths in a steamer, and every niche once contained one or more bodies. These vast excavations once formed the ancient Christian cemeteries of Rome. They were begun in the apostles' time, and continued to be burying-places of the faithful till the capture of the city by Alaric, in the year 410. In the third century the Roman Church numbered twenty-five or twenty-six of them, corresponding to the number of her titles, or parishes within the city, and besides these, twenty others of smaller dimensions, isolated monuments of special martyrs, or belonging to private families. It is agreed among men of learning, who have had an opportunity of examining these excavations, that they were used exclusively by the Christians as places of burial and religious assemblies. Modern researches have now placed it beyond a doubt that they were originally assigned for this purpose, and no other. In most of these chambers, and sometimes in the galleries themselves, are one or more tombs of a more elaborate kind, hollowed out in the rock, or built up with masonry, and closed by a heavy slab of marble lying horizontally at the top of it.

The fact that the early Christians were always anxious not to burn their dead, but to bury them in these rock-hewn sepulchers, was probably owing to the remembrance that our Lord was himself laid "in a new tomb hewn out of a rock," and perhaps also, for this reason, the bodies were wrapped in linen cloths and precious spices, of which remains have been found in the tombs.

In the road leading to Surbam is the entrance to the Jewish catacomb. It is entered by a chamber opened to the sky, floored with black and white mosaic, which is supposed to have formed part of a pagan dwelling. The following chamber has the remains of a well. Among the most remarkable paintings is Elijah ascending to heaven in a chariot drawn by four horses, and a portrait of our Lord.

Owing to the desire in the early Christian Church of saving the graves of their first confessors and martyrs from desecration, almost all the catacombs were gradually blocked up, and by a lapse of time their entrances were forgotten. In the fourteenth century very few of them were still open. In the fifteenth none remained except this one at Sebastian, which continues to be frequented by pilgrims. A little more than a mile from the gate the road reaches the Basilica of St. Agnes, founded by Constantine in honor of the virgin martyr buried in the neighboring catacomb. It retains more of an ancient character than most of the Roman churches. The approach to the church is by a picturesque staircase of forty-five ancient marble-steps, lined with inscriptions from the catacombs. Beneath is the shrine of St. Agnes, surmounted by her statue—an antique of ancient alabaster, with wooden head, and hands of gilt bronze. The mosaics of the tribune represent St. Agnes between two popes of the seventh century. Beneath is an ancient episcopal chair. So ancient is the worship paid to St. Agnes that next to the evangelists and apostles there is no saint whose effigy is older. It is found on the ancient glass and earthen vessels used by the Christians in the early part of the third century, with her name inscribed, which leaves no doubt of her identity. St. Agnes suffered martyrdom by being stabbed in the throat, under Diocletian, in her thirtieth year, after which, according to the expressions used in the acts of her martyrdom, her parents "with all joy" laid her in the catacombs. One day while they were near the body of their child, she appeared to them surrounded by a great multitude of virgins, triumphant and glorious like herself, with a lamb by her side, and said: I am in heaven, living with these virgins, my companions, near Him whom I have so much loved." By her tomb also Constantia, a princess, sick with hopeless leprosy, was praying for the healing of her body, when she heard a voice saying: "Rise up, Constantia, and go on constantly in the faith of Jesus Christ, the Son of God, who shall heal your diseases." And being cured of her evil, she besought her father to build this basilica as a thank-offering. On the 21st of January a beautiful service is celebrated, in which two lambs, typical of the purity of the virgin saint, are blessed upon the altar.

The catacomb of St. Agnes is entered from a vineyard about a quarter of a mile beyond the church. It is lighted and open to the public on St. Agnes' day. This is one of the most interesting catacombs to visit. The entrance is by a staircase attributed to Constantine. The most interesting features here are a square chamber hewn in the rock, with an arm-chair cut out of the rock on either side of the entrance. In the central compartment is our Lord, seated between the rolls of the Old and New Testament. Above the arcosolium, in the place of honor, is the Saviour, as the Good Shepherd, bearing a sheep upon his shoulders, and standing between other sheep and the trees. In the other compartments are Daniel in the lion's den, the three Hebrew children in the furnace, Moses taking off his shoes, Moses striking the rock, and nearest the entrance the paralytic carrying his bed. A neighboring chapel has also remains of an altar, and well-preserved paintings—"The Good Shepherd;" "Adam and Eve, with the tree between them;" "Jonah under the Gourd." In the farther part of the catacomb is a long, narrow chapel, divided into three parts, of which the farthest, a presbytery, contains an ancient episcopal chair, with lower seats on either side for priests. In the extremity of the catacombs, under the Basilica of St. Agnes, is one of its most interesting features. There the passages become wider and more irregular, the walls sloping and unformed, and graves cease to appear, indicating one of the ancient arenaria which have formed the approaches to the catacomb, and beyond which the Christians excavated their cemetery. The graves throughout almost all the catacombs have been rifled, the bones which they contained being distributed as relics throughout Roman Catholic Christendom, and most of the sarcophagi and inscriptions removed to Lateran and other museums.

I have devoted more space to St. Agnes because of the importance attached to her name and memory than almost any other saint, and that we have a school named in honor of her in the city.

The Santa Scala—Roman Funeral—The Pantheon.

Among the many places of interest in Rome is the Santa Scala, erected by Fortuna, for Sextus V. We must of course go to see this remarkable relic of antiquity as well as credulity, which is supposed to be that of the stairs of the house of Pilate, ascended and descended by our Saviour. It is said to have been brought from Jerusalem by Helena, the mother of Constantine the Great, and has been regarded with special reverence by the Roman Church for fifteen hundred years. Clement XII. caused the steps to be covered with a wooden casing, which has since been repeatedly worn out by the knees of the ascending pilgrims. Apertures are left through which the marble steps can be seen, two of which are said to be stained by the blood of the Saviour. Between two statues the pilgrims kneel to commence the ascent, which, by the way, I should suppose, from what we saw when there, was not only a very tedious, but a laborious operation.

Numerous indulgences have been granted by different popes to those who ascend it with a prayer at each step. There is no day on which worshipers may not be seen slowly ascending these stairs, but during the Holy Week the concourse is at its height, and on Good Friday this structure is completely covered by the multitudes paying penance. Martin Luther went to accomplish the ascent of the Santa Scala. He slowly mounted, step after step, the hard stone, worn into hollows by the knees of the pilgrims for an indulgence for a thousand years. Patiently he crept half-way up the staircase. He suddenly stood erect, lifted his face heavenward, turned and walked slowly down again. He said, as he was toiling up, a voice as from heaven seemed to whisper to him the old well-known words which had been his battle-cry in so many a victorious conflict: "The just shall live by faith." He seemed suddenly released from his bonds and fetters, and with a firm step he went away. Ascending one of the lateral staircases—no foot must touch the Santa Scala—we reached a chapel so intensely sacred that none but a pope can officiate at its altar, and as Victor Emmanuel has stopped his officiating, it is probable it will be some time before service will be had in that chapel again.

Our company did not seem to feel much of the sacredness of this place, or its performances. Those who were going up were in good earnest, and we could but admire their perseverance while doubting their judgment.

A Roman funeral is a sad sight, and strikes one with peculiar solemnity. After death the body is entirely abandoned to the priests, who take possession of it, watch over it, and prepare it for burial; while the family, if they can find refuge anywhere else, abandon the house, and remain away a week. The body is not ordinarily allowed to remain in the house more than twelve hours, except on condition that it is sealed up with lead or zinc. At nightfall a sad procession stops before the house of the dead. They are dressed in a black cap, covering the head and face as well as the body, and two large holes cut in front for the eyes. Four carry the bier, and are furnished with wax candles, for no one is buried in Rome without a candle. If the person is wealthy the funeral takes place late at night, and the procession is long. I presume the one I saw was not of that class, for although there was a long procession, there were no carriages, and it was early in the night. I believe no carriages are allowed but at State funerals. Every one takes off his hat, or makes the sign of the cross, or mutters a prayer as the body passes. All these we failed to do, as we were not then posted in regard to these regulations.

The Pantheon.—The first time I saw this most perfect pagan building was the evening of our arrival in the city. There was an immense crowd there, and the soft, mellow light from the ceiling made one think it "grand, gloomy, and peculiar." The Pantheon was not originally as it now is, below the level of the plazza, but was approached by a flight of five steps. The portico, which is one hundred and ten feet long and forty-four feet deep, is supported by sixteen grand Corinthian columns of Oriental granite, thirty-six feet in height. The interior is a rotunda, one hundred and forty-three feet in diameter, covered by a dome. It is only lighted by an aperture in the center, twenty-eight feet in diameter. Seven great niches around the wall once contained statues of different gods and goddesses, that of Jupiter being the central figure. The world has nothing like the Pantheon. Every thing makes an impression of deep solemnity, which St. Peter's itself fails to produce.

St. Peter's—The Vatican—Sistine Chapel—Michael Angelo, etc.

St. Peter's.—The first church which existed on or near the site of the present building was the oratory founded A.D. 90 by Anacletus, Bishop of Rome, who is said to have been ordained by St. Peter himself, and who thus marked the spot where many Christian martyrs had suffered in the circus of Nero, and where St. Peter was buried after his crucifixion.

In 306 Constantine the Great yielded to the request of Pope Sylvester, and began the erection of a basilica on this spot, laboring with his own hands at the work, and himself carrying twelve loads of earth in honor of the twelve apostles. The great apostle is said to have been exhumed at this time, and reinterred in a shrine of silver, inclosed in a sarcophagus of gilt bronze. I wish here to state that it is a question about which there is a great difference of opinion, as to whether St. Peter was ever at Rome, Protestants contending that he never was, while the Romanists are fully established in the belief that he was here crucified and buried. I neither know nor care which is correct. I attach not the least importance to it, but I am giving only what is there believed, and about which they think there can be no possibility of doubt. I leave them to fight their own battles, while I proceed to say that the early basilica measured three hundred and ninety-five feet in length, by two hundred and twelve in width. Its nave and aisles were divided by eighty-six marble pillars. Though only half the size of the present cathedral, still it covered a greater space than any cathedral except those at Milan and Seville, with which it ranked in size. The building of the present St. Peter's extended altogether over one hundred and seventy-six years, and its expenses were so great that Julius II. and Leo X. were obliged to meet them by the sale of indulgences, which led to the Reformation. The expense of the main building alone has been estimated at ten million pounds sterling ($50,000,000). The annual expense of repairs is over forty thousand dollars. The *façade* of St. Peter's is three hundred and fifty-seven feet long, and one hundred and forty-four feet high, bearing statues of the Saviour and his twelve apostles. Near the central entrance is the Loggia, where the pope is crowned, and where he gives, or has given, the Easter benediction. On entering this largest of all churches you feel at first disappointed. You can't see it all from any one place, hence it does not fully meet your expectations. I was there several times, and each time was more impressed with its immensity. It appeared like some great work of nature, for we can scarcely realize that it is the work of men. You may lose your way in St. Peter's. There are so many chapels where divine service is performed and chanted that you come upon them before you are aware of it. The angels in the baptistry are immense giants, the doves colossal birds of prey. You lose all ideas of measurement, every thing being of gigantic proportions. As you enter the front door a cold wind strikes you which makes you feel like you needed an overcoat in summer. It is said the temperature does not change; in the coldest weather it is like summer to your feelings, and in the most oppressive heat it strikes you with a delightful sensation of cold.

The enormous size of the statues and ornaments in St. Peter's does away, to some extent, with the impression of its vast size, and it is only by observing the living, moving figures, that one can form an idea of its colossal proportions. A line in the pavement is marked with the comparative size of the other great Christian churches. I stepped its length, and found it over two hundred yards. Its exact length, as given by Mr. Hare, from whom I copy largely, is six hundred and thirteen and a half-feet; St. Paul's, London, five hundred and twenty and a half; Milan Cathedral, four hundred and forty-three; St. Sophia, Constantinople, three hundred and sixty and a half. The height of the dome in the interior is four hundred and five feet, and the exterior four hundred and forty-eight feet. St. Peter's is a grand aggregation of splendid churches, chapels, tombs, and works of art.

The Vatican, the first residence of the popes, was erected in A.D. 498–514, near the court of old St. Peter's, and here Charlemagne is believed to have resided on the occasion of his several visits to Rome. The Vatican Palace was used only on State occasions, and for the reception of any foreign sovereign visiting Rome.

The principal entrance of the Vatican is at the end of the right colonnade of St. Peter's, and is the nearest way to the collections of statues and pictures. On the right is the entrance of the Pauline Chapel. The Crucifixion of St. Peter, under the large window, and the Conversion of St. Paul, are tolerably distinct. There is a long train of soldiers seen ascending in the background. Christ, surrounded by a host of angels, bursts upon your sight from the storm-flash. Paul lies stretched upon the ground, a noble and finely-developed form. His followers fly on all sides, or are struck motionless to the ground.

The arrangement of the groups is excellent, and some single figures are very dignified. On the left of the approach from the Scala Regia is the Sistine Chapel. The lower part of the walls of this wonderful chapel was formerly hung, on festivals, with the tapestries executed from the cartoons of Raphael. The upper portion is decorated in fresco by the great Florentine masters of the fifteenth century. It was intended to represent scenes from the life of Moses, on one side of the chapel, and from the life of Christ on the other, so that the old law might be confirmed by the new—the type by the typified. The following is the order of the frescoes—type and antitype together: "Moses in the Bulrushes"—"Christ in the Manger;" "Moses on the way to Egypt"—"Baptism of Christ;" "Moses and the Israelites passing the Red Sea"—"Calling the Apostles;" "Moses giving the Law"—"Christ's Sermon on the Mount;" "Last Interview of Moses and Joshua"—"Resurrection of Christ." The avenue of pictures is a preparation for the surpassing grandeur of the ceiling. It contains the most perfect works of Michael Angelo in his long and active life. There his great spirit appears in its noblest dignity, and in its highest purity; the most important events in the Book of Genesis—the creation and fall of man, and its immediate consequences; the sitting figures of the prophets as the foretellers of the coming Saviour. A great number of figures are also connected with the frame-work. They may be the best described as the living and embodied genii of architecture. It required the unlimited power of an architect, sculptor, and painter to conceive a structured whole of so much grandeur; to design the decorative figures with the significant repose required by the picturesque character.

The pictures of the Old Testament are: "The Separation of Light from Darkness;" "The Creation of the Sun and Moon;" "The Creation of Trees and Plants;" "The Creation of Adam;" "The Creation of Eve;" "The Fall, and Expulsion from Paradise;" "The Sacrifice of Noah;" "The Deluge," and "The Intoxication of Noah."

The lower portion of the ceiling is divided into triangles, occupied by the prophets. They sit in twelve throne-like niches, more like presiding deities, each enwrapt in self-contemplation, than as tributary witnesses to the truth and omnipotence of Him they are intended to announce. They thus form a gigantic frame-work around the subjects of the creation, of which the birth of Eve, as the type of the nativity, is the intentional center.

The Sistine Chapel is associated in the minds of all the Roman sojourners with the great ceremonies of the Church, but especially with the Passion Week.

The small portion of the Vatican inhabited by the pope is never seen except by those admitted to a special audience. As our time was limited in which to see the wonders of this most remarkable of cities, we had none to spend in the preparations to see his holiness. We learned that it required some three or four days, after a good recommendation (which we do not know that we could have obtained), to be admitted into his sacred presence. A suit of clothes, made after a certain style, is one of the requirements in order to see him. We made no effort to get to see the man who, though he regards himself as a prisoner, wields more influence still in Europe than any crowned head in the land.

Leaving the city.

ROME, July 30, 1873.

I sent you a letter day before yesterday, giving a hasty sketch of my impressions of this ancient city of Rome. Since then we have been going from 7 A.M. to 9 P.M., nearly all the time, with Professor

Wood, a celebrated archæologist, an Englishman, who has resided in Rome for nearly a quarter of a century. He has taken us through the old city excavations, showing the present city to be fifty feet above the ancient one. Sometimes we find a building directly over one below it, and sometimes the third one below both the others. These excavations have been going on since the commencement of the present century, more or less, as the means could be obtained to prosecute them. Louis Napoleon purchased of the ex-king a portion of them, and has been for many years expending some fifty thousand dollars annually in this work.

A great many things have been found which belong to other ages, demonstrated by the inscriptions found on them. Some of the most important were found last August. These we have met with in the Vatican and other places. Napoleon sold out his possessions here to the Italian government, and they are now engaged in these excavations, expending large sums of money for the removal of the rubbish. I have taken down some sixty pages in my note-book, but have not time to look over them. I shall not say any thing of them now, for we are to be off this morning for Pisa. At present I have only time to sketch our route, and the objects that impress me most at the time, just as they come up in my mind, when I can find a few moments to write them.

We had heard much of the heat of Rome, but we have found it very pleasant. In the sunshine for a few hours in the day it is very warm, but not near so hot as with us. The nights are cold and refreshing. We have had no warm weather to make it unpleasant yet, and as we are now going to Switzerland, we do n't expect to suffer with it in the mountains. All our party keep well, and in good spirits.

Leaving the City.

Our ladies pack their baggage when necessary, which is often, like heroes. They are nearly all teachers, and are learning that which will qualify them better for their duties. Then their natural curiosity stimulates them to rush ahead to see all they can. One will see, perhaps, ten times as many people on the streets at night as in the day-time. The squares are filled with idlers, who have a free and easy way of spending their time. I have counted seventy performers in a brass-band. Everybody seems to enjoy themselves in their nightly amusements. They do n't have their beer-gardens, like the Germans, nor do they seem to drink any thing much but lemonade, publicly. They are a much more intellectual-looking people than many we have seen. They look more like our Southern population than any we have met with in Europe. They do not remind us, however, of our hotels. They study economy closely. They have meat only once a day, and that done up in "Italian style," sometimes repulsive to me. We make a clear sweep of all they give us that we can eat, and that is enough. Upon the whole I like these Italians. They are republican in their feelings, and some day they will cut loose from civil and ecclesiastical despotism. In fact, there has been a great improvement in these matters within the past few years. The pope's bulls seem to create no sensation among the people, so far as we could learn. Religious and civil liberty seem to be enjoyed as much here as in any country we have visited. This is the first place on the Continent in which we have not been able to spend the time we desired; but the "Eternal City" attracts us, and soon we are to be off for romantic Switzerland.

CHAPTER XIII.

Letters from the Rev. A. B. Whipple, President of Lansingburgh College, New York.

VENICE, July 22, 1873.

TUESDAY at 6 A.M., after twenty-three consecutive hours in the cars, we were glad to get into gondolas and wend our way through water-streets, or canals, to the Hotel Victoria, for breakfast in Venice, "the bride of the sea." In its best days it had a population of 200,000; now about one-half as many, and one-fourth of these helped as paupers. Fifteen thousand houses and palaces constitute Venice, built on three large and one hundred and fourteen small islands, formed by one hundred and forty-seven canals, united by three hundred and seventy-five bridges. The city is surrounded by a shallow bay twenty-five miles long and nine wide, protected from the open sea by long sand-hills, converted into bulwarks by solid masonry averaging thirty feet in height and forty-five in width. There are two kinds of bays, or lagoons—living or dead, or those in which the tide rises and falls, and those shallow and unaffected by the tides. Most of the houses rise immediately from the water, and all expeditious traveling is done in gondolas. There are many places of interest, chief of which is the Piazza of St. Mark and its surroundings. "Piazza" means a large open space; small ones are called "*campi*." This is five hundred and seventy-five feet in length, two hundred and sixty-eight in breadth on the east, and one hundred and eighty-five feet on the west side. On three sides it is inclosed by imposing structures, forming one vast marble palace, blackened by age and the elements, and looking, in fact, very much as if seen through a stereoscope. On the east is the Church of St. Mark and a small piazza, called Piazzetta, on the west of which is the ancient library of St. Mark. On the south is the Lagune, or "live bay." In this part of the piazza are two lofty granite columns—one surmounted by the winged Lion of St. Mark, the tutelary saint of Venice; the other column supports St. Theodore, on a crocodile, the patron of the old republic. You can easily infer what these emblems are designed to teach. On the north are the *procuratia*, or palaces of the "procurators," the highest officials in the republic, and on the west the Atrio, or new palace, erected by Napoleon in 1810, on the site of a former church. All these buildings surrounding the Piazza have their ground structures of arcades, in which are the *cafés* and shops, the grandest in the city. This Piazza is the focus of public life in Venice. Here rich and poor, on summer evenings, gather to enjoy the band of music, lemonade, cigars, conversation, sight-seeing, and purchases.

I do not wonder that in this warm climate, and with such narrow streets and small accommodations, most of the people live out of doors as much as possible. Even in the winter the band plays here in the open air from 2 to 4 P.M., and then this is the promenade of the fashionable world.

Rather than try to give a running account of the whole city, let me in this letter be more special than hitherto, and confine my description to St. Mark's Church. I can do this, because I tarried in and around it longer than any other church in Europe.

Some years ago a very rich man died, and left a very large sum of money to be annually expended, and perpetually, in one hundred masses per day for three days. One of these days we were there listening to the service, employing the best singing talent of the Italians. Not being a critic of the music, I let my eyes roam around the church, and read the Latin inscriptions under every painting and statue. (In parenthesis let me say, in all the churches and most of the galleries of paintings and art, we find Latin inscriptions, and he who can read them need not wait for a guide to explain in very poor English what he can read for himself.) I have mentioned St. Mark as the tutelary saint of Venice. This church was begun in 976, and finished in 1071, and lavishly decorated, with oriental magnificence, in after centuries. In form it is a Greek cross; has equal arms, covered by a dome in the center, and one at the extremity of each arm—five domes. Inside and outside, the church is adorned and supported by five hundred marble columns, with capitals in every variety of style. Mosaics of the tenth century cover forty thousand square feet, and the interior is lavishly decorated with gilding, bronze, and eastern marble. The conjoined effect is picturesque, or fantastic, rather than seriously impressive. Without, and over the portal, are four horses in gilded bronze, some five feet high, made in the time of Nero, well executed, and valuable as the sole specimen of an ancient four-horse team, pictured before a chariot. They once adorned the triumphal arch of Nero, next that of Trajan. Constantine took them to Constantinople, and Dandolo captured and brought them to Venice in 1207. Then Napoleon captured the place, and took them to Paris in 1797, and placed them on top of the triumphal arch in the Place du Carroussel, and in 1815 the Emperor Francis brought them back to

Venice, and they are now in their former position. Few horses have traveled so far, or had so many royal horse-thieves to run them out of one country into another, and, in common parlance, "show their oats so well." Mosaics below the horses and in the arches represent the Last Judgment, the embarkation at Alexandria of St. Mark's body, and its disembarkation at Venice, and on the left the veneration of the saint, and the church into which his relics were conveyed in the thirteenth century. The vaulting of the entrance-hall, entirely of mosaic, represents Old Testament subjects, beginning on the right with the creation; the new part, New Testament scenes; while over the entrance is St. Mark, from a design by Titian; and the capitals of the columns are said to be from the Temple at Jerusalem. The interior is fifty-eight by two hundred and ten feet, and over the entrance-door is one of the oldest mosaics of the church, done in the eleventh century, representing Christ, Mary, and St. Mark. Approaching the altar, on the right and left are two pulpits of colored marble, and above, in mosaic, the genealogy of Mary. On the screen are fourteen statues in marble of Mark, Mary, and the Apostles. On the arches each side of the choir are five bronze reliefs from events in the life of St. Mark. Beneath the high altar, as the marble slab says, repose the relics of St. Mark. Back of the high altar is another slab, with four spiral columns of alabaster, two of which are semi-transparent, and are said to have belonged to the temple of Solomon. In the right aisle, near the west portal, in the center, is the baptistery, a large bronze fount made in 1546, and above it is John the Baptist. The stone above the altar is said to be from Mount Tabor. Left of the altar is the heart of John the Baptist, a work of art, and beneath it the stone on which he is said to have been beheaded. In the right transept one enters the Treasury of St. Mark, where is shown the cover of the Books of the Gospels, brought from the Church of St. Sophia, at Constantinople, decorated with gold and jewels; a crystal vase with the "blood of the Saviour;" a silver column, with a fragment of the "True Cross;" a cup of agate, with a portion of the "skull of St. John;" an episcopal throne of the seventh century, said to be that of St. Mark; and other equally curious things.

Thus far I have noticed some of the most noteworthy objects within and about this wonderful church, now the Cathedral of Venice. I have failed to describe the "thousand-and-one" paintings which also adorn it—Bible history to repletion; every prophet, priest, and king; every evangelist and martyr, and a tree full of eager Zachariahs; mothers and children, clothed and unclothed, without number. At these strange works of genius, trying to express in colors verbal pictures from Holy Writ, I sat and gazed, while the music was rolling through vaulted aisles and corridors and domes, and thousands on bended knees about me were joining in a service lavishly paid for to help a soul out of purgatory; while the very Saviour so many times pictured above and around us all, is ever inviting all to come to him, without money and without price. I would find no fault with all these beautiful churches and their wonderful artistic adornment; nor do I wonder that in this land, educated to it, these people are devout Catholics. To tear them away from all their beautiful churches and the service in which they take delight and have faith will require more than mere human power. Nor can I wonder that Oliver Cromwell, that stern old Puritan, when he saw the devotion of the people to their churches and works of art, thought it needful to demolish them. Yet I do not think it would be wise to make a grand crusade against all works of art. Rightly educated, people will learn that love of the beautiful and love of the holy are two distinct things, and that we may have both, and so worship God with the heart and with the understanding. I have seen no church or picture yet which I should be willing to bow before and worship. Yet, every day, as I see so much, in spirit I am grateful to Him who gives to men such privileges and powers.

GENEVA, August 2, 1873.

Once more I find a few moments' leisure to write to friends 4,000 miles away and tell them that since last writing I have been for the best part of five days in Rome. Of this city it is somewhat difficult to speak; for it is *"multum in parvo,"* or *" e pluribus unum;"* i.e., there is much in one place, or there are many cities grown out of one. Hence, in a description of Rome, one is led to ask, Which Rome shall be described? For here is the old pagan Rome, as founded by Romulus, with a portion of its wall remaining; the very place also where, in the midst of sacred games instituted for the purpose, he seized the Sabine virgins, and also the battle-field where, to prevent farther bloodshed, these same seized women rushed between the armies, stayed the contest, formed a union of Romans and Sabines, and so rendered the original walls needless. This is the Rome founded 753 years B.C., or, to be exact, 2,527 years ago, on the 23d of last April. The rapid growth of the ancient city must be attributed greatly to its situation, the most central in the peninsula, alike adapted for a great commercial town and for the capital of a vast empire; for then, with small vessels, it had large intercourse with the Mediterranean. To describe this Rome is to speak of it as a kingdom. On the Palatine Hill was the walled city of Romulus; on the Quirinal sprang up the city of the Sabines, afterward united, as mentioned above, each retaining its peculiar temples and sanctuaries, with the Forum between them and common to both, an assembly focus for the entire State. Around these twin hills, on five others, as suburbs, extensive settlements sprang up, increasing in population both by increase of business and because conquered Latin towns were frequently transplanted thither. Such was the earliest Rome. Out of these mixed elements, a new civic community took its origin toward the close of the period of kings; and the Servian wall much larger; the remains of this wall show a moat without and a rampart within of great solidity, surrounding the seven hills, some seven miles in circumference. While thus strengthening the city against invasions from without, the kings were no less anxious to embellish the interior with handsome buildings. To this period belongs the Circus in the valley between the Palatine and Aventine hills. The Circus is a kind of a race-course, with elliptical course, in a long valley, with seats on each side for spectators, enough to accommodate 120,000. Here took place athletic exercises and various games for the amusement of the people, and the exhibitions of wild animals brought from conquered countries. You will remember that there were no pictures of animals then, as now, nor Barnum's menagerie, and so the greatest curiosity was excited when a victorious army from Asia or Africa brought the wild animals, as well as kings and slaves, and exhibited them to the thousands gathered on either side the Circus to gratify their curiosity and, no doubt, hurrah for the Roman soldiers returning victorious. Then, also, was built the Cloaca Maxima, or great sewer or drain, which made available the swampy site of the Roman Forum. Through this massive construction we could see the rushing waters, while far above, and over the road of the ancient Forum, more modern sewers are emptying the dirtier waters of a later Rome. These grand developments of the ancient, and still admired city, were due to the energy of the Tarquinian kings, whose last king, Tarquinius Superbus, was expelled in 509. So we have noticed two Romes, both now the deep foundations of still later Romes. Most of what I now describe has been brought to light by the last Napoleon, who purchased the gardens of the Palatine hills, simply that he might excavate, and so certify himself of facts, when he was compiling a history of Cesar. After the expulsion of the kings came the third Rome, or the Republic. During the first century, the Republic had a hard time in establishing its supremacy, and once, with the exception of the capitol, was wholly destroyed by the Gauls. It was only a transient loss to the prestige of Rome, but produced a marked change in the external features of the city. The work of resurrection was begun with zeal and pride of industry rather than of beauty; for the streets were narrow and crooked, and the houses poor and unattractive, and Rome was then far from being attractive or handsome as a city. Her steady increase in power could not fail to have a good influence on her architecture. During this period the first aqueduct was made, traces of which remain, and the first high road, the Appian Way. Down to the Punic wars, Rome had not extended beyond the walls of Servius Tullius. The overthrow of Carthage made Rome the mistress of the world; and the wall had to give way for new buildings. Speculation was now active, and real estate and rents greatly advanced; fortunes were made, and palaces were constructed with fabulous magnificence and luxury. Claudius, for instance, Cicero's opponent, paid nearly $700,000 for his palace. In the last century B.C., Rome began to look like the world's capital—streets were paved, hitherto not, and the ambition of the opulent nobles was to erect sumptuous public buildings, whereby to perpetuate their names. So Cato built the first Basilica, or Court-house, in the Forum. Remember, the Forum is not a building, but a large public assembly-place, where various business was transacted; but constantly improved and adorned with works of art and the like; then with columns and arcades, then the Basilica, etc. Theaters were all out of doors, like the Circus, till Pompey founded the first one of stone. A change, from a republic into a military despotism, involved a new period of architecture. Usurpers generally exercise their energies in destroying the works and monuments of their predecessors, and then try to outdo them, and such were Cesar's plans; and now, of all the ruins of ancient Rome, the buildings of Augustine rank highest in number and importance. Take the Pantheon, for instance, the only building entirely preserved of ancient Rome—a huge circular structure, with vast colonnades and strikingly imposing in aspect; walls of brick-work, covered with marble and stucco, formerly five steps above the pavement, it is now below. The portico has fifteen columns of granite, thirty-eight feet high, eight in front; the others form three colonnades, vaulted and terminating in niches in which colossal statues of Augustus and his son-in-law, M. Agrippa, stood, with an inscription on the frieze showing the edifice was erected B.C. 27. It is illuminated wholly by an aperture in the center of the dome, producing so pleasing an effect that, even in ancient times, it caused the belief that the temple derived its appellation, *Pantheon*, from its resemblance to the vault of heaven. Within were seven large niches, containing statues of Mars, Venus, Cesar, etc. The entire roof was covered with gilded bronze tiles, which Constantine II. removed to Constantinople, and Gregory III. replaced them by lead. Eleven thermæ, or bathing houses, were also built, each large enough for 15,000 bathers, with warm and cold water; these were huge buildings, with magnificent rooms in mosaics and marble, and richly decorated with statues and paintings. We were shown through the remains of one, grand in its ruins, covering forty acres. During this age no less than eighty-two temples were restored, and other works in proportion, so that Augustus boasted that he found Rome a town of brick and turned it into marble. Up to about one hundred years B.C. marble quarries were not known near Rome. Future history brings its destruction, and fire leaves its devastations, till again the glory of Rome has departed, and the palaces of the Cesars, in their mighty ruins, remain to suggest their past grandeur; and we get some idea of Cesar's ample palace, when we learn that in its completeness it occupied more ground than all the area inclosed within the city walls first built by Romulus. I have written thus of early Rome, because as a teacher it is Latin, not Italian, Rome about which we study, and to which reference is so often made in school-books and learned essays. We had as guide Mr. S. Wood, twenty-two years a resident of the city, and one of the most reliable archæologists of the present time. He has watched the excavation during the past years, and could tell all the history of the past, and how he could tell by the brick or by the impressions to what age any structure belonged. Of modern Rome, its 365 churches full of old relics and adorned with fine paintings, of the Coliseum and St. Peter's Church, of the Vatican and its magnificent works of art, of its present busy street life, this letter can only hint; for you know I shall want something to talk about on my return. This I can say for the hotel where we stay, we get the least food for the most money of any place we have yet seen.

Letter from Rev. C. W. Cushing, President of Auburndale College, Massachusetts.

LONDON, August 21, 1873.

To write a letter upon Rome which shall give even an outline of the interesting ruins which have been brought to light by recent excavations would make an epistle quite too long for a newspaper; so I shall speak of but very few of the objects of interest upon which we looked with wonder. First of all I want to dispel the popular illusion that it is fatal to visit Rome in the summer months, on account of the malaria which is so prevalent there. Our company, consisting of forty-five men and women—a large majority of them women—went from Florence to Rome, July 25th, and left on the 30th. During these days we were all in perfect health, though we disregarded all the precautions which had been given us in regard to night air, and remained out on the Campagna or elsewhere until ten o'clock at night, or even later.

When we arrived in Rome, Professor Shakspeare Woods, who has resided in Rome for twenty-two years, advising and encouraging the excavations, met us at the hotel, and promised us every possible assistance during our stay. He also assured us that we need have no anxiety in regard to malaria. He told us that, as head of the health department, he had received weekly reports for the last two years, which showed Rome to be the healthiest city in Italy, and that there were but two cities in Europe as healthful. Professor Woods is reputed the best living archæologist, and whatever statements I shall make in regard to the ruins of Rome will be upon his authority. He assured us that whatever statements he should make concerning the age and identity of these ruins would be upon authority and evidence which were unquestionable. With these assurances we started on our explorations, with him for our guide, at seven o'clock in the morning of the 28th of July, and continued with him two full days.

Our first point was the ancient palaces of the Cesars, one of the principal parts of which is the Palace of Tiberius. This palace was enlarged and changed by successive emperors, until it covered an area which is almost fabulous. The location is on the ancient Palatine, the spot on which ancient Rome was founded on the 23d of April, 2,627 years ago.

In looking at these ruins, one is impressed at the outset with the grandeur of the old Roman character. The public buildings were on a scale of magnificence never equaled. But they are buildings *upon* buildings. Indeed, Rome is a city upon cities.

Standing on the Palatine, three arches mark the site of the old Basilica of Constantine, which was erected on the site of the ancient Temple of Peace. Before you, looking southward into the valley below, was the great Circus Maximus, between the Palatine and Aventine, where the games of Romulus took place. The building would accommodate 485,000 persons. Here was where the rape of the Sabines took place. Near this, on the Palatine, is the famous Arch of Titus.

The ruins of the house of Domitian were traversed; also the great entrance hall, where emperors after Domitian received embassadors. Portions of the beautiful marble floor still remain. Lying about in different directions were portions of the immense porphyry columns which were in the adjoining dining-room. In a large open court, into which the dining-room opened by spacious windows, were the remains of large fountains, elaborate in plan and profuse with ornament, which were kept in play to cool the air in the dining-room. The pavement in the room of the fountains, portions of which still remain, was of Oriental alabaster. Near this were the remains of the house of Augustus. The walls on which the foundations of these buildings rested were of great height, often seventy-five to a hundred feet, built up from the valley below, and of immense thickness. They were strengthened by arches, which were built in all through them. The bricks in these walls are as perfect as when first laid.

From this point, in full view just over the hill, was the Appian Way, and the gate where Paul entered Rome. To see it, we stood on the ground floor of the portico, built by the Emperor Septimus Severus, two hundred years A.C., for the purpose of extending his palace. It was at least seventy feet above the valley below. One room was found in this palace which was originally lined entirely with silver, set with gems.

Near this were portions of the original wall built by Romulus, soon after founding Rome. The walls are very thick, built of stone—mostly tufa—fitting very closely, and laid without mortar. Recent excavations have removed all doubts from the minds of archæologists in regard to the founding of Rome, and have confirmed the statement so long regarded mythical, that Romulus was the real founder of Rome.

In the ruins of the Palace of the Emperor Caligula, the stucco on the ceilings, and a marble railing forming a balustrade to a balcony, were very perfect and beautiful. The large portico where Caligula used to walk sleepless nights is still complete, and the original mosaic pavements are well preserved.

We next entered the house of Tiberius Claudius Nero, the father of the Emperor Nero, built one hundred years B.C., and anterior to the Palace of the Cesars. The paintings on the walls are very perfect. In many instances the colors are as rich and brilliant, and the features on the faces as perfect, as if painted yesterday. There is no marble in this building, as it was not used for building purposes until one hundred years A.C. The wreaths of fruit and flowers, with elaborate friezes, are still fresh and beautiful, though they have been buried for centuries. These private buildings have been exhumed within a few years, some of them within a few months, from beneath the foundation of the Palace of the Emperors. They were filled up in order to raise the foundations to a greater height.

The palace, or palaces of the successive emperors, which were erected upon these foundations, covered at least thirty acres. The marble and granite of which they were built were all brought from Egypt.

The Baths of Caracalla were next visited. These were built by the emperor whose name they bear, 216 A.C., entirely for the use of the people. They accommodated 1,600 persons at once. There were eleven of these baths in the city, for the accommodation of the people. The floors and walls of this one were covered with the most beautiful marble. Its size was 750 by 500 feet, inclosed by walls one-fourth of a mile in length, and containing forty acres. Besides every kind of bath, from Turkish to swimming, there were gardens, a stadium, and rooms for exercise and intellectual culture. The methods of heating the rooms and baths were fully as perfect as those of the best baths of modern times. The niches in the walls were filled with statues of the most beautiful workmanship. The celebrated statue of Hercules leaning on his club was found here. Many of the best statues now scattered through Europe were taken from these ruins. Shelley's Prometheus unbound was written on the overhanging point, at least sixty feet above where we were standing. I measured the brick walls and arches, and found that they were five feet and nine inches in thickness. On each story was a floor in porphyry, serpentine, and marble, wrought in most beautiful figures of mosaic. Scattered through the rooms here and there were immense porphyry columns, brought from Egypt. For the foundation of these baths, Caracalla filled in and destroyed villas two stories high, the ruins of which are apparent by the excavations which are still going on. The workmen were uncovering large columns and rare statues the day we were there.

We next visited the Coliseum. These are the most perfect ruins in Rome. Although the stones and brick have been removed from this magnificent old building for centuries almost without limit, until not more than one-third of it now remains, still the value of the material remaining is estimated by an architect at one-half million pounds sterling, or two and a half millions of dollars. All of the 365 churches of modern Rome were built out of the ruins of ancient Rome, and all the statuary in these churches was taken from these ancient buildings, and the Coliseum furnished its full share.

Barbarina Palace, with all its ornaments, was built entirely from the Coliseum. In the seventeenth century, Pope Benedictine XIV. built all around upon the inside of it little stations or chapels, and dedicated it to Christ and the blood of all the martyrs, so that it became sacred, since which the vandalism has ceased.

The Coliseum was built by order of the Emperor Flavius Vespasian, on the site of the stagnum of Nero's garden. It was built originally for the exhibition of wild animals brought from different countries as trophies of war. It was opened by games of one hundred days, in which 5,000 wild beasts were slain. These were driven around the ring and then slain in sight of the spectators. In later days these beasts were made to fight together, and then with gladiators. There were large rollers all around the outside of the ring, so that when the beasts attempted to jump out they would inevitably be rolled back.

The building was a masterpiece of architectural skill, both in plan and construction. Its form is an oval, 1,900 feet, or nearly two-fifths of a mile in circumference. Its greatest diameter is 658 feet, and its shortest 558, while its height was 202 feet. The seats, which were arranged around the building, tier above tier, each tier receding from the one below it, were covered, wherever it was desirable, by an awning, which rested upon masts fastened to the walls. The building rested upon rows of arches, through which were the entrances. There were eighty of these entrances, so that the building could be emptied in the shortest possible space of time. The outside tier of these arches was of stone and the rest of brick. On measuring the piers on which these arches rested, I found them to be nine feet square.

The building seated 87,000 persons, and furnished standing room for 20,000 more. This makes modern coliseums look small, and yet the seats were so arranged that every person in the building could see what was taking place in every part of the ring below. The whole of the outside tier of arches was taken away, excepting a small place on the northeast side, before the stripping was forbidden. One stands amazed before the ruins of such buildings, and wonders at the public enterprise which constructed such magnificent monuments. We think of the men who could accomplish such marvelous works more as a race of demigods than of men.

The ruins of the Golden Palace of Nero on the Esquiline, next claimed our attention. This is far removed from the other palaces of the emperors; and yet constitutes a part of the great palace, and was connected with them by underground passages. This building is nearly 1,800 years old. It was built in matchless magnificence. The ceiling of the dining-room was made to revolve, so as to shower perfumes on the heads of the guests as they sat at the table. Trajan filled this building with rubbish and arches, which he built all through it, regardless of its magnificence, to make a foundation for his baths, which he built on top of it. The baths have been demolished for centuries, and a vegetable garden flourishes on the site, while the ruins of this golden palace, which have been buried and forgotten for ages, are just brought to light. Some of the frescoes on the ceiling are still very brilliant, and the figures are surprisingly perfect. The building is of immense proportions, and the walls very high.

Another class of ruins is of special interest to Christians. Among these stands first the Church of St. Clement. This is of the Basilican form, and very antique. It has been supposed, since the time of Jerome until within fifteen years, that this was the church built upon the house of Clement. But by excavations it was found that there was another church under this; and a large church, complete in every part, with the most elaborate frescoes, and paintings representing scenes in Christian history well known to the fathers, all preserved with almost miraculous perfection, was brought to light, directly under the church in which they had worshiped for centuries. Many of the rooms in this old church have been entirely cleared, so that we could wander through them with our wax tapers without any obstruction. The paintings and mottoes on the walls prove beyond doubt that this is the original church of St. Clement.

But it was known that this church was built upon the house of St. Clement. So with our wax tapers we prepared again to descend, and soon found ourselves wandering through the damp halls of the very house where Paul was entertained by St. Clement. In it was the prison-like chapel in which they doubtless worshiped before the erection of the church. This was subsequently confiscated, and consecrated to the worship of Mithorias. The altar still stands in the center, on which are the carvings representing this worship.

Here, then, is an ancient church, standing upon the top of another church, and this upon the top of what was once a private house, and all in the most perfect state of preservation.

And this is a brief glance at some points of interest in ancient Rome as it is to-day. What Rome will be, time and work only can tell.

CHAPTER XIV.

Switzerland—From Rome to Geneva—Scenes by the wayside—The indescribable splendor of the Alps—On the shores of Lake Geneva.

GENEVA, August 2, 1873.

I WROTE you the morning we left Rome, inclosing the publication of the pope, issued the day previous. Some of our party were not well pleased with the hotel there, and knowing they were to have no dinner until we arrived at Pisa, at nine o'clock that night, were disposed to make a "square meal" of their breakfast. You must bear in mind that only one kind of meat (beef) is furnished for breakfast. It is cut up in pieces about three inches long and two wide. One of these is all that is allowed one person. Those who took more had to pay extra for it—one of them, five francs. The fact is, their whole system seems to be to furnish as little as possible, and get as much for it as they can. Notwithstanding the heat, we would like to have remained a day or two longer in this city. Our time is out, and we are off in a circuitous route around the suburbs, recognizing the pyramid at the Protestant cemetery, St. Paul's Church, and the place where he was beheaded.

The country, after we leave the immediate vicinity of Rome on this route, is very poor. The mountains on one side, and the Mediterranean on the other, with the fine sea-breeze, made it a very pleasant trip. We pass the island of Corsica, where the great man whose influence was felt all over this country was born; also, the island of Elba, where he spent some time after his reverses, previous to his final overthrow. Here, too, another man of distinction arises. The discoverer of America was born at Genoa. We stop awhile at Leghorn, one of the most pleasant cities in Europe. It is the great emporium of foreign goods and manufactures consumed in this part of Italy. The squares and streets are regular and well paved, clean and nice. We spend the night at Pisa, one of the most ancient and beautiful cities in Europe. Soon after breakfast we take carriages to see the four great sights of the city.

The Cathedral was begun in 1063. It is of the nave form, and double aisles, two hundred and ninety-two feet in length, with galleries over the aisles. The dome is of white marble, with black and colored ornamentation. The church was consecrated by Pope Gelasius II., in 1118. There are a number of fine paintings, and some superb mosaic-work. The refitting commenced in 1153, but was not completed till 1278. It is a beautiful structure of marble, of circular form, surmounted by a conical dome one hundred and seventy-four feet high. The interior rests on eight columns and four pillars, adorned with beautiful marble rosettes. The pulpit, which is said to be the finest in the world, is borne by seven columns, representing the Annunciation, Nativity, Adoration, Presentation, Crucifixion, Last Judgment, and Martyrdom of John the Baptist. The place for baptizing, both for adults and infants, is a most wonderful piece of workmanship, brought from Constantinople.

The Tower, commenced in 1174, and completed in 1350, rises in eight stories, with half columns and colonnades. Its oblique position (twelve feet) out of the perpendicular height (one hundred and fifteen feet) gives it the name of the Leaning Tower. We ascended by two hundred and ninety-four steps to the top, where we had a fine view of the city and its environs—the sea to the west, and mountains on the east. The tower contains six bells, one of them weighing six tons, suspended on the side opposite the overhanging wall of the tower.

The Campa Santa, or burying-ground near by, was founded between 1188 and 1200. After the loss of the Holy Land, the Archbishop brought fifty-three ships' load of earth from Mount Calvary, in order that the dead might repose in holy ground. The tombstones form the pavement around the tombs or vaults, out of which the bodies had been taken. The sarcophagi are inscribed with the names of persons who once occupied them, some of whom were royal Romans. On the walls are some of the largest paintings I have ever seen, among which are Paradise, Purgatory, The Last Judgment, Hell, and others—the three latter being most frightful to look upon.

Pisa became a Roman colony 180 years before the Christian era. In the middle ages it attained considerable eminence, and became the rival of Venice and Genoa. It has now only about fifty thousand inhabitants.

The country from here to Florence is beautiful—mountains on either side, with a valley highly cultivated with olives and vegetables. We dine at Florence, and are off in the evening for Turin. For some distance the country is very hilly, with numerous tunnels, after passing which we emerge out in a fine country, perhaps the most productive in Italy.

This place was founded by Hannibal, B.C. 218. It was formerly the capital of Italy. From 1859 to 1865 the king resided here. It is evidently on the decline. It has, however, a fine old university, with two thousand students. It has an obelisk seventy-four feet high, erected in 1854 to commemorate the abolition of ecclesiastical jurisdiction and the establishment of the Constitution, and was erected with the consent of the king and chambers. The names of all the towns and provinces which voted for the suppression of the Spiritual Courts are inscribed on the column.

Here we can see the cloud-capped mountains, covered with snow, and the smoke ascending from the summits of a number of them, and the white clouds hanging around them—all together forming a spectacle that is inexpressibly grand and beautiful.

The bell rings for breakfast, and I leave this for another time.

Being desirous of writing up to this place, I resume.

We pass Chamborg, the capital of the Department of Savoy, with twenty thousand inhabitants. It was here that, in 1248, a great land-slide descended and overwhelmed sixteen villages. This portion of the Alps is where Napoleon built a road in 1802; and it has been the principal channel of communication between France and Italy, and is one of the safest of the Alpine passes. The summit is 6,848 feet above the sea-level. We pass through Mont Cenis tunnel, which is the longest in the world, being eight and one-eighth miles. It took us about half an hour to run through it. It was built by the French and Italian Governments. The latter progressed more rapidly, owing to the softer nature of the rock, and completed their portion in November, 1869, while on the French side it was not finished till 1871. It is the grandest undertaking of modern times. It is lit up so that you can see the sides and the arch above.

You can see the crystal streams leaping from these mountains, hundreds of feet, almost perpendicularly, from the melting snow above. Altogether, it is the grandest display of "mountain upon mountain piled" that I have ever seen. Sometimes the fleecy clouds which hang around their summits seem to mingle with them in delightful splendor, picturesquely magnificent. No words can adequately describe this Alpine country.

As we pass into Switzerland an officer of the government demands our passports. This is the first time they have been called for. In looking for mine he saw a letter addressed to me, and asked me if that was my name, which was all he required. On entering France, a few hours before, we simply told the officer we had them, when he examined, or rather marked, our baggage. For the last two or three days we have found a crowd of travelers. Most of them, I believe, are Americans, sight-seeing, and traveling for health.

We arrived at this place last night, and are pleasantly situated at the Hotel de Russe, within a few feet of the lake. Rev. Dr. Speer and myself have a room opening on the lake, which is as clear as crystal, and running as rapidly as a mill-tail. It is forty-five miles long, and varies in width from one and one-half to eight and one-half miles, containing an area of two hundred and sixty square miles. At this point the lake emerges into the Rhone, which causes the rapid current, as it is only about two hundred yards wide opposite our hotel. The river divides the city into two halves, which are connected by six bridges. The lake is surrounded by mountains towering away up among the clouds. I stand in my door and look away in the distance, and see Mont Blanc, with the smoke ascending from its summit. This is a grand old town—not much to attract attention in the way of cathedrals, statuary, and painting; but it has Nature's sublime attractions spread all around, above and below, with a cool, refreshing breeze from the lake, invigorating the body, and cheering to us, who have been in Italy ten or twelve days, and for the last twenty-six hours on the road. This is the most inviting place we have seen in Europe. Then the government and people are what we desired to see. They seem to be more like Americans at the hotel than at any place we have been. We met here another section of the party, who are to leave this evening; also, Brother Witherspoon, who has been in Switzerland while we went to Italy. His health is greatly improved.

My sheet is full; so I will close, leaving what I may have to say of Geneva until after I go out to look around at it from other points than the elevation of the seventh story of the hotel on the lake.

Picturesque Switzerland—The watches and music-boxes of Geneva—Rambles afoot.

GENEVA, August 4, 1873.

I wrote on Saturday, giving some items about this place. Having gone over the place, I sketch some things I saw before leaving here.

Geneva is celebrated for its watches and musical boxes. The watchmakers have the greatest repute of any in the world. We got a ticket of admission to enter one of the most extensive manufactories, to see the process of making watches, from the commencement to the completion of them. This establishment employs over three thousand hands. Each man has his special work to do. They carry one thousand watches through at the same time, all precisely the same size, each watch containing about one hundred and fifty pieces. This manufactory is well worth seeing.

We also went to the music-box manufactory. The works are not very large, but require great skill and genius to make what they do.

This city was the residence of John Calvin after the reformed religion was established by law. At the Academy, founded by him, is a reading-room containing thirty thousand volumes.

Here, also, was the residence of Voltaire.

The arbitrators of the Alabama claims, between England and America, sat here last year, holding their meetings in the Turn Halle.

Saturday evening we walked up the lake some distance, where we had a better view of the mountain scenery, especially Mont Blanc. It is perfectly white, as it is covered with snow. It is outside of Switzerland, on the border of French Savoy and Italy. It is among the highest points in Europe

This is, no doubt, one of the most healthy countries to be found, and is a great place of resort by travelers. From the number of American hotels and newspapers here, one can scarcely realize that he is so far away from home. There are quite a number of boats running in the lake, making trips to different points at regular intervals.

The city has wide, well-paved streets, kept very clean. I passed through the manufacturing portion, and found it to be kept in fine order. Take it all together, it is the most romantic, picturesque city we have seen. The commingling of mountain and lake, snow and green foliage, streets extending across lake and river, bath-houses and washerwomen, islands and shrubbery, with a busy multitude by day and night, is beautifully spread out from where I write. The rising and setting sun is never seen here, because of the mountains rising far away above the horizon, nor does it shine so intensely as in Italy.

Sabbath morning a number of our party started, soon after breakfast, to hear Père Hyacinthe preach. After missing our way several times, we found the place, but missed the preacher, as he did not officiate yesterday. We then went to the Greek-Russian Church; but there was no service. Most of the party returned to the hotel. I found a Waldensian service, after which I went to the English church. There was but a small congregation. Dr. Gray, of the Presbyterian Church of Scotland, preached there at twelve o'clock to some sixty or seventy persons, nearly all Americans or English. Bishop Foster, of the Methodist Episcopal Church, who had been holding a Conference in Germany, was there. I had known him for many years, and was glad to meet him. This was John Calvin's Church, where he preached and where he lived. His chair is kept as a sacred relic. There were quite a number of ministers who sat down in it. On our way to the hotel we went into the American Episcopal Church. The Sabbath is better observed here than at any place we have been in Europe.

From all I can see and learn, Protestants are doing very little in this country. We have attended their service everywhere, but have never seen any place where they seem to be effecting any thing of consequence. I made the acquaintance of a Methodist minister; but he had no service yesterday.

The people here have more liberal views of politics and religion than in any place we have been. Civil and religious liberty are enjoyed here, perhaps, to a greater extent than under any of the other European governments. They seem to be an intelligent, industrious people; but they have but little territory, and that, to a great extent, mountainous. There is no room for expansion. If half of them would come to our country, they would improve themselves and give more room to those who remain. It seems to me, if proper efforts were made, thousands of them would go where their energies would have room for development, and their genius be appreciated.

We leave on a lake boat after breakfast for Lausanne, thence by rail to Berne.

Beautiful Berne—The Swiss love of home—Life and habits of the Bernese—The wonderful clock of 1191—The Lake of Geneva.

BERNE, SWITZERLAND, August 5, 1873.

We had a most delightful sail up Geneva Lake. The mountains slope down to the valley, which is in the highest state of cultivation. We pass several villages which look like they had seen several centuries pass over them. The lake is of a deep blue color, and is said to have twenty different kinds of fish, highly esteemed by the people. This beautiful lake has been the theme of writers for centuries. The magnolia and the cedar grow in great luxuriance, while the vine-clad hills look beautiful to their summits. One of the Rothschilds has a fine residence here. At Aven is an ancient castle of Roman style, with five towers, built in the twelfth century. We leave the steamer at Lausanne, capital of the Canton de Vand, 26,000 population. It is most delightfully situated on the terraced slopes. Mont Josat overshadows it by its cathedral on one side, and its castle on the other.

The Swiss Homes.—There we take the cars; and such a country we have never seen before, and never expect to see again. The steep and lofty mountains and valleys, all covered with evergreens or cultivated with vines, vegetables, or grain, with the sloping valleys, giving views sometimes as far as the eye can reach, become grander. As the train proceeds, the amphitheater of mountains, like a magnificent panorama, passes before you in such rapid succession, that one can scarcely realize the fact that it is not an illusion. Having exhausted my vocabulary of description, I cease to attempt it by saying, no wonder the Swiss love their mountain home, and that their officers, in time of war, will not suffer their songs to be sung while away from them.

We arrive at Berne, and find a fine hotel. At Geneva, Rev. Dr. Speer and myself were in the seventh story, where we had a fine view of the lake and mountains. Here, our room is on the first story, and yet we are one hundred feet above the valley. We look over the tops of the houses, and see the sloping mountains in the distance, and near by the Swiss cottages with their busy occupants. We arrive a little before 5 o'clock, and some of our party saw the first striking of the great clock, of which I will speak before I close.

An Arcadian City.—This city joined the Confederacy in 1353, and is still the most important of the Swiss Cantons. It is built on a peninsula of sandstone rock, formed by the windings of the Aar. The houses are built on arcades, in the principal part of the city, beneath which the pavement for foot-passengers runs. We took walks in several directions, and find the stores, shops, and dwellings all have these arcades. The men work here, and the women sew and do their work here, and here the children play. It seems that this is the place where they have light and air. Along their streets at suitable distances are fountains, where they all obtain their supply of water near their houses. These fountains are adorned with statues. The bear—the heraldic emblem of Berne—is a constantly recurring object. Bruin appears equipped with shield, sword, banner, and helmet.

Two gigantic bears keep guard over the pillars of the west gate. Others support a shield in the pediment of the corn-hall, which, till 1830, always contained a store of corn, in case of famine, beneath a spacious wine-cellar. A whole troop of bears go through a performance at the clock-tower. At

11*

three minutes before every hour a cock gives the signal by clapping his wings and crowing; one minute later the bears march around a seated figure, and a harlequin indicates the number of the hour by striking a bell. The cock then repeats his signal when the hour strikes. The seated figure—an old man with a beard—turns an hour-glass, and counts the hour by raising his scepter and opening his mouth, while the bear on his right does the same by an inclination of his head. At the same time a stone figure in the tower strikes the bell with a hammer. The cock concludes the performance by crowing the third time. This remarkable clock was built in 1191, and for nearly seven hundred years it has been attracting the attention of the people. We went twice to see it, and may go again. The ancient Egyptians had not a greater veneration for their Ibis than these people have for the bear, which would seem to be a tutelary deity, as well as a heraldic emblem of the Canton. Here Bruin has been supported, according to immemorial usage, at the expense of the public, who are prohibited from making him any other offering than bread or fruit. On the night of March 3, 1861, an English officer fell into one of the dens and was torn to pieces by the male bear, after a long and desperate struggle.

Three thousand feet high—The illuminated falls at interlachen—Seas of ice—The Bernese Alps—Up among the coolnesses of Switzerland in August.

LUCERNE, August 7, 1873.

We took the cars again, and came to Interlachen, situated between the mountains, which tower up in the clouds on either hand. Away in the distance are seen some whose summits are covered with snow. The sunset here was glorious. The yellow sunshine for some distance below, then the white snow in the shade, with the evergreens surrounding, was sublimely beautiful. Here, for the first time, we see the glaciers. This is the third highest of the Swiss mountains, and is in full view of our hotel. This place may be said to combine tasteful quiet with magnificent scenery.

Early in the morning we are off in carriages to see the glaciers. The road is between three and four hours' drive through a romantic country, settled by Swiss peasants. Leaving the carriages, we go on foot a mile and a half still farther up, a most fatiguing walk, to view the splendors of nature. A grotto is cut in the ice for some distance, inside of which two girls are playing on some queer instrument and singing. We pay our fifty centimes (ten cents) and go under the ice—above, below, all around, how far no one can tell. These grottoes are, many of them, eighteen or twenty miles long, and from one to two miles wide, and from one hundred to six hundred feet thick. The glaciers of Switzerland are supposed to form a sea of ice more than a thousand miles long. They melt at the bottom and sides and slide down slowly in a body. The waters rush in torrents down the mountain sides in roaring cataracts. The next winter the space is again filled with ice to go through the same process. This water forms lakes, where there is space enough to contain it, and runs off by rivers between the mountains. This place is situated between Lakes Brienz and Thun. The water in the latter is said to be over two thousand feet deep.

We take one of the steamers near Interlachen, and pass through the beautiful lake filling nearly all the space between the mountains and Griesbach.

We walk up through a wilderness of evergreens, over a thousand feet, to the hotel to spend the night, and see the illuminated falls. As we pass up, an animated scene presents itself. A stream of considerable size comes tumbling, roaring down, you know not from where, but rushing on down the precipices to the lake. You see the noisy torrent by your side, winding its way in silvery foam through the verdant slopes, while far beyond are seen the majestic Bernese Alps, aspiring above the whole, and casting their shadows in the deep caldron.

After supper these falls are illuminated. There are four falls. The impression made by these different colors will never be erased from our minds. I cannot describe its transcendently beautiful appearance. The roar of these falls, and the bracing atmosphere of this three thousand feet elevation, gave us a refreshing night's repose. This place—formerly inaccessible—became known in 1818. It has now become one of the most delightful and popular resorts in Switzerland. The series of cascades—seven in number—falling from rock to rock, from a great height (1,148 feet), harmonize with the character of the scenery so as to enhance its attractions.

We breakfast 5:15, and descend to the boat which takes us across the lake, where we take diligences to cross the Alps. Here an interesting scene occurs. Crowds of passengers to go, six to the smaller diligences, and perhaps double that number to the large ones. Tourists of many tongues, guides, porters, horses, drivers, all mingled in the utmost confusion. I go with two young ladies from Oxford, Mississippi; one from Virginia, and Revs. Messrs. Witherspoon and Richardson.

We ascend for miles a circuitous way, to look down on the place of our ascent, seemingly less than a mile below us. The mountains now appear in all their majesty, covered with snow, on the higher peaks of the summit, with dazzling whiteness.

The ascent becomes so steep that some of us walk for miles, taking nearer routes up the mountains.

There have recently been some of those terrible avalanches of ice and snow. Along these mountain-slopes are hundreds of cottages, with small patches of garden and orchards. The descent is rapid, with locked wheels.

We pass some fine Swiss houses near the lake, and a town of some size, with churches. The road is all smoothly paved with blue marble, beat up. Workmen are removing the stones and earth brought down by the avalanches. This has been one of our most interesting days of travel.

We take steamer at Lucerne, unsurpassed for the grandeur of its scenery. We arrived at this city in the afternoon.

Top of the Alps—A view of three hundred miles from Rigi—One of Nature's grandest displays.

Rigi, Top of the Alps, August 8, 1873.

Here we are on the highest accessible point of these far-famed mountains. We took the steamer at Lucerne this morning, and went to the far end of the lake, passing a number of places of natural as well as historic interest. Of these I cannot now write, not even of the most remarkable railroad that brought us up these mountains. If there were inspiration to be had from one's position and surroundings, then certainly this place possesses more to inspire one than any place I have ever seen. This view far exceeds my expectations. I realize more fully than ever before what the Alps are—their extent and grandeur. It is estimated that three hundred miles may be taken in a view, on a clear day, from this summit. The mountains we had seen from the lake now look like a plain. The houses in the towns look like toys. The cultivated ground seen in the distance, cut up in patches, looks like bed-quilts. The power of vision seems lost in the distance, or seen only in the most diminutive form. Thus it is as seen before us. But what can I say of that above and around us, as seen in the distance? There is no humbug in this upon which we now gaze almost in bewilderment. It is Nature's grandest display of her most sublime magnificence. No words can convey to the mind a correct idea of what I behold spread out below, above, around, everywhere, from the position which I occupy while I write. The lakes below, as they are seen in their serpentine course between the mountains, look like a creek, and the mountains themselves, with the little houses upon them, seem to be a valley. Every thing seen below is diminished. The towns and villages have dwindled into insignificance, and what we thought a very mountainous country looks like one of the most lovely, picturesque plains we ever saw. We seem to have ascended into the heavens, and it is winter. The surrounding mountains are covered with snow, while the fleecy clouds hang below them in glorious grandeur, overwhelming us with the omnific power of Nature's God, as seen around everywhere.

This day winds up our sight-seeing in Switzerland. We quit at the right place. Nothing else in this line could interest us. I shall leave this mountain filled with emotions of the commingling of all that is magnificently grand, combined with that which is most beautiful in nature. Even under the everlasting snow grow the lovely flowers, born to blush unseen, and shed their fragrance on this mountain air. Many varieties are collected and pressed in books, to be sold to visitors, who press by thousands to see the wonders of nature from this Rigi of the Alps. Two or three hundred more than can be accommodated at the hotels throng there daily to see that which can only be witnessed by the aid of steam, applied by the most skillful engineering.

We remain till near night to see the setting sun from this lofty eminence. Some of our party stay to see it rise.

Romantic Switzerland—Impressions of the most interesting country in Europe—An amusing dinner-table experience—The need of an interpreter—Sketch of Lucerne—William Tell—A mountain railroad—Farewell, Switzerland.

LUCERNE, August 9, 1873.

We return on the steamer to this place. After nine o'clock to-day we leave this romantic Switzerland for Paris.

I will give my impressions in regard to the Swiss country and people. In some respects it is the most interesting country in Europe. It is about two hundred miles from east to west, by some one hundred and sixty or seventy miles. Two-thirds of the country are lofty mountain-chains, and valleys with lakes. The language of the people is a mixture of French, German, and Italian, or rather French-Swiss, German-Swiss, and Italian-Swiss. Having a conductor who understands all the languages of the people among whom we have traveled, we had but little difficulty.

On our arrival at the top of the Rigi, nearly all of the party went directly to the hotel to get their dinner before they went out sight-seeing. I was much more intent on seeing than eating, and, having no baggage, I did not enter the hotel, but went from place to place for an hour or two, to see all that I could as soon as possible. The hotel is within a few steps of the highest point. After looking from there I went to the hotel, and found that some of our party had been sitting at the table, waiting for their dinner, ever since their arrival.

Strategy.—I did not attempt to speak to the waiter, but wrote what I wanted, which he took to some one who understood English, and soon my wants were supplied. Not so with those who sat near me. Some of them, being teachers, seemed determined to make them understand what they wanted; but they failed to a great extent. We laughed long and immoderately. This, no doubt, confused the waiters, and when they went after any thing, they seemed to forget to return to our end of the table. When they did get back, they brought that which was not ordered, and failed to bring that which the teachers thought they had ordered, each one laughing at the other's mishaps. Finally, they ate such things as they could get. On to the "confectionery." Next, the professor went and got some for his wife; but before the others got a chance to make signs that they wanted some of the same, she had eaten it up, and then they were out at sea again. The husband had left to see the mountains; but his wife, enjoying this, remained to see the end of it. They jabbered away, and made signs for the confectionery, but it was not to be had. After all patience was exhausted, and all had enjoyed the joke to the fullest extent but the waiters, they concluded to give it up and quit. But here comes another difficulty. Every thing here is upon the "European style." You pay for what you order. This seemed to be impossible. The waiters could not understand a word, nor could the teachers understand them. A new source of amusement arose, which cannot be described. Their dinner-coupons were worth four francs (eighty cents); but they could not get, and had not eaten, the worth of their money, and the waiters could not give change for them. After much parleying, two would put their orders together, and one pay for both. One of the ladies said it took them longer to settle for than to eat their dinner, *minus* the confectionery, which could not be obtained for love, signs, speech, coupons, or money. Thus ended the most amusing dinner I have ever seen, and shows the necessity of having a conductor in this country.

I was going to speak of Switzerland, but was led off by the dinner mishaps until my sheet was full. This is a remarkable country in many respects. It has been a republic longer, and has a freer government than any other country in Europe. Its population is only about 2,500,000. It is divided into many Cantons—about twenty, I think. It reminds me more of our country than any other on the Continent. Their railroads are made like ours. You are not locked up in their carriages, as in other countries. At their hotels they are willing to set meat before you, and not limit your allowance at every meal, as in other countries. They have orchards like ours, and flowers are seen in most of their windows, in pots. The vine grows luxuriantly in their valleys and on their hill-sides. Their climate is cold in winter, but most delightful in summer. Millions of money are spent among these people by seekers of health and pleasure. Their principal manufactures are of carved wood, watches, and music-boxes, in which they excel the world.

I have deviated a little from my plan of giving a running sketch of our trip. I must, therefore, go back to Lucerne, which is situated at the head of the lake of the same name. The "lion" of this place is cut out of a solid rock, twenty-eight by eighteen feet, and stands in a garden. It is commemorative of the Swiss Guards, who may be said to have suffered in defense of the King of France, at the beginning of the French Revolution. The spear is sticking in his side, and he is dying, yet seeking to protect the shield of France. Lucerne is the residence of the Papal Nuncio. It became independent in 1332, and joined the Swiss Confederacy. Its history dates from the eighth century. It was taken by the French in 1798, and was, for that time, the capital of the Helvetian Republic.

On our way to Rigi we passed several places of interest in the vicinity where William Tell performed his exploits. A chapel is built by the side of the lake, said to be on the spot where he shot the apple off his son's head. It is said to have been built thirty years after his death.

There are four Cantons on the shores of this lake. One of these, with a population of but one thousand, has maintained its independence for four hundred years. In the town-hall is this inscription: "Received into the Confederacy, 1315. Purchased its freedom, 1390. It was taken by the French in 1798." There is near this place what is called the "Devil's Bridge," seventy feet high. The whole scene around is one of savage grandeur. The railroad by which we ascend to Rigi has a central iron rail, with cogs, into which runs a wheel, like a ginwheel. It took over an hour to ascend the mountain. The railroad has only been in operation since May, 1871. Three trains are now kept busy with the thousands of visitors visiting the place.

We leave this mountain country with the most pleasant associations, feeling that we have been amply compensated for our week spent in the Republic of Switzerland.

Letters from Rev. T. W. Hooper.

GENEVA, July 19, 1873.

The bells have chimed 6 A.M., and here I am, dressed and at my window, writing to you from the home of Calvin. But how can a man sleep with such scenery bursting all around him! From my window I look down upon Lake Geneva, just across the street, and the rushing of whose waters, as they form the Rhone at this point, was the first sound that greeted me this morning. Just a few yards to the right of my window is the beautiful stone bridge that spans the river, with a foot-bridge extending to Rousseau's Island, now used as a beer-garden. Across the lake is the body of the quaint old town, with its turreted cathedral (now used by the Presbyterians of Scotland), while overlooking all is a range of magnificent mountains, over whose towering crags we gaze in rapt wonder upon the everlasting snow of Mont Blanc.

Could you write with such a scene as that to look upon, while under you is the continual rattle of Swiss market wagons, with fruits and vegetables, mingling with the escaping steam from the steamer Winkbried, whose smoke-stack is just under my window? But beautiful as it is to-day, it was still more so on yesterday, and especially at the "Chateau of Rothschild," to which we rode, and from whose beautiful park we had an almost unclouded view of Mont Blanc and the surrounding mountains of Savoy. No wonder that Byron selected this lake for one of his scenes in "Childe Harold," for it must have set his poetical genius on fire by its placid beauty. Last night we sat long and gazed upon its waters, from whose smooth surface thousands of lamplights glittered, and while music floated in the balmy atmosphere, memories came trooping from the glorious past.

It seems to me that John Calvin must have been a Calvinist, living in the substantial stone house which he occupied, and studying Romans and Ephesians in that straight-back arm-chair in which I sat on yesterday, and surrounded by those everlasting mountains.

Oh! but how about the burning of Servetus?

Well, I have seen the very spot where the poor fellow was burned—but if your readers had seen as many places as I have where the 11th chapter of Hebrews was reënacted on Presbyterians, they would not think so strongly of poor old John Calvin's consent to the burning of one poor heretic. They must remember that our Baptist brethren had not yet come into existence to clamor for "soul liberty;" episcopacy had not even emerged from the thraldom of Rome, and the remnant of primitive Presbyterians were still "earnestly contending for the faith once delivered to the saints" in the valleys of Piedmont.

But I must quit this moralizing—a small amount of which I trust is excusable in such a Calvinistic atmosphere as this. Apart from its associations and its beautiful scenery, there is nothing remarkable about this ancient town, unless you except its representation for watch-making and jewelry. Yesterday we went all through one of the largest manufactories, and you may form some idea of its size, when I tell you that this one firm employs three hundred hands in the building, and keeps three thousand others constantly employed on job work outside. They sell their watches "in pieces," or completed, all over the world, and are famous as manufacturers wherever people are enough civilized to know the time of day by mechanism.

But now, going back a little, I would say, we left the beautiful city of Paris Thursday night at 8:40, and arrived here at 10:30 yesterday morning, having traveled over four hundred miles on a road as smooth as a bowling-alley, and the latter part abounding in striking and picturesque scenery.

We also got quite a correct idea of peasant life as we drifted along among their "cottages," as tourists call them, but which we regarded as very indifferent negro cabins. The family seem to dwell in one end and the horses and cattle in the other, while dogs and cats and goats lie around loose wherever it suits them. It was harvest-time, and we saw it in all its reality, without the poetry—men cutting wheat with a scythe or a hook, and women, with short blue cotton dresses of scant pattern, and without stockings or pantalettes, picking it up and tying it into bundles. We also saw the first Indian corn growing that we have seen since we left America; and everywhere the universal Irish potato. The fact is, we have scarcely seen a farm or sat down to a table, since we landed at Moville, without this famous vegetable; and while we have eaten many strange mixtures which none of us could recognize, either by name or in reality, we are all acquainted and feel at home with this homely old vegetable, which seems to be regarded as a sort of *sine qua non* among the rich as well as among the poor.

And now, I want to make one assertion which may strike some of your readers with surprise. I traveled yesterday through some of the finest and most fertile valleys of France, but I saw no land as rich as the Roanoke Valley, no scenery more beautiful than that around Liberty, and no farm-house as beautifully located or as pretty a private residence as Mr. Langhorne's, at Shawsville. "Distance lends enchantment to the view," and historic associations cast a halo of glory around these scenes through which we have been passing; but dissipate this misty vail of the dim and hoary antiquity, and I will pick out a hundred more picturesque and more beautiful scenes among the mountains of Virginia. Just here, my brother waked up, and I asked him what he thought of that last sentiment. "It is correct," said he; "for as I look out of that window I can easily imagine that I am looking down the Goose Creek Valley."

Shades of Rousseau, Calvin, Byron! what a sentiment, so near the spot where Servetus was burned! The Peaks and Mont Blanc! Savoy and Bedford! the Rhone and Goose Creek! Lake Geneva and Buford's Mill-pond! How long would it take such a genius as his to develop into a second Byron, and produce another "Childe Harold," amid such scenery?

I think, after this, I'll let scenery alone, and would respectfully refer all your readers to the ordinary guide-books for the fiction, and to Mark Twain for the reality. By the way, he had only one oracle in his party; but we have two, and they furnish us a constant source of amusement as well as disgust, and by some curious streak of fortune they are room-mates. Yesterday, as soon as we came in sight of Mont Jura, they commenced discussing the point as to "where Hannibal crossed the Alps," which some one stopped by asserting that Hannibal didn't cross the Alps at all. They both think they talk French; and whenever we want fun, we get them to ask a Frenchman a question, and watch his countenance and the shrug of his shoulders, while they scream louder and louder, thinking that he must be deaf.

"The marms" have somewhat subsided, under the influence of travel, and mixing with a people to whom, every time they speak, they show their ignorance. Not one of them speaks French, and only one pretends to; but she prefers the English, and so do I. Really, I am tired out with this continuous jargon, and shall be glad when I get back to England, and gladder still when I get back to Lynchburg.

We leave by steamer this morning for Lausanne, Berne, Interlachen, etc.

INTERLACHEN, July 21, 1873.

I am afraid your readers will think I am getting almost too prolific in letters, as I wrote day before yesterday. But the fact is, that in my case, which is "early to bed," it is sure to result in "early to rise," and at five o'clock this morning I was awakened by the glorious sunlight, giving promise of another beautiful day in the Alps. This is not always the case, and I have heard of parties having to wait for days without a glimpse of Mont Blanc or the Jungfrau; while not a cloud obscured either, when we got near enough to see them. And now that I am up, and we are to make an early start for the glaciers, I have concluded to write to my various friends through you, as it saves time, which is precious, and postage, which is high, though not as high here as in France.

As this is Monday, and the time for our ministerial conference, I shall give some account of the sermons which I heard on yesterday, after giving you a hasty sketch of my trip here.

We left Geneva at half-past seven on a cup of coffee and cold bread, and glided up the Lake Leman, or Geneva, to a little place called Ouchy. As I was quietly gazing on the mountain-peaks that rose all around us, and the intervening valleys, green with the growing crops and dotted over with beautiful villas, I heard some one say, "Brother T——, this scenery is going back on Goose Creek." I felt that he had made reparation for the poetic slander of the morning; and I, too, must confess that I had not fully reached the picturesque sublimity of the Alps when I compared it to Bedford; but there is a most striking similarity in many of the scenes to those along the Virginia and Tennessee Railroad.

At Ouchy, we got breakfast about twelve, in one of the grandest hotels I ever saw—large, airy, handsomely frescoed, and surrounded with a flower-garden and park that is worthy of a count, or a duke at least.

Mounting the omnibus, we climbed a considerable height around a macadamized road to the ancient town of Lausanne, where Gibbon finished his "History of the Decline and Fall of Rome." Here we took the train, and a little before five we landed at the quaint old town of Berne. In an incredibly short time Mr. Cook had us seated in "cabs," and whipped off to see the famous clock. We got there just in time to see the performance. True to the Guide-book, at three minutes before five a wooden rooster clapped his wings and crowed; a minute later the bear turned his head, while the harlequin rang his bells, and the old man turned his hour-glass and opened his mouth just as the iron figure above raised his hammer and struck off five on the old bell in the tower. We then drove on to see the bears (kept at public expense), and then to the Parliament House, where we visited the senate and representative chambers, both of which are republican in their simplicity, and accord well with the grand Lutheran cathedral, which has all the simplicity of Roman architecture, and shows that it was intended for real worship, not for mere Romish mummery.

Returning to the depot, we took another train, on special first-class cars, and about seven o'clock came to Lake Thun, where we again took steamer in the midst of the wildest Alpine scenery; and after ten minutes' ride on the cars again, we were safely deposited at the magnificent Hotel Victoria, the largest and finest of all the numerous hotels at this famous summer resort, where three thousand visitors congregate during the summer months. . We are surrounded on all sides by giant mountain-peaks which seem to pierce the very heavens, while the Young Virgin, or Jungfrau, rises over thirteen thousand feet, just in front of us, and is covered with perpetual snow. With a glass, this snow gives us all the colors of the rainbow; while without it, the dazzling whiteness blinds us, and stands in striking contrast to all the green of lower peaks.

Yesterday we were glad to recognize another Sabbath, and to have a day of rest in this quiet, peaceful valley, instead of all the sights and sounds of some large city. At eleven o'clock we attended service at the Scotch chapel, where a minister of the true Church holds a service every Sunday during the summer months. It furnishes a rest to the minister and a chance to see the world, and at the same time furnishes the gospel to those who need it in their travels. The minister in this case is Rev. James T. Stuart, of Kelso, Scotland, and I never heard two more excellent, spiritual, evangelical sermons, while the Scotch accent gave me a peculiar relish and delight.

At 11 A.M. he preached on "My beloved is mine, and I am his." It was the language of the Church, or the Christian, in regard to Christ, who has looked in at the lattice and is now gone to heaven. This language, he said, implied—1. Mutual choice —Christ first chose us, and then we chose him. 2. This choice was based on love—his love of pity and complacency and benefit—producing in us a love which has as its elements gratitude, delight, and desire to please and to serve him.

At 4 P.M. I heard him again on "Trees of Righteousness." He first quoted a list of names by which God, as a fond and loving father, calls his children, and then discussed the subject under two heads: 1. The similitude between a Christian and a tree. 2. How they both grow. Under the first head he brought out these points: The tree must have a root: first, to sustain it; and second, to supply it with nutriment. So the Christian has his root in Christ by faith, which both sustains and supplies him. Then, as the tree has a trunk and foliage and fruit, so the Christian has his spiritual life, leading to profession as foliage, and good works as the fruit. Under the second head he brought out these points: The tree and the Christian both grow—first, by expansion from within; secondly, by assimilation; third, by circulation. He closed with a most excellent and fervent practical appeal to vital godliness. Your readers generally may not see the drift, but the preachers will see the heads of two capital sermons. I am sure that we all enjoyed it, after so much French and German jabber all around us.

I used to tell my people, when I wanted to shame them into regular attendance at church, that I would like to send them out by detachments for six months into the country, when they would ride ten miles and hear a sermon once a month. But hereafter I shall wish to send them to France or Germany, where they will have fanciful singing, see the mass conducted by well-fed, sensual-looking old priests, and only hear the gospel occasionally from some Scotch or English minister.

But I must close now, as I do not intend to close this, but shall wait for the Grindelwald Glacier.

Lucerne, July 23, 1873.

I intended to complete the above at Griesbach, but it was too late when the illumination of the falls was over, and too soon a start the next morning when we started for this point. But now, as some of us are resting, while others have gone to the Rigi, I will finish it.

We went by mistake to Lauterbrunnen, where

we saw the famous Saublack Fall. It is caused by a small stream running over a precipice one thousand feet high, and breaking into a complete mist before it strikes the rocks below. It is really one of the most wonderful and beautiful scenes that we have witnessed in this fairy-land of Switzerland.

But, retracing our drive several miles, our carriage, with its six passengers and driver, drawn by two horses urged by a hundred horse-flies each, slowly dragged its way up to the glaciers of Grindelwald, while the beautiful white Wetterhorn stared us in the face, and kept us on the *qui vive* for avalanches. But while we heard them thundering around the mountains, we did not get a view of them, and had to content ourselves with sound and fury.

We got a splendid view of the glaciers, and then came down the mountain at a fearful rate to Lake Brientz, where we took a steamer about ten miles to Griesbach, and spent the night. The hotel is on a cliff one thousand feet from the wharf, which we climbed around a graded walk, admiring the seven falls formed by a large stream leaping hundreds of feet from one rock to another, dashing the white foam in all directions, and sounding like one continuous roar of thunder.

After an excellent supper, we walked down in front of the falls to witness the illumination, which takes place every night during the season. We saw the lanterns as they darted in and out among the trees like will-o'-the-wisps; and when the highest fall was reached a rocket shot up, and this was answered by another at the bottom, and then as a third exploded it threw balls in the air, and the falls blazed out at once with lights of amazing brilliancy, that gave the trees and the water the appearance of an "Arabian Night's Entertainment," and these lights suddenly changed to pink and green and yellow, and then one by one went out, leaving the darkness darker by reason of the wondrous contrast.

The next morning several of us climbed up to the very top of the topmost rock, at imminent peril of life and limb, passed under one of the falls, and caught the dashing of the spray as we stood upon the narrow bridge that spanned those yawning chasms.

At ten o'clock we descended to the wharf, and at Brientz took private carriages provided by the thoughtful Mr. Cook, instead of lumbering diligences, as they are called, for the sake of contrast, I suppose. It was a weary, weary day of heat and dust and flies—first for three hours up the Bruni Pass, and then at a brisk trot down again to Alpnach, where we took, first, our long-lost letters from home, and then the steamer on this charming Lake Lucerne to this town of the same name. The scenery over the Bruni is grand, wild, and romantic beyond all conception. Beautiful valleys, dotted with cottages of the Swiss peasantry, and watered by dancing streams, lie basking in the sunlight; while bold and rugged mountains, some covered with verdure and some with snow, lift their giant heads above the clouds, and sparkle with hundreds of riverets that dash over their sides and scatter into spray, fulfilling those beautiful lines of Lord Byron,

> That left so late the mountain's brow,
> As though its waters ne'er would sever,
> But ere it reach the plain below
> Break into drops that part forever.

By the way, we passed by the old castle said to be the scene of Byron's "Manfred," and also the castle of "Bluebeard."

We have also had the pleasure of hearing a genuine Swiss horn, with its splendid echoes among the mountain-peaks. It is about four feet long and about five inches in diameter at the muzzle, straight nearly to the large end, where it makes a slight upward deflection. The old man who was blowing it had it resting on a kind of fulcrum, and blew as if he were certain of good pay. But there is only one of our party who carried a "sou," and while he paid, another tried to step it on the fantastic toe. No puns intended, except for the initiated.

We had rare times coming up the mountain. One of the party was good on "dog-German," and his conversation with our driver, who only talked Dutch, was exceedingly amusing — especially the driver's.

Letter from the Rev. A. B. Whipple, President of Lansingburgh College, New York.

PARIS, August 11, 1873.

Greetings once more to my friends from this side the Atlantic. My last letters have been local, or descriptive of one place only. This shall be a running comment on things seen between Rome and this place.

Leaving Rome July 30, at 11 o'clock A.M., we were soon outside the walls and passing the spot where St. Paul was executed, and the church in which they say is the very stone on which he was beheaded. Within the city we had visited the house where he dwelt, the prison in which he had been confined, and the house of his friend Clement, where he was permitted to preach. Of this house I may have more to say hereafter; for the present, suffice it to say, every place mentioned, and every place possessed of some sacred relic or legend, is invested with as much legendary history as the most devout will be willing to believe. Passing on, we follow up the valley of the "Yellow Tiber"—rendered so by the great amount of soil washed along with its rushing waters. Dry, doubly dry, is the country through which we pass—no rain having fallen here since April. Every farm, however, seems to be supplied with a large tank of water brought from the mountains. Cattle are in groups near the water, as if in consultation about something to eat, as well as drink. Hardly a green thing is visible except weeds uneatable and trees unreachable by cattle. The cattle are all white, the tips of their noses, ears, horns, and the bush of their tails being black. They are of the wide-spreading horn species, and look quite unlike our own. White, certainly, is a desirable color in a country of such intense heat, if it be true that black draws the heat, or even retains it. On we go, until the blue waters of the Mediterranean greet our eyes. We watch it, and the vessels upon it, as for miles we speed along its shores. Nothing worthy of note till we reach Pisa, at ten o'clock at night, to eat supper out of doors, and uncomfortably warm at that. We slept as people do very warm nights. How the other 49,999 slept I cannot affirm. This I do know: the other one was not any too much rested to start early in the morning to spend an hour or two in sight-seeing. The Piazza del Duomo, the Cathedral, the Baptistery, the Campo Santo, and the Leaning Tower, were all the places we could visit. A minute description I cannot now give. Of course, the Duomo is a church entirely of white marble, with black and colored ornamentation, with solid silver altar, and other things in keeping. What most interested me was the moderate swaying of the same bronze lamp, suspended from the lofty nave, that once suggested to Galileo the idea of a pendulum as time-keeper. The Baptistery—a beautiful circular structure, surrounded by half columns below, and a gallery of small detached columns above, and surmounted by a conical dome one hundred and seventy-nine feet high—was commenced in 1153. It has a wonderful echoing gallery; and when one of the guides sang a few strains we could hear them reverberating around and above us, till all were ready to cheer through admiration.

The Campanile, or clock-tower, as the Leaning Tower is called, begun in 1174, and finished in 1350, rises in eight different stories, and, like the Baptistery, is surrounded with half columns and colonnades. It leans twelve feet out of perpendicular, and whether built so on purpose, or whether it has settled, is still a matter of discussion. It seems as if built so. Two hundred and ninety-four steps enable us to reach the top, and look down the leaning side with a feeling that it is falling. A fine view of the country is seen from the top, the sea some six miles to the west. It contains six bells; the heaviest, weighing six tons, is on the side opposite the overhanging wall.

The Campo Santo, or burial-ground, is in many ways remarkable for paintings, statuary, etc., but chiefly to me for fifty-three ship-loads of earth brought from Mount Calvary, and deposited here for a sacred burial-place; so I have walked upon the soil of Mount Zion.

Florence was the next place of interest; for from it have emanated, almost exclusively, the Italian language and literature. Here, also, the fine arts have attained the zenith of their glory. A vast profusion of treasures of art is here, such as is found in no other place within so narrow limits—reminiscences of all Europe, imposing monuments, and the delightful environs of the city—altogether making Florence one of the most delightful places in the world. Besides wandering through vast and numerous halls of the fine arts, we also traversed the elegantly-furnished rooms in the palace of Victor Emmanuel, and, while admiring the beauty and grandeur of the soldier-guarded palace, could not help thinking how the millions toil that a few may revel in luxury.

Leaving Florence, we have twenty-seven hours' ride to Geneva, passing Turin, a city once destroyed by Hannibal, B.C. 218, now with a population of over one hundred and eighty thousand. Shortly after leaving this city we began the ascent of the Bernese Alps, winding through beautiful valleys, climbing up the sides of mountains amid grape-fields without number. Wilder and more picturesque the scenery becomes—cottages in seemingly inaccessible places on steep mountain-sides; red-tile covered hamlets far below us; snow-covered mountain peaks far above us—and so for many an hour we wend our way upward through tunnels too frequent to count them, till finally we enter the famous Mont Cenis tunnel, seven miles through, requiring twenty-eight minutes in the passage. Then descending through like Alpine scenery, we reach at length the river Rhone, and then again begin our ascent, passing through ever-varying scenery, over rivers, under mountains, around lakes clear and beautiful in their deep valleys—still onward and upward, till, in the midst of a thunder-storm, at 10 P.M., we enter Geneva, glad to have something to eat and a bed. Saturday morning is clear, and we spend the day delighted with the place and its surroundings, in a most beautiful valley at the end of the lake, whose waters are pure as spring water. Around are lofty mountains as background to fine houses, while, forty miles away, concealed under a vail of clouds, we are told, lies or stands Mont Blanc, the monarch of mountains. All day long, at intervals, I turned my eyes in that direction, hoping to see it. At length toward sunset the clouds lifted, and revealed the coveted sight. Clear, cold, and lofty, stood his bared head leaning, as it were, against a clear, blue sky. As the sun sank lower and behind lesser mountains, the snowy peak of Mont Blanc caught his setting rays and sent them back to us in golden colors. Higher and higher climbed the sunless shade, till on the summit rested, as it were, the golden crown of setting day; then, as its last color left his royal head, the silver moon appeared from behind, caught the last tinge, and with serene majesty bore it aloft into the mid-heavens. So ended the week.

Sunday morning found me, at half-past eight o'clock, wending my way to hear the famous Père Hyacinthe preach, and at eleven o'clock I was in the American Chapel to hear once more a sermon in plain English.

Monday morning we steamed across the beautiful Lake of Geneva, past the palace of Baron Rothschild, past the prison-castle of Chillon, and on amid enchanting scenery to Lausanne; then took cars, and about 5 P.M. arrived at Berne, the capital of Switzerland. Berne means *bear*, which seems to have been the deity of the Swiss in ancient times. Bears take the place of men and lions as statuary. Churches are adorned with them, houses and temples ornamented with them, and even a den of live ones is kept at the city's expense. Here, also, is a famous clock, in a tower built between 1100 and 1200. When about to strike the hour, a cock flaps his wings and crows (pretty well for a cock seven hundred years old). Then a procession of bears, on foot and horseback, march out around, and back again. Next, old Father Time, seated above, turns his hour-glass and waves his scepter; then a man above strikes the hour; a bear one side of him turns his head and listens to each blow; then, away up in the belfry, an iron man rings out the hour for the city; the cock once more flaps his wings and crows, and for an hour the show is ended.

A few hours more, and we are at Interlachen, the Saratoga of Switzerland. Hotels, rather than churches, are the objects of attraction—sumptuous within, and beautiful without, and around a small rich valley, surrounded by very lofty mountains, between two of which, in the background, rises white and cold, the Jungfrau, next to Mont Blanc, the mountain-wonder of Europe. The sun gilds it in his setting, and the moon silvers it in her rising, and we drink in the grandeur of the scene.

Next morning at 7 sharp, we took carriages to Grindelwald, fifteen miles away, with two added on foot, to see, and feel, and enter a live glacier. We have seen the frozen river of ice, entered its grotto, seen its wearing action on the rocks beside and beneath; and now, according to traveling custom, are entitled to wear white scarfs on our hats—said to be a sign of having seen a glacier. None of the "Educated Tourists," as our party is now called, has yet put on the white scarf. We enjoy mountain scenery and Swiss cottages all the way, as well as snow-peaks and glaciers.

At 5 P.M. we cross Lake Brientz to Griesbach, and in the most cosy and elevated dell spent the night. Beautiful for situation is the hotel and all its surroundings of high mountains, and the lake, eight hundred feet below us. Chief among the attractions is a fine cascade coming over the rocks fifteen hundred feet above us, and in seven successive leaps reaching the lake below us, and in very nearly a straight line. At half-past nine we were summoned by a bell to seats directly in front of the cascade. Torches were seen winding among the dark spruce evergreens bordering the stream up above us and down below us. Presently a rocket from the uppermost part shot out into the sky; soon it was answered by one at our feet, and instantly, from lake to crest, Roman candles flashed on the foaming waters and from the caverns behind, illuminating the whole surroundings; anon red lights intervened, then white. The uppermost cavern gleamed like a burning volcano; the midmost one, lighted back of the water, was brilliantly beautiful, while the lurid glare from the deep gulf below us was suggestive of a burning lower world. Not the water only, but the trunks and branches of the bordering and overhanging trees, lit up by the strong and mingled red, green, and white Bengal lights, presented a combination of natural and artificial beauty seldom witnessed by pleasure-seekers.

Next morning we crossed the lake again, and took diligences over the Alps by what is known as the Bruni Pass, going thus from the valley of the Rhone into the valley of the Rhine.

Crossing Lake Lucerne, we enter a city of the same name, pleased with the wild mountain ride, and made tired by the same. Next day we spend upon the lake—the most beautiful and historic in Switzerland — the Lake of the Four Cantons. Among other places, the Tell Platz may most interest my readers, being the place where William Tell sprang from the boat, pushing his jailers back into the stormy waters, and escaping up the mountains. The event of the day was the ascent of Mount Rigi in cars, five thousand feet—an average ascent of one foot in four all the way. From the top we can see more than a hundred snow-capped mountain-peaks, seven beautiful lakes, and villages and valleys of rarest beauty.

Again we bid adieu to scenes of loveliness, descend the Rigi, and steam it across the moonlit lake to Lucerne. Another morning finds us gazing at a huge monument cut in the side of a mountain. It is known in history as the Lion of Lucerne—cut in the rock as a memorial symbol of many brave men who died in defending the liberty of the Swiss. It represents a dying lion with his forefoot on the shield of the enemy, with a broken spear in his side, indicating the cause of his death. There is both pain and pleasure in his dying looks. The whole is cut in relief in a perpendicular face of sandstone rock. It is twenty-eight feet in length, and every way well proportioned. Beneath is a little lake, or pond, around which is kept a beautiful garden, amid many shade-producing trees. This is our ante-breakfast trip; for, after eating, we leave for Basle, at which place we stop and eat again.

There is nothing remarkable about this place, save a former curious custom, for hundreds of years, of keeping their clocks all one hour in advance of the true time. Various reasons have been given for this custom, one of which is that the people were so slow in all things that it was needful to keep the time ahead; another is that the town was once saved from capture by their enemies by the clock striking one instead of twelve. Twelve was the signal agreed upon by the enemy; but, hearing the clock strike one, thought themselves belated, and the citizens on the watch for them, and so retreated. Still another reason is, that once the clock in the tower was struck by lightning, and set forward an hour, and the superstitious people long afterward refused to have it changed, and so kept their time by it. Be this as it may, for the last sixty years the clocks keep the proper time. The place is on the river Rhine, and the last of our Switzerland cities.

A few moments' ride brings us into France, on the border of which we stop to have our luggage examined by polite French officials, after which we speed our way some three hundred and twenty miles through the domain of France, some fifty miles of the distance being through that portion lately taken from France and added to Germany. Night comes down upon us, and our view of the country along to Paris is mostly by moonlight.

By seven o'clock Sunday morning we are in nearly the center of Paris city—hungry, of course, having had nothing to eat since four o'clock on Saturday. Our first day here, then, is Sunday, and we see shops open as on any other day. We walk along the Boulevards in the afternoon and evening to see the gay turn-outs of pleasure-seekers—to see Punch and Judy shows at every turn. Circuses, shows, and concerts have many visitors; all is gayety, and one would not have reason to think it was the Lord's-day. A city of two million people cannot be seen in a day; so we shall tarry here nearly a week, and then, perhaps, material enough for a letter may be gathered, and a whole letter from Paris greet your many readers. Meanwhile, be patient, if a week goes by without a letter. There is an old proverb, "A patient waiter is no loser."

CHAPTER XV.

"Paris is France."—Views on the wicked, beautiful city—Strolls in historic localities, some of which have been baptized in blood of saint and sinner.

PARIS, August 12, 1873.

MY last left me finishing up Switzerland at Lucerne. Leaving there at ten o'clock, we passed through a beautiful country to Basle. This is one of the finest cities in Switzerland. The buildings are of a more modern style. The greater part of the city is on the left bank of the Rhine. Our hotel being on the river, we had to pass through the best portion of it from the depot. Owing to its situation at the junction of the frontiers of France, Germany, and Switzerland, it maintains its position as a place of great commercial activity. The cathedral—a monster—is the chief attraction of the place for tourists. It is built of red sandstone. The older portion dates from 1010, and is of the Byzantine order; but in 1356 a considerable part was destroyed by an earthquake, and it was rebuilt in Gothic style. Among the relics of the ancient structure are the statues of Christ and St. Peter, and the wise and foolish virgins. Great Roman antiquities have been found in this vicinity. It has a population of forty-five thousand. We spent only a few hours here, after partaking of a good dinner at a fine hotel on the margin of the river.

Leaving Basle at five o'clock, we soon enter what was the territory of France. The late unfortunate war with Prussia took this country from her dominion. It was one of the best and richest departments. We had several hours of daylight, and our train, running some forty miles per hour, gave us a good opportunity to see France. There are but few fine houses, only in the cities. The land here, as almost everywhere we have been, is cut up in small patches, and cultivated by those who live in the adjacent villages.

The full moon shines brightly, and we sit up to look at this remarkable country, and the places which have witnessed so many changes. Sunday morning opens upon us some five or six miles from this city. The first persons we see are the reapers of wheat, now being harvested. No Sabbath is recognized in town or country, only as a holiday, while many pursue their daily avocations as usual.

Paris is seen in the distance. All are anxious to get a view of this great city as we approach its environs. At the depot we learn that the hotels are full and we must be divided, as rooms cannot be obtained for so large a party at either of those assigned us. I have comfortable quarters at the St. Petersburg, with about half our party.

After arranging some things, we are off to the Scotch Presbyterian Church, near the Tuileries. Some thirty-five persons only are present. As we were near the place about which I have read and heard so much, it was the place I most desired to see. What a mass of ruins is here! At one end all was burnt that could be consumed. The new buildings, extending to the magnificent passage in front of the bridge of St. Peter's, were injured but little. The roofing of the apartments of the ex-Prince Imperial only was damaged. The sculpture, statues, groups, and ornaments of these magnificent buildings have not been injured. We passed through the former, went across the bridge, and remained for some two hours viewing the most extensive building I ever saw. After dinner we visited a large church in which people were worshiping, and from the front of which there rushed streams of water.

Paris is the best-planned city we have seen. The extensive boulevards running around and through the city, beautifully shaded, and leading to the focal points, make it easy to comprehend. They run one into another in such a manner that you need not miss your way through the city. It seems to have been arranged for military defense better than any I have ever seen. It has had more occasion to use those streets for that purpose than any in modern times. No place in the world can boast of such thoroughfares as Paris. It is greatly indebted to Louis Napoleon for its magnificent boulevards.

Monday morning we take a large open carriage, containing twenty-four persons, and spend the day with a guide. The first object of interest is the church La Madeleine, begun by Louis XIV., continued by Napoleon, who intended it as a temple. After the restoration it was finished as a church. It is a beautiful structure, raised on an immense platform three hundred and eighty-eight feet in length by one hundred and thirty feet. Forty-eight Corinthian columns fifty feet high surround it, having the shape and style of a Grecian temple. It is one of the finest edifices in Europe. As it is near our hotel, I have visited it again and heard its organ.

We next view the Tuileries, and the immense space where the Exchequer was burned by the Commune; then the gardens, statues, and fountains; then the triumphal arch of Louis Philippe and the triumphal arch of St. Martin; the new theater of 1871, the old Bastile of 1798, the prison of 1830, and the column of Charles X., over the canal, running six miles; this the Commune endeavored to blow up by a boat running under it, but it exploded too soon. Here we see cannon-shot all around, and here the last of the Commune were shot themselves. Here immense quantities of goods were burned by the Commune. Here is the vicinity of the insurrections of Paris, and on this immense column are put inscriptions commemorative of the three days of fighting in 1830. Mercury crowns the column, and an inscription, "To the glory of the citizens who fought for liberty," in memory of the revolution of 1830.

We then go to the famous prison where the archbishop and nine others suffered by the guillotine. It is the place where executions now take place. It is famous for having been where the royal and ecclesiastical blood has been shed freely.

We also visit the Zoölogical Gardens, which are very extensive. Every plant, flower, and shrub in the world is said to be here. The animals were eaten during the war, but have been replaced by others. They excel those of London.

We spent some time viewing Notre Dame, a church commenced in 522—the most ancient church in Paris. Napoleon and Josephine were crowned in it. The Archbishop of Paris was killed at the foot of the column, in 1848, while attempting to pacify the tumult. It is in the form of a Latin cross, with three naves and twenty-four chapels. The cushion on which the crown was deposited when Napoleon was crowned, a solid gold cross, and two Russian banners, are among the sacred relics that adorn the church.

Near this church is the place where those people who are drowned, or are found dead, are kept until recognized. It was solemn to see it. Our guide would not go, but told us to do so if we desired, while he waited for us.

Our visit to the cemetery was full of interest. Many names with which we were familiar are seen here—in the department of literature, science, and war. I took the names of many, but have not time to transcribe or comment upon them. Napoleon's marshals sleep here. I plucked a flower and an evergreen from Marshal Ney's grave. As I looked at these marshals' graves, I could but reflect upon the vanity of earthly glory. This is a great city of the dead, some four or five miles in extent.

Napoleon's Tomb.—We go to Napoleon the First's tomb, at the Chapel of the Invalides. This I desired to see above all others. A tower crypt occupies the center of the dome, and in the middle stands the sarcophagus containing the emperor's remains. The circumference forms an open gallery, the pillars of which are decorated with embossed figures bearing palms, and bearing the symbols of the emperor's victories. The second part of the monument is an altar raised on a basement opposite the dome. It is adorned with four columns surmounted with a rich canopy. This work, including the columns, is of black marble from Egypt. The third part of the monument is a chapel, constructed under the ground of the dome—a veritable subterranean crypt, lighted with a lamp on a slab of black marble. These immortal words of the emperor are traced in his testament: " I desire that my ashes may rest on the banks of the Seine, among the French nation I loved so much." The sarcophagus measures four yards in length, two in breadth, and four in height, and is formed of four blocks of Fontainebleau quartz of antiquity, which is inestimable. It required a steam-engine to polish it. The last chest, which has received the cedar and leaden coffin brought from St. Helena, is of a material called *algila*, coming from Corsica. On the 7th day of May, 1861, the mortal remains of this most remarkable man were brought from their resting-place and deposited here, in presence of the dignitaries of State. It was on the 12th of May, 1840, that the Chamber of Deputies determined to remove them from St. Helena. For twenty years they were deposited in St. Jerome Church of the Invalides Hotel, and now finally rest in a manner no monarch ever did. It is the most gorgeous monument I ever saw. The dome of the church, covered with gold, shines out from every point where you can see the city. The opened part of the crypt is lighted by twelve bronze lamps, the models taken from Pompeii. The succession of basso-relievos is of black marble, and is called the Sword-room. It contains various relics, and the banners taken from the different nations which he conquered—the golden crown voted by Cherbourg, and sixty banners, coming from the victories he achieved over his enemies. The monument has cost three millions. Crowds go to see it daily. We met a great many—or rather, saw them—as they passed out at another gate. These people glory in the name of Napoleon.

We ascend the triumphal arch erected in honor of his many victories. There are twelve avenues meeting here. From the top of this arch we have the finest view of the city and its surroundings I have seen. For miles far away in every direction you can see down these avenues the most magnificent buildings, the finest parks, gardens, statues, fountains—in fact, every thing of grandeur and magnificence that the imagination can well picture, to make the most beautiful city in the world.

I now realize more fully than ever the expression that "Paris is France." The French glory in their splendor and gayety. In this city they have much to stimulate their national pride, much of ancient art and modern improvement in science.

They must have amusements, and they have them to a greater extent than any other people of whom I have any knowledge. To walk out of an evening on any of their boulevards, especially about their gardens, one will see more of some things than in any other place I have ever been. There are many places where they have concerts of various kinds in open air. We were passing one of these last night, and we stopped awhile and saw quite a variety of things, as well as heard some very fine music, vocal as well as instrumental. The French feel deeply their present humiliation, at times. We see them in national mourning for their misfortunes. A young lady, dressed in mourning, came out and sang one of their national airs, which moved the crowd to such an extent that, though I did not understand a word she said, yet I found the unbidden tear stealing from my eyes in sympathy for them.

France will yet recover her lost glory, and, whenever the time comes, will show that there are recuperative energies within her that can and will restore her to the position she has occupied among the nations of earth.

I did not intend expressing opinions, but merely to give a running sketch of what I have seen as I pass hurriedly through the cities and countries of Europe.

Lingering in Paris—Sight-seeing in the finest city in the world—Versailles and its antique remains of royalty—The Tuileries—Pantheon—St. Cloud—Gobelin.

PARIS, August 14, 1873.

Our third day was spent in Versailles, some twelve miles from Paris. This was formerly the second town of France, having 100,000 people, mostly nobility and gentry. The splendor of this city under Louis XIV., who had Mansard to build him the palace and lay out the parks and gardens at an average cost of forty million pounds sterling, ceased with the unfortunate Louis XVI., for Paris. Louis Philippe had it devoted to a museum for the glories of the illustrations of France. The palace is divided into three great divisions. We went through some of these once famous buildings, which are filled with the most wonderful collection of paintings, relating to the history of France. The chapel is one of the finest we have seen. The ceiling is eighty-six feet high, with magnificent frescoes and a mosaic pavement of great beauty.

The Grand Trianon is a small palace four hundred feet long, built by order of Louis XIV. in 1683, in the grounds of the park. It was the favorite residence of Napoleon I., and is the usual residence of Queen Victoria when in Paris. Here are to be seen many of the relics of the former monarchs of France, showing what royalty was in the days of her glory.

President MacMahon and the Assembly are now in session here, but we could not even look in upon them. Soldiers are seen drilling, cannon are pointing out, and the surroundings seem warlike.

The gardens are the most extensive and magnificent I have seen. Sixty miles of ground are occupied by them and the parks. There are eighty fountains, some of them the largest ever made. These play only on Sundays—others only once a month, and the whole of them only once a year. The gardens are kept in fine order, but the hundreds of groups of statuary around them are neglected, and moss is growing on them. We felt "like one who treads alone some banquet-hall deserted," whenever we went over these antique remains of royalty, yet they are grand in their loneliness. The orangery, which was planted as far back as 1421, is artistically arranged in large inclosures, so as to move them in the houses during winter.

We return to the city by the tramway railroad, which is a large two-story omnibus running within an iron railing. On the top of this we had a fine view of the country along the Seine. It is densely populated, and a good part of the way is a village.

We pass St. Cloud. It is a pretty little town, celebrated for its palace, which was destroyed during the war. It was the favorite resort of Napoleon I., and has a park ten miles in circumference. As we pass the gate into the city, a halt is made, to see if there is any thing contraband among us. This is a fine boulevard for miles, extending into the city.

The Siege and Bombardment.—Yesterday morning we went to see the panorama of the siege and bombardment of Paris. This is the most astonishing thing we have seen. You go into a large building, ascend a winding staircase, and come out on top of what seems to be a hill overlooking the city, where the battle is raging. You see no painting, no moving of scenes, but the heavens above, with the clouds obscured by the smoke. Around you is the fort the French are defending. Some of the buildings near are in flames, and appear as natural as if real. The artillery playing upon the Prussians, belching out flames and smoke. The dead and wounded spread out before you as real (seemingly) as if you were in a few steps of them. The Prussian camps are seen in the distance. Other forts, also, are attacked. Other buildings are on fire. The fort where you are is in ruins, as perfectly natural as if really before you. Yet you see no painting anywhere, but all is open, as if you were looking on the strife all around you. The city is seen about as it looks from other directions. We are bewildered—overwhelmed with amazement. Can this be artificial? It is the triumph of art—a delusion such as we have never expected to see. The earth, we know, is real, the broken shells around us are real—and yet the others near it are not. One of the banks of sand-bags was said to be real, but the others seemed as natural as it did. Some one threw a penny near the cannon, and we heard it strike the rock and saw it afterward. This settled the question of there being some things that were not illusions, but the whole scene far surpasses any thing we have seen in this line. Every one who visits Paris to see should see this.

We go to the Palace of Industry, built in 1854, for the Universal Exhibition. Here are paintings and statues of men eminent in art and science.

We have passed the Palace of the Tuileries several times—a terrible mass of ruins, but now being rebuilt. In front is a noble arch of Napoleon, erected in 1806. Here we see a chariot drawn by four horses, copied from those of St. Mark's, at Venice, to which I have referred. Here is a palace constructed by Julian the Apostate, or by his ancestor Constantius, toward the close of the fourth century.

We spent some time in the Pantheon. Louis XV. laid the foundation in 1764. The Assembly (in 1790) converted it into a temple to receive the ashes of the great men of the country. In 1822 it was restored to a church, to become in 1830 a secular institution, and in 1848 the scene of desperate combat between the insurgents and the troops. It is three hundred and two by two hundred and fifty feet, its summit being four hundred and fifty feet high. In the vaults are the tombs of Voltaire, Rousseau, and several of Napoleon's best officers.

Gobelin Tapestry.—Tapestry work is done in Paris as at no other place. Some two hundred years since it was invented by a Frenchman named Gobelin. The emperor bought the right, and named the establishment after him. Our guide had permission from the authorities to take persons in to see the manufacture of it. We were taken through the rooms where the most exquisite work was being performed. There were carpets requiring ten men twenty years to make, and paintings copied so as to be exactly like the originals. These works are never sold from this establishment, as they are used only for royalty, or presented to such.

We visited a number of churches and other places of which I cannot now say any thing. I thought Paris needed street railways, but when I went on the steamboats of the Seine, passing swiftly by and stopping at convenient distances, circling through the city, and the many lines of omnibuses, running all around and through the city—sixteen miles for ten cents—I see they have locomotive facilities as cheap as any city I have seen. I took those trips to-day by river several miles, and around the city, at a cost of less than twenty cents. The railroad runs sometimes above the houses, giving a fine view of the city from several points of observation. I think there are twenty-six stations in the circle. When it is above the houses, there are five large stone columns across the road, on which the double-track road is built. Under it is a fine arcade, which can be used for various purposes.

Upon the whole, I consider Paris the finest city I have ever seen. Nature has done much for the location, and countless millions have been spent to beautify and adorn it. The Academy of Music, near where I am writing to-night, is said to be the finest building in Europe. It is rapidly recovering from the devastations of the war, and, if MacMahon proves successful in his government, will soon regain its former prosperity. The motto, "Liberty, equality, fraternity," is seen all over the city on the public buildings and many other places.

The position of Paris is very much the same as that of London. The Seine, over which are built twenty-five bridges, divides it in the same manner that the Thames divides London. The form of Paris is nearly circular. It is entirely surrounded by a fortified wall, at the different gates of which the customs are collected. It has twelve palaces, forty Roman Catholic churches, sixteen Protestant churches, one hundred ornamental fountains, thirty-eight markets, and twenty hospitals. Its population is about two millions, one-third having been added in the last twenty years.

For those whose inclination leads them to fashion, amusement, music, and gayety, Paris affords more facility than any other city. The citizens are intelligent, polite, affable, and partial to Americans, who were under many obligations to France for assistance in the time of her greatest need. I gazed on the portrait of the noble La Fayette the other day with much interest. Well do I remember seeing him when he visited our country in 1824, when he was welcomed everywhere as the friend of liberty. He stands prominent in a large painting of the surrender of Yorktown.

We leave here in the morning for London. I may say something more of Paris before I close these sketches, for much may be truthfully said of this city without exhausting the subject.

This is not only the gayest and most fashionable, but the most beautiful city in the world. The hotels, I think, are not so good as in some other European cities. Furnished apartments are said to be much cheaper than the hotels.

One of the most interesting monuments in the city is the triumphal arch dedicated by Napoleon I. to the glory of the French armies. It was commenced on the 15th of August (which, I think, is his birthday), 1806. The work was interrupted in 1814, but was continued in 1833, but not completed till 1836. Twelve wide boulevards terminate at it, as a focal point. We ascended to the summit, where we had the best view of this magnificent city we could have. It is delightfully grand in every direction.

The Egyptian obelisk, given by the viceroy Mehemet Ali, and taken from the ruins of Thebes, is, perhaps, the oldest thing of the kind of which we have any knowledge. It once ornamented the entrance of a palace constructed by Rameses II. (sixteen centuries before Christ). It was brought to Paris in October, 1836.

The most frequented and deeply-interesting place in Paris is the garden of the Tuileries, containing about seventy acres. Here congregate tens of thousands nightly, to hear the music and witness the performance of many things that interest this fun-loving people. All that money, taste, and genius can do seems to have been done to render these places attractive to all classes who visit them.

Foremost among the churches of Paris is Notre Dame. This cathedral was commenced in 522; was continued, on a much larger scale, to 1160. It is the most ancient church in Paris. In the revolution of 1789 it was made a wine-store, and afterward a hay-loft. In 1802, when Napoleon ratified the concordat with the pope, it was reëstablished as a church. It was in this church that Napoleon and Josephine were crowned by Pope Pius VII., in 1804. The Italians are not the only people who have fabulous stories about relics. In this church a piece of the real cross and crown of thorns are to be seen, having been brought by St. Louis from Palestine. They were first placed in the Sainte Chapelle, built for that purpose in 1825, and afterward moved to the cathedral for greater safety. The time for such stuff, I think, is rapidly passing away, never more to return among intelligent people; but as I am simply giving a sketch of things as they are, this is one of the many ways by which the ignorant masses have been blindly deluded to attach importance to the possession of relics. The interior of the cathedral is of the greatest magnificence. The vaulted roof, the three naves, the twenty-four chapels, the high altar, the paintings, the massive pillars and columns, each a single block, will excite the admiration of every beholder of taste. It is in this choir that most of the kings and queens, their sons and daughters, have been baptized, married, and crowned. In the sacristy are to be seen the coronation mantle of Napoleon I., and the cushion on which the crown was deposited during the ceremony of their coronation; also, a solid gold cross, presented by Napoleon on that occasion; two Russian banners, taken in the Crimea; and a silver virgin, presented by Charles X. This magnificent church was condemned by the Commune, but was saved by the students of the Hospital, with the assistance of the inhabitants of the island of the city, in the center of which the cathedral stands. Six hundred Communists took possession of it on Good Friday, 1871, at three o'clock in the evening, while the preacher was in the pulpit. Fortunately, the troops of Versailles arrived just in time to prevent its destruction. It was set on fire the night the troops were entering Paris.

The Pantheon is one of the most magnificent buildings in the city. Its foundation was laid by Louis XV., in 1764. By a decree of the Assembly of 1791, it was converted into a temple to receive the ashes of the great men of the country. In 1822 it was restored as a church, to become, in 1830, a secular institution, and in 1848 the scene of some desperate combats between the insurgents and the troops, who ravaged the building by firing artillery at the revolutionists. In that dilapidated state the emperor, in 1852, caused the necessary repairs to be made, and restored it to ecclesiastical use. It is three hundred and two feet long, by two hundred and fifty in breadth at the transept. The cupola is two hundred and sixty feet above the ground. The lantern, which crowns the summit, is four hundred and fifty feet above the Seine.

The Palace de Luxembourg was begun in 1615, and finished in 1620. It was much enlarged in 1804, and great additions made between 1831 and 1841. It has served successively as the habitation of princes, as a prison under the first revolution, then as a palace of the Directory and of the Consulate; as a palace of the Senate under the first empire; as a palace of the peers under the restoration and under Louis Philippe, and again as the palace of the Senate under the second empire. There are several noble saloons in this palace, the principal ones being those of Napoleon I.

The Palace of the Tuileries was built more than three hundred years ago, but underwent, as did a large portion of Paris, many alterations under Napoleon III. This is in front of the Triumphal Arch of Napoleon I.; but this, and the whole of the Tuileries, were entirely destroyed by the Commune, in May, 1871, but are now being rebuilt. I stepped the width, and found it to be about a quarter of a mile; the length about one-third greater.

The Palace of Themis was constructed by Julian the Apostate, or by his ancestor, Constantine, toward the end of the fourth century. The part of the palace which remains consists of some subterraneous passages, altars, urns, and sculpture.

The military bands play select pieces of music every day, from four to six o'clock, in the principal squares, parks, and wards of Paris, from the second month of spring to the last month of autumn.

The damage done by the Prussians was small, in comparison with that done by the Commune. The ruins of the Tuileries, the Palais Royal, the Ministere de Finances, the Hotel de Ville, and many less important buildings, remain to bear witness of their blind fury. Whole streets, which were razed to the ground, have now been entirely rebuilt, and thousands of houses, which were more or less injured, have been so repaired that not a trace of the ruinous condition they were once in can be seen. Eighty square yards of the Gobelin tapestry were consumed, with the building in which it was kept, and the unique collection of tapestries of the time of Louis XIV., was also destroyed by the Commune. The city and country are recuperating more rapidly than any which has been so much devastated by the horrors of war. One would not suppose, only when he was looking at some of the ruins, that this gay city had been so recently suffering from foreign war, and, far worse, from the dissensions of her own people. Paris will soon be herself again, without a peer, or scarcely a rival, in the world of beauty, grandeur, and glory.

Farewell to France—Back in London—Dr. Cummings—Billingsgate—The Tower—The docks and the shipping.

LONDON, August 19, 1873.

Although I have written you three letters from Paris, I feel, as some of our party did, that I am not ready to leave it yet. To go through and around the city and see the devastations made by the Commune after the Prussian war was over, makes one's heart sick to think of such destruction by their own people. France has the desire for a republic without the capacity to sustain one; and although there seems to be peace, I think there are elements of discord, which will soon be manifested publicly. The more intelligent do not desire a republic, but a limited monarchy. If MacMahon does not fill their bill, I think they will have some one in whose veins flows royal blood to reign over them. This party is now in the ascendant, and is increasing its influence, so that I cannot believe the present government will continue long. I inclose you an editorial from the London *Times*, which, I think, takes a proper view of the present *status* of politics in France.

We left Paris on Friday morning. There is something captivating about that city. Some of our party remained. Two young ladies from Oxford, Mississippi, will be here some months.

The railroad time here is regulated to suit the tides. Our train was detained a short time. The boat waited, but the tide would not, and we had to await its movements. This is the first detention we have had. It gave us an opportunity to see the whole of the country in daylight.

Rouen is the most important city on this route. Here, and through all this part of France, we see manufactories of various kinds. The land is not so good as it is in England, nor is it in so high a state of cultivation.

We spent a few hours at the place of embarkation to cross the Channel. It is an old town, with many who make a living by fishing. We saw the mackerel-fishing process, with nets. Women are fishers as well as men. It was a grand holiday in France—celebrating the Assumption. We went to a very large cathedral, said to be the oldest in France, to witness the ceremonies. White seemed to be the style of dressing for the occasion. Old women with white caps, young ladies with white head-dresses, young girls in blue and white. They sang with a vim I have never heard in a Catholic church before. They then formed a grand procession, and marched through the streets.

At six o'clock we sailed from France. I looked back to her chalk bluffs, extending all along her coast, reminding me of our bluffs, and sighed for France. The sunset, bar, and light-house were the last we saw of that land of revolution and commotion.

We have to wait for the train, so that we pass through this part of England in the morning. Here large herds of cattle, and flocks of sheep are seen, as the train passes at the rate of forty miles an hour. And soon it brings us back to London again. This seems like home. They are our people, and like Americans. Sunday I went to hear Dr. Cummings in the morning, and a celebrated Episcopalian at St. Paul's, in the afternoon.

Yesterday we passed through that celebrated place, Billingsgate, on our way to the Tower of London; thence to see the docks and shipping, and from there to the British Museum.

I have not time to say any thing farther, but may before I conclude these sketches. It is breakfast-time, and other matters press upon me. I hope to see my friends in Memphis soon.

Letter from the Rev. T. W. Hooper, of Lynchburg, Va., written for the *News*.

HOTEL ST. PETERSBURG, PARIS,
July 16, 1873.

Here we are, at last, in this beautiful combination of Sodom and Gomorrah—beautiful in spite of all that the Communists have done to destroy it; and as we walk its wide and shady boulevards, or promenade the magnificent Champs Elysées, we cannot wonder that some enthusiasts should write, "See

Paris and die." There is one thing certain, and that is, that many of the heroes of the past have seen Paris and died in the streets. We have visited the Place de la Concorde, which marks the spot where the beautiful and virtuous Marie Antoinette was beheaded; and did not grieve much when we remembered that the brutal Robespierre there plunged into that eternity which he had passed with his victims, who are now ministers to his everlasting remains. But it is not worth while to moralize; for were I to attempt it, just think of the scenes which in three days I have seen, to awaken suggestion—the Madeleine, the tomb of Napoleon, the Column of July, the Tuileries (in ruins), the Champs Elysées, the Column of Victory, the Column Vendome (in ruins), the Louvre, and a hundred other places of historical interest and association, which would set a salt on fire with enthusiasm, and exhaust all my French quicker than you can snap your fingers.

Think of my hearing Catholic music at Notre Dame, where the great Napoleon was crowned emperor! Think of my looking at the private apartments at the palace of Trianon, and also at the private bed-room and furniture of the deserted Josephine—at the carriage in which she rode away in disgrace, while near it was the one in which he and his new wife rode into Paris on the occasion of the nuptials! Think of my visiting St. Cloud, where the last Napoleon had his favorite residence, and wandering along those shaded, flowering drives where the beautiful Eugenie once rode in all the beauty and dignity of her imperial splendor! When I think of all these things, mingled as they are with visible marks of the Prussian invasion and the subsequent "reign of terror" under the anarchy of the Commune, I seem to have been floating in a dream of the past, and can hardly realize that I am actually here in the flesh, and that all around me are these wonderful palaces and promenades and boulevards that are read about at home.

But this is certainly Paris—there is no mistaking it. None but Parisians can jabber in such uninterpretable lingo. The men, women, and children all talk French. The horses and dogs understand French. The babies cry in French; and if I were to live here about a year, I think I could talk enough to learn my way about from one place to another without carrying a map or employing a guide. As it is, we have a jolly time, and have had many ludicrous adventures with these people, who *will* imagine that we can speak French, and whom *we* imagine must be deaf, because they shake their heads and mutter something when we talk to them.

But, seriously, American French does n't pass in Paris much better than greenbacks, and I have not seriously regretted the want of such a language. When I want to study it, I will come over here and get the genuine article. Indeed, I have gotten along remarkably well, for their English is just as bad as my French, and between us we manage with signs, which serve every purpose — with them to cheat, and me to be cheated.

I am confirmed every day in my impression that Mark Twain is the only man that is fit to write a guide-book, and that what he writes about Paris is true to the letter. We hired his "Fergerson," or one of the family, yesterday and the day before, to guide us. The first day, he charged us five shillings apiece, and packed twenty-four on top of a kind of circus band-wagon, and rode us around, to the evident amusement of all Paris. Every now and then he would stop to wet his whistle, and then talk—rather loosely, as might be imagined. He was evidently disgusted, as were some of us, at the tomb of Abelard and Héloise; though some of the

13*

ancient "marms" almost went into hysterics, and even went so far as to steal flowers from the inclosure, which "they had n't ought to have done."

But, after all, beggars must n't be choosers; and Scotch guides, that speak English, know the ropes, and have to tip a penny to see the great dining-halls and private chapel at Trianon, like our man Cunningham, are not to be despised. And then, he has such a dogmatic way of taking down Yankees, who, he says, are the most selfish, uncompromising, dissatisfied set of people he ever saw, that you are obliged to admire him. And to us, who are so miserably grum, he has proved himself almost invaluable; and I would earnestly recommend him to all future tourists who are fortunate enough to travel with our kind and attentive friend Mr. Cook, who, by the way, has done all that a man could do for our comfort and convenience.

But I must close this hastily-written note, scribbled at an hour which I have snatched merely to give our readers some idea of the scenes we have visited while we have been in Paris.

I would also say, that last Sunday we heard a capital sermon from Rev. Mr. Hitchcock, of the American chapel; but at night I never saw such a Sabbath desecration. The Shah of Persia, who is quite a sharp-looking, gingerbread darkey, is here, and wherever we go we find the people in a stir. Sunday night the city was illuminated in his honor, and millions of gas-lights were blazing all over the immense crowds that swayed in every direction, and crowded all the avenues to get a look at his august majesty. I saw him, and was satisfied that I could beat him on looks at any of your tobacco-factories.

Letter from the Rev. A. B. Whipple, President of Lansingburgh College, N. Y.

LONDON, August 19, 1873.

If I remember rightly, my dear friends and *Gazette* readers, I indirectly promised to write a letter concerning Paris, the capital of France, and, as the French think, the capital of the world. It really is a beautiful city, embracing a population of more than two millions. It contains public places and buildings of historic interest, so numerous and so varied as to render a selection for description quite a puzzle; more especially when that description must be quite precise, to enable the reader to see it as the writer does; add to this, all must be condensed, not into a guide-book, but the narrow columns of a newspaper.

Let me take you, first of all, right into the midst of the city to the Arc d'Etoile, the largest and finest sculptured arch in Europe, built by order of Napoleon to commemorate his victories of 1805. We pause a moment to admire its size, design, and workmanship, and read the names of the places where his victories were won; we see the engraved honors, but not many of the horrors of war. We learn that its solid concrete underground structure is twenty-five feet in thickness, and that all above is solid stone. Learning so much, we seek its summit by two hundred and forty steps, and find the top is one hundred and fifty feet above the ground, and the ground a hill; and so Paris lies spread out like a huge living map below us. We are not long in perceiving that the Triumphal Arch is in a conspicuous position. Twelve boulevards, like spokes of a wheel, radiate from it. Down these grand, doubly-lined and tree-shaded avenues, far into the city, we look with pleasure; and from these same boulevards the glory-loving Frenchmen can cast their eyes up to this Triumphal Arch, and in heart bless the author, and only wait a few months to place the young prince in power, and shout "Vive l'Empereur!" The French love the Napoleons.

Let us look along one boulevard at a time. Adown the avenue we see myriads of seemingly happy people. On the right we see a grand building: it is the Industrial Palace—the Crystal Palace—rebuilt for annual home exhibitions. Farther down is the broad street called the Champs Elysées (Elysian Fields), covering some forty acres, and bordering on the Seine. It is finely shaded with horse-chestnut trees laid out in walks, cut through by the avenue bearing its name. Along this the aristocratic drive, going to and returning from the park beyond the Arc. Here, too, are the amusements for the people—singing, coffee-houses, theaters, circuses, and mimic shows in splendid variety. At the lower end of this avenue is the Place de la Concorde, an open space with fountains and fine statuary; and in the midst the great red-granite obelisk of Luxor, brought from Thebes, in Egypt, at immense expense. It is one granite piece, seventy-five feet long, well proportioned, and with Egyptian hieroglyphics. It has been known more than three thousand years. It stands on the very spot where, during the early Reign of Terror, stood the guillotine on which were beheaded Louis XVI., his sister Mary Antoinette, and twenty-eight hundred others. Well may a *red*-granite obelisk cover the spot! Beyond this, in the same direction, are the gardens of the Tuileries—extended and beautifully-shaded grounds, lying immediately in front of the palace. Within are fountains and statuary of rare merit, altogether forming one of the favorite promenades to Parisians of all classes and ages—for here children and their nurses do greatly abound. Still farther on is the palace of the Tuileries, now mostly in ruins; the building itself, of great extent and many historical associations, also the late imperial residence, was destroyed in 1871 by the Communal authorities, for a short time in power in Paris. Adjoining the Tuileries is the Louvre—a palace and great national museum. It was partly destroyed by the Commune. Many of the halls remain, and in them are some of the finest pictures in the world; not paintings only, but statuary of all ages and nations; models of naval and marine architecture, from early ages to the present; ethnological specimens, embracing the peculiar costumes and implements of all nations—as, for instance, the idols, temples, and car of Juggernaut; halls of vases, halls of medals, halls of dishes, halls of ornaments, halls of arts of all kinds, through which one may travel twelve miles without going over the same hall the second time. I tried it, and it took me all of one day. My eyes were never tired of seeing; but my legs, long ere the day was done, complained bitterly, inasmuch as marble floors and oft-repeated granite steps made even slow walking very hard—and even now my knees tremble at the sight of stairs.

Still farther on we may enter Notre Dame, one of the architectural glories of Paris and the world. It has two immense square towers. The whole front and portals are elaborate, and within are some of the finest Gothic arches in Europe. It has a wealth of stained-glass windows, splendid side-chapels, and a most magnificent high-altar, at which Napoleon and Josephine were crowned. As an ecclesiastical object, it is the most impressive in Paris, and in grandeur and historical associations it can hardly be excelled in Europe. Across the Seine, to the right, we find an immense structure, built by Louis XIV. for military hospital purposes, and afterward used by Napoleon for the same purpose.

It is called the Hotel des Invalides. Besides the living remains of many old and scarred veterans, there are old pictures of old wars—a little real and much imaginary. In the chapel are rotting battle-flags, from the oriflamme of St. Louis to those taken at Sebastopol. Back of this chapel is a church called the Dome of the Invalides—so named, perhaps, from its conspicuous gilded dome, enabling one to see it and know it from afar—more noteworthy for what is within and immediately under the dome. In a sunken, circular space, in a large red-granite sarcophagus, surrounded by his moldering battle-flags, between a number of weeping marble maidens, lie the remains of Napoleon Bonaparte. White marble and nice workmanship make the church very beautiful within; and the high-altar, colored by the light streaming through glass stained with golden color, is rendered peculiarly beautiful. Around in the church are monuments containing the remains of Vauban, Turenne, and Joseph Bonaparte. Two empty rooms indicate the places selected by Napoleon III. and Eugenie as their last resting-place. Whether recent events in French history will keep them out remains to be proven. My judgment is, that ultimately they will be honored with a place among their illustrious relatives, whom at heart the nation loves. Here, as all through Europe, men of great fighting ability are honored after death with admission to the churches, and worshiped as heroes, if not canonized as saints.

My dear readers, I have only, as it were, run a little way down one avenue in Paris, with brief touches. The gay out-door life, the busy industry, splendid markets, stores, etc., need mention; but I have used my last sheet.

CHAPTER XVII.

Loitering in London—Prince Albert's memorial monument—Description of its beauties, its grandeur, and sculpture.

LONDON, August 20, 1873.

London's Immensity.—The time allotted for this great city has nearly expired. I feel inclined to say something more of a few things here. The longer I remain here, the more I am impressed with its immensity. It is the only place we have visited that we have not been able to comprehend. Having been composed of quite a number of towns by filling up the intervening space between them, it does not present that uniformity which it would have done had it been built as one city. This complicates the ability to grasp its proportions. It has thus increased its population to about three and a half millions. The wealth and intelligence concentrates in the cities, as well as the population.

I was more impressed with this after visiting the memorial monument erected to Prince Albert, in Regent's Park. We went out by the underground railroad, and returned by two lines of omnibuses. In this vicinity are the Exposition buildings, and the South Kensington Museum. Here are the historical paintings of England, embracing portraits, not only of her kings and queens, but many of other nations; also, their great men in theology, science, art, and literature. Here I saw many with whose names I have been familiar from my boyhood. Wesley's was taken at manhood and in old age. There is scarcely a prominent man in English history whose portrait is not to be found in this gallery.

There are a great many specimens of printing in the different stages of its progress, and thousands of things collected from England's colonies, showing the vast resources of her territory, on which the sun never sets.

I am not surprised that Englishmen are proud of their country. They have much of which to boast in her past history, present condition, and future destiny. They have in their government all the civil and religious liberty that they think is necessary. Their House of Commons, elected by the people, have a controlling influence in their parliament, so that it may be said the people rule.

Memorial Monument.—But I am wandering. I started to say something about the most magnificent memorial monument there is perhaps in the world. It is to honor the husband of their queen. The monument is elevated upon a lofty and wide-spreading pyramid of steps. From the upper platform rises a continued pedestal surrounded by sculptures, representing historical groups or scenes of the most eminent artists of all ages of the world, the four sides being devoted severally to painting, sculpture, architecture, poetry, and music. The figures are about six feet high. This forms, as it were, the foundation of the monument, and upon it is placed the shrine. This is supported at each of its angles by groups of four pillars of polished granite, bearing the four main arches of the shrine. There are one hundred and sixty-nine full-sized marble statues. The whole structure is crowned by a lofty shrine of rich tabernacle-work in gilt and enameled metal, continued in a cross one hundred and eighty feet high. Beneath this vast canopy, and raised upon a lofty pedestal, will be placed the statue of the prince. Besides the sculpture already mentioned there are, on pedestals, groups illustrating the industrial arts of agriculture, manufacture, commerce, and engineering. Above these, against the pillars, are statues which represent the greater sciences and the Christian virtues. At the angles of the pyramid of steps from which the monument rises are four large pedestals, being groups allegorically relating to the four quarters of the globe and their productions. The figures in the niches idealize the four great Christian virtues—faith, hope, charity, and humility. The four statues at the angle of the second story represent the four great moral virtues—fortitude, prudence, justice, and temperance. The four angels immediately over these niches suggest aspiration after heavenly glory. The monument is intended to commemorate his royal highness the Prince Consort, first in rank and station in the United Kingdom, except the sovereign, as the great promoter of art, science, and the social virtues. It is the most magnificent thing of the kind in the world. It was all made of materials found in England, and by her own artists. It was paid for by the spontaneous contributions of the people.

If I had time, I would like to give a description of the eight groups of sculpture—four representing the four continents, the other four the industrial arts—but it would take too much space. I will say, however, that the four lower groups represent Europe, Asia, Africa, and America. The figure representing England is seated on a rock, against which the waves are dashing. France, as a military power, is shown holding a sword in the one hand and in the other a wreath of laurel. Germany, the great home of literature and science, is represented in a thoughtful attitude, with an open volume on her knee. Italy is shown as awakening from a dream, in allusion to her recent union into one kingdom, the broken column on which she is sitting referring to her former greatness. Asia is represented by a figure seated on an elephant, and in the act of raising her veil from her face. The poet represents Persia with his pen and writing-case. In brief: China holding his specimen of porcelain; the warrior of India and Central Asia with his weapons, and the Arab merchant sitting on his camel's saddle with the Koran beside him. A general feeling of repose seems to pervade this group. Africa is represented by an Egyptian princess seated on a camel. On her right stands a Nubian, his hand resting on a half-buried statue, in allusion to the monumental glories of the past. The negro, leaning on his bow, is the representative of the uncivilized races of that continent. The camel was chosen for this group, as it is indispensable in the African deserts, and is used universally as a means of communication by traders, and has at all times been characteristic of Egypt.

America is placed on the north angle. The group consists of a central figure of America as a quarter of the globe, mounted on a bison, charging through the long grass of the prairie. Their advance is directed by the United States on the one side, while Canada attends them, pressing the rose of England to her breast. In the other figures of the composition are represented Mexico rising from a trance, and South America equipped for the chase. The figures of America are of the Indian type, in native costumes and feathered head-dresses; the eagle for the United States, the beaver for Canada, the lone star for Chili, volcano for Mexico, the alpaca for Peru, and the cross for Brazil. In the composition of this group present progress and general onward movement are expressed, and form a contrast to the other three continents, which are more tranquil in their arrangement. It is the most expressive marble I ever saw. On it you may look for hours with intense interest. It is in Hyde Park, containing three hundred and ninety acres, beautifully laid off, and containing the statue of Wellington, whom England delights to honor. Take it altogether, it far surpasses any thing of the kind that has ever been erected.

Sacred to John Wesley.—A number of our party, who had not visited the City-road Wesleyan Chapel and Cemetery, desiring me, I went with them once more to that hallowed place, made sacred by the life, labors, and triumphant death of one of the most remarkable men in English history. John Wesley not only commenced an organization which has become the largest Protestant Church, but the influence of the doctrines he preached has been felt by the Church of England and other Churches. Here his remains rest in the rear of the church in which he labored, and within a few steps of the house in which he passed from earth to heaven. I am glad the church, parsonage, and his house remain as they were in his day. I bought some stereoscopic views of them, some books, and memorials made out of that part of the pulpit which was taken off when it was lowered five feet. If I venerate any man, and the place where his remains sleep, this would be that place. I saw and heard much of St. Paul's prison, beheading, and burial, both in St. Peter's and St. Paul's Churches in Rome, but I know not whether the places are really the ones they claim to be, but here I know sleep those whose words and works have shaken the world. Dr. Clarke and Richard Watson and others, whom Methodists esteem as pillars of the church, are here together, moldering to their common elements, while they—in the better land—have met countless thousands who have been aided in their upward march by their writings. John Bunyan, whose "Pilgrim's Progress" has been read by more people than any book save the Bible, sleeps just across the street, near the mother of the Wesleys. Some Baptists along, no doubt, felt toward him as I did in regard to those to whom I have referred.

I have visited several other places of interest since I wrote, but I find I shall spin this letter out too long if I give any account of them. My time is swiftly passing, and soon I must leave this world's metropolis for home. I may, however, sketch some items of places and things that may, perhaps, be read with some interest, as they belong to that people from whom we descended, and to whom we, as a people, sustain the most important relations, commercially, socially, and morally. They feel toward us as brothers, and manifest the most lively interest in our welfare, thinking that—next to themselves—we have the best country and government in the world.

Letters from the Rev. A. B. Whipple, President of Lansingburgh College, N. Y.

H. V. I., October 14, 1873.

One day while in London I started to find the Patent Office, as I wished to see the models of the many curious machines kept there for sight-seeing and study. I found the office only to learn that the models were kept in the Museum of Arts, at South Kensington. A pleasant ride of an hour brought me there; and many an hour was spent in looking at the skill of man, as shown in his inventions. Models of almost every contrivance of man are gathered here in various halls and departments. At home I may tell of some things I saw inside the halls of art.

My purpose in this letter is to describe a work of art which (in its completeness) surpasses any thing else I saw in my journey; and I fear a single letter will be insufficient to give a full account; nevertheless, I will begin, and your interest in the subject shall be the token of continuance or discontinuance. What I am about to describe is called the Prince Consort National Memorial.

In constructing this, two objects seem to have been intended—one to commemorate the love of the nation to the prince; the other, to commemorate the great interest taken by the prince in the advancement of the arts and sciences. To him England is greatly indebted for the World's Fair of 1851, and the present Crystal Palace described in my last letter. As a study, it is hoped that this memorial will stimulate the development of the decorative arts, and so, practically, illustrate and realize the object to which the prince incessantly devoted his energies. I will try and picture the monument in words, asking only that you will use your fancy somewhat in trying to fill out the picture.

Fancy you see the base of a granite pyramid two hundred feet square; walk up about twenty-five steps, and you are on the base of the monument. From this upper platform rises a continuous pedestal, surrounded by sculptures representing historical groups of the most eminent artists of all ages of the world—one side devoted to painting, one to sculpture, one to architecture, and one to poetry and music. The figures, carved in stone, are six feet high, and in number one hundred and sixty-nine—forty-two or forty-three on a side, with the most famous in the center—in poetry, Homer; in painting, Angelo; in architecture, Christopher Wren; in music, Beethoven. All these form, as it were, the foundation of the monument on which the shrine is placed. This is supported by groups of four polished granite pillars, supporting the four main arches of the shrine. Each side terminates with a gable, in the tympanum of which is a large mosaic picture.

The intersecting roofs are covered with scales of metal richly enameled and gilded. The whole structure is crowned by a lofty spire terminating in a cross one hundred and eighty feet above the ground. Under this vast canopy, on a lofty pedestal, in a sitting posture, is the statue of the prince.

In addition to the sculpture already mentioned, there are, on pedestals projecting from each angle, groups illustrating the industrial arts of agriculture, manufactures, commerce and engineering. Above these, against the pillars and in the angles of the gables, are statues representing the greater sciences, and in the work of the spire are figures of angels and of the Christian virtues. At the four corners of the pyramid of steps, from which the monument rises, are four large pedestals, each bearing an allegoric group representing the four quarters of the globe and their productions. These I will more minutely describe, believing that a specific description will please and instruct more than a general one.

The group at the south-west corner is called Europe. It is composed of five female figures seated. The central one, typifying the continent, is seated on a bull, in allusion to the ancient mythological fable; in her right hand a scepter, in her left an orb, indicating the influence exercised over the other continents. The figure of England is seated on a rock, against which the waves are dashing; in her right hand a trident, her left hand resting on a shield with the united crosses of St. George and St. Andrew.

As a military power, France is holding a sword in one hand, and a wreath of laurel in the other.

The home of literature and science, Germany, is in meditative attitude, with an open volume on her knee.

Italy seems waking from a dream, signifying her

recent union into one kingdom; she is seated on a broken column, alluding to her former greatness; and the lyre and the palette acknowledge her excellence in the arts of music and painting.

The group at the south-east angle represents Asia, the central figure only being a female. She is seated on an elephant, and is in the act of removing her veil. The prostrate elephant signifies the subjection of brute force to human intelligence; and the poet of Persia, with his pen and writing-case; the art-manufacturer of China, holding a specimen of porcelain; the warrior of India, with his weapons; and the Arab merchant, resting on his camel-saddle—all suggest learning, industry, courage, and enterprise, the combined elements of Asia's greatness. A characteristic of this whole group is the spirit of repose resting, as it seems, on a civilization unchanged for ages, and never hinting of the past, nor anxious for the future.

On the pedestal, at the north-east, is placed Africa. On a camel is seated the principal figure, an Egyptian princess, for the reason that Egypt was the first African power, and forerunner of civilization. At her right hand stands a Nubian—her easternmost dweller—his hand resting on a half-buried statue, in allusion to her past monumental glories. On her left is a seated figure of her northern merchant, with his native products and objects of commerce near him. As the representative of the uncivilized races of his continent, the negro stands leaning on his bow, listening to the teaching of a female figure, indicating kindly effort to improve the race; while at his feet the broken chains show the part England took in the emancipation of the slaves.

At the north-west, as it should be, America mounts the pedestal. The group consists of a central figure, America, mounted on a bison, charging through the long prairie-grass. Their advance is directed by the United States on one side, while on the other Canada attends them, pressing the rose of England to her breast. Other figures represent Mexico rising from a trance, and South America equipped for the chase. A detail of the emblem is as follows: The figure of America is of the Indian type, and in native costume, with feathered head-dress, while the housings of the bison are a grizzly bear's skin. In her right hand is a stone-pointed, feathered lance, with Indian "totems" of the gray squirrel and humming-bird; and on her left arm she bears a shield, with blazons of the principal divisions of the hemisphere—the eagle for the States, the beaver for Canada, the lone star for Chili, the volcanoes for Mexico, the alpaca for Peru, and the southern cross for Brazil. In the rear, aroused by the passage of a bison through the grass, is a rattle-snake. The features of the United States are of the North American Anglo-Saxon civilized type. Her tresses are surmounted by an eagle's plume and by a star, which is repeated on her baldric—a richly-ornamented belt—at the point of the scepter in her right hand, and on the bracelet round her left arm; in her left hand is a wreath formed by the leaves of the evergreen oak. At her foot lies the Indian's quiver, with but an arrow or two left in it. Her dress is partly thin and partly of a thicker texture, indicating the great range of climate.

Canada, dressed in furs, has a more English type; woven into her head-dress are the maple-leaf of the mainland and the May-flower of Nova Scotia. In her right hand are ears of wheat; at her feet a pair of snow-shoes and the cone of a pine-tree. Three distinct types of womanhood are thus represented by the artists. Mexico has a somewhat Aztec face, a Mexican head-dress, staff, feather cincture, and the cochineal cactus at his feet. He seems rising from his panther's skin, restless and disturbed, yet looking forward with hope.

South America is represented by a half-breed type—Indians and Spaniards—seated on a rock, habited in a sombrero, poncho, and Indian girdle; in his left hand the short horseman's carbine of the country; in his right, a lasso. By his side is an orchid of the forests of Brazil, and at his feet a horn of the wild cattle of the plains, and also a blossom of the giant lily of the Amazon.

In comparing this American group with the others, one can hardly fail to notice that it is quite unlike the others. There is not so much of repose, but more of an onward movement, expressed—a kind of visible unrest quite in contrast with the other more tranquil continents.

I could not more briefly describe these four geographical groups, and do them justice. They form a very interesting study, and do honor to the four different artists who designed and executed them. Instructive as they are, they form only a small part of the many allegorical statues and mosaics introduced into the whole monument; whether I shall describe the others will depend largely on your interest in what you have now read.

H. V. I., March 2, 1874.

In my last letter I partly described the Prince Albert Memorial, ending with an account of the four lower groups, representing the four quarters of the world.

Ascending the steps to the podium, we find four more groups of statuary, typifying agriculture, manufacture, commerce, and engineering. The first occupies the south-west corner, having, as the principal figure, Agriculture, crowned with a wreath of corn, and directing the husbandmen to the improvements in farming implements caused by the steam-engine and chemistry; she is pointing from the primitive plow on which the farmer leans, to a steam-cylinder and chemical retort lying below. Seated on the left of Agriculture is a woman having her lap full of corn as a result of the improved means; on the right is a shepherd-boy, with a lamb in his arms and a ewe by his side, suggesting the rearing and breeding of cattle.

At the south-east angle stands the second group, having the genius of Manufactures for the principal figure. She is pointing to a bee-hive as the emblem of industry, while an hour-glass indicates the value of time as important in all manufacturing operations. Beside her is a smith, indicating the importance of the iron industries to the country in aiding the manufacturer. On the other side is the weaver, and in front the potter, exhibiting their textile and fictile manufactures.

On the north-east of the podium is the allegorical group of Commerce. The chief figure holds in her left hand a cornucopia showing the result of commercial enterprise. In her right hand she holds a balance—emblem of trade—and also a purse and ledger. A ground figure in front brings corn—the great necessity of life—and an oriental merchant has a casket of jewels, indicating objects of luxury imported by means of commerce.

On the north-west is the fourth group. The genius of Engineering stands above the other figures, resting her hand on a steam-cylinder. In front a youthful figure, with compasses in hand, is noting a design spread on the ground before him. The great agent of all engineering operations, the navvy, is seated on one side, while on the other kneels one holding a cog-wheel, showing that engineering is aided by machinery. Back of the group is a steam-hammer, a blast-furnace, and the Britannia and Menai bridges—triumphs of the engineering art.

Above the podium, on four large pillars, stands the vaulted memorial. On the outer side, and near the base of the pillars, are four bronze statues, each about eight and one-half feet in height. One represents Astronomy, having her head surrounded with a fillet of stars, and holding in her hand a globe—symbol of the science over which she presides. The second statue is Chemistry, having in her hand a retort, one of the most important chemical instruments. The third is Geology, with hammer and pick-ax in her right hand, and in her left the earth partly excavated. At her feet are various ores and the remains of antediluvian animals. Geometry stands at the south-west, holding in one hand the compasses, and in the other a tablet inscribed with geometric figures.

Above these, in the four niches of the canopy, are four more bronze statues. The one at the south-east is Rhetoric, with head bent forward as if reading a speech which she holds in her hand. In the north-east angle of the canopy is Medicine, holding a cup in her left hand, and a serpent in her right—emblems of Hygeia, the daughter of Esculapius. Philosopy occupies the north-west angle of the canopy, having in one hand an open book, to which she points with the other, suggesting the development of philosophy by means of literature. The remaining angle of the canopy is occupied by Physiology, having a new-born babe on her left arm, to teach the highest development of perfect physiological forms. Her right hand points to a microscope as the means of investigating minute organisms.

Above these, and on the spire, are eight bronze-gilt statues—four in the great niches, and four in the angles of these niches. The four greater, or

Christian virtues, are—Faith, with her chalice and cross; Hope, with upraised look, standing beside her anchor; Charity, a crowned figure, uncovering her bosom with her right hand, and in her left holding the burning heart; and Humility, fully draped, looking down, and holding in her right hand a lighted taper. The four lesser or moral virtues are Fortitude, armed with a shield and club; Prudence, holding the serpent-emblem of wisdom; Justice, holding the sword and scales; Temperance, with a bridle in her hands. Immediately above these, with drooping heads, are four angels, in attitudes suggesting the resignation of worldly honors; while still higher, and at the base of the surmounting cross, four other angels, with uplifted heads and hands, indicate aspirations for heavenly glory.

Underneath the vault of blue mosaic ground, inwrought with his armorial bearings, is the bronze statue of the Prince Consort, for whom this national memorial has been constructed. He is represented in a sitting posture, in attitude and expression embodying rank, character, and a responsive intelligence, showing active interest in every thing indicated by the surrounding groups, figures, and relievos. In his right hand is a catalogue of the works collected for the International Exhibition of 1851. The dedicatory inscription is in mosaic, the letters of blue glass with black edges on a ground of gold-enameled glass: "Queen Victoria and her people to the memory of Albert, Prince Consort, as a tribute of their gratitude for a life devoted to the public good."

From this description, thus minutely given, and yet containing only a small part of the whole, one can easily see the great amount of study, as well as work, required to create and execute this remarkable memorial. The learning of all ages and climes is here expressed in symbols appreciated by every visitor in proportion to his knowledge. The whole becomes what artists call a study, and reveals the character and attainments of the prince so honorable and honored, and of the men and nation designing and constructing it. More and more will it become the honored resort of the learned traveler. If you have read the description carefully, you may have noticed that not a soldier or warrior or great military hero has any mention or symbol to illustrate his usefulness to the world. The peaceful arts, the moral and Christian virtues, all aim upward and terminate in the cross—a significance which the race would see realized.

Letters from the Rev. T. W. Hooper, of Lynchburg, Va., written for the *News.*

LONDON, August 11, 1873.

Here we are, once more in this great metropolis, enjoying again the pleasant sound of our mother-tongue, and somewhat familiar with its streets and noted places, from our former visit. You cannot imagine how pleasant it is to us all to get out of the range of French and German, and understand what is spoken at the depots and on the streets by those who are talking to each other or to us.

We left Brussels Saturday morning, by rail, and spent several hours very pleasantly at Antwerp, waiting for the steamer. We visited the cathedral, which is most famous for containing the finest paintings of Rubens. We saw his masterpiece, The Descent from the Cross, and another not much inferior, in my judgment, The Elevation on the Cross. Both are worthy of his genius, and the citizens of Antwerp are proud of the fact that such a man as Rubens was born there. His statue in the public place represents him as one of the finest-looking men, with a most intellectual brow. At 4 o'clock P.M. we bade adieu to the continent, on the steamer Pacific, in the midst of a fearful thunderstorm, and glided down the Scheldt, between Belgium and Holland, watching with great interest the entrance to the great ship canal that leads up to Rotterdam, the tremendous sea-walls along the shore, which keep back the water from the lowland, with its sluices for drainage at low tide, and its windmills for pumping purposes, where the land is lower than the tide, and at about dark we passed Flushing, where we exchanged pilots, and floated out upon the waters of the German Ocean. In the meantime the storm had passed away, and, much to our surprise and gratification, the dreaded ocean was as calm as a Scotch lake, and we slept as soundly as we could have done on shore.

This evening we reached Harwich, where we landed, and after a formal examination of baggage, we came on rapidly by the cars to London. On reaching the St. Pancras Hotel, said by the proprietors to be the largest in the world, we were pleased to be so cordially greeted by the second and third sections, who had preceded us by a few days. It was delightful to meet with these friends, from whom we had parted a month ago, and exchange views as to the different places we had all seen at different times and under different circumstances. But I am sure that all of us are more than delighted with what we have seen, and it is a mystery to us all how Thos. Cook & Son could show us so much, in such a time, and at such a small cost, when we compare notes with other travelers. I have no hesitation now, after a thorough trial, in advising all my friends who propose a European tour hereafter to purchase Mr. Cook's coupons, and I can conceive of nothing more pleasant in the way of travel than for twenty friends to form a party under his personal superintendence, or conducted by one of his own conductors. We have no trouble about our baggage, or rooms at hotels, or payment of bills, or securing seats (extra cars when required). We have sometimes found our trunks in our rooms on our arrival at the hotel, and our rooms are always ready to receive us, and the meal awaiting us when we arrive.

I am inclined to think, too, that preference has been given to us where there was a crowd, and I am sure that the Messrs. Cook and our conductor, Mr. Tuttshell, have done every thing that lay in their power for our pleasure and our comfort.

But yesterday! What pen can describe the pleasure of Protestant worship in a Christian land, after even two Sabbaths on the Continent? As we expect to spend a week or ten days here, we had already secured rooms (four of us) at Mr. Cook's boarding-house, just opposite the British Museum, so we moved around Saturday evening. It may be that the quiet, home-like place, in contrast to busy, bustling hotels, had something to do with it; but yesterday was a calm, beautiful, sunny day, and we certainly made the most of it. At 11 o'clock A.M. we mingled with the 6,500 worshipers at Mr. Spurgeon's Tabernacle. The house is elliptical, with the pulpit, or stand, in one focus, and a double gallery all around. Large as it is, I thought as I stood in the pulpit that my voice would fill it as easily as it does my own church at home. By the kindness of a member we had a seat near the center of the main auditorium, Mr. C. having secured tickets for the whole party. A little ticket also secured to us admission to the communion-table in the lecture-room below, after the services, and for the first time in my life I had the pleasure of eating the Lord's Supper with my dear brethren of the Baptist Church. I remembered those at home, as well as the dear people of my own charge, with whom I communed the Sunday before I left home, and with one of whom, at least, I shall meet no more, until I meet her in heaven.

Mr. Spurgeon was more portly than I expected to find him, and his whiskers gave him a different appearance from the picture that I have in my study. His manner is plain, simple, earnest, and at times impassioned. His voice is strong, clear, well-modulated, and capable of almost any inflection. He preaches to his vast congregation just as we common men talk at our prayer-meetings. There is the same self-possession, colloquial simplicity, directness, point, and homeliness; while now and then come the flashes of genius, and all along is the deep earnestness of a man who wants to save souls and to comfort believers. He is bold in the statement of doctrine, but not dry; unqualified in his renunciation of error, but not personal; candid in the statement of his own trusts, but charitable to those who differ from him. His text was from Isaiah lx., and the subject, "Praising God for his loving kindnesses." After the Communion we went up to shake hands, and found him a really pleasant, jovial, warm-hearted Christian man, glad to see everybody from America, and with a warm grasp of the hand, said: "God bless you, my brother, and take you all back home in safety."

As we still had several hours before us, we strolled on down across the Thames at London bridge, up through by the monument where the great fire was stayed, through Poultry lane, and other places familiar to every reader of English literature, to the Cathedral of St. Paul, where Canon Lyddon was to preach at 3:15 P.M. We entered the grand old cathedral along with an immense concourse, and secured chairs in the middle aisle just under the dome, and not far from the pulpit, which was placed against one of the central columns. To the music of a splendid organ there came in a long procession of men with white gowns on, who turned out to be the choral service performers, and who chanted the whole service bodily, including the Lord's Prayer, two or three times. This, I must say, I did not think in good taste, not to mention the absence of all that was spiritually beneficial to the people. The boys sang well, but the old man that led reminded me of a Hard-shell Baptist preacher, with his long, whining drawl. I wondered what Brother C. would think of such a performance in another St. Paul's, and hope the day will never come when our brethren there will imagine that this is the way to worship God "in the beauty of holiness." But after this display of musical praying, amid the burning of tapers, we had a splendid hymn or anthem—the most of it a solo—and then the sermon. It must be a miserable place to preach in, for the speaker's voice echoed among the arches equal to an Alpine horn; but he had preached there before, and knows how to control it. The sermon was based on the lesson of the day—"The unjust steward"—and was a splendid specimen of highly-finished, classic, ornate eloquence, splendidly delivered, and anywhere else and to any other audience would have produced a profound impression. But the nobility are not good listeners, and the cathedral, with its stillness, is inviting for a drowsy repast, and I am afraid several of the lords and ladies I saw were not wide enough awake to take the solemn admonitions which were reënforced by the recent sudden deaths of the Bishop of Winchester and others, to whom the speaker alluded.

Last night we started too late for the whole service, for it commences at half-past six, but we were directed through several narrow lanes near Covent Garden, to the quaint old church of Dr. Cummins. We found him preaching in his old Scotch gown, in a little inverted wine-glass of a pulpit at the side of the church, to, not a large, but seemingly a very select audience. Indeed, he told me afterwards, when I met him in the "lecture room," that the most of his people were in the country, and those were strangers. He was preaching on "God forbid that I should glory," etc. His style, too, is plain, simple, colloquial, and his sermon very suggestive and rich in illustration.

But my paper is out. I hope to hear him and Spurgeon again next Sunday, and by that time I shall have made up for the two Sundays I lost on the Continent.

Although it is after 9 o'clock P.M., and after such tramps as I have taken I ought to be in bed, still, as all of our immediate party are out sight-seeing, and I am weary, I have concluded to write what may be my last letter to you on this famous tour. The fact is, on such a trip as this a man sees so much, and he becomes so weary with the sight, that it is almost impossible to find time or inclination to write, nor does he know what to write about.

What interests one person will not interest another; and, indeed, in our party of four, we find it more pleasant to go out separately, and just wander about as inclination may suggest. But as far as I am personally concerned, I enjoy wandering along the streets and looking in at the windows about as much as any other amusement. The retail shops here are small, and sometimes, I think, nearly the whole stock will be displayed in the windows. I have just been wandering up and down Tottenham Court road, as it is called, where there are thousands of people promenading in the brilliant gaslight and looking in at the brilliant windows, where are displayed all kinds of articles, from a "ha'penny box of matches" to a hundred-dollar gold watch, or from a Scotch herring to the largest salmon. I have spent hours in this way, every day, with great satisfaction. But of course we have not confined ourselves to this kind of amusement.

On Monday night, by special invitation, we were all regaled at the rooms of the British and Foreign Sabbath-school Union, where a member of parliament presided, and where we had some good Sabbath-school music that reminded me of home, especially the song, "Work while the day," etc. We also had some good speeches, and closed with a refreshment of ices, cakes, wines, etc.

Yesterday, J. T—— and I took a stroll down Chancery lane to Fleet street, Ludgate hill, King William street, etc., until we came to London bridge. Here we had our pictures taken, and met with some very pleasant people who were about to sail for Norfolk *via* Allan Line, and thence to Atlanta. They were very inquisitive about our country, and we referred them to our friend Major Robertson, as there was a young lady in the party. We then went on down through Billingsgate, of which you have heard before. As the market was almost closed, it was too late for much "cussing;" and amid numerous smells we went on through the old city to the Tower. Stopping long enough to visit the Jewel-room, where we saw all the crowns, scepters, etc., and the famous Koh-i-noor diamond, we continued our walk to London Dock. Here we found vessels from all quarters of the globe, and stores of merchandise (assafetida included) sufficient to stock a large city. We also went into the famous port-wine vault, where there are at this time twenty-two thousand casks of the best port. We tasted it, of course; and from its effect I am sure I must be constitutionally a "Son of Temperance." We then walked through the tunnel under the

Thames, and crossing at London bridge, we took a "bus" and came on home pretty well used up.

This morning, I again strolled down to the old city, passing Pudding lane, Threadneedle street, Cheapside, etc., all of which are familiar names to the readers of English literature, went by Newgate Prison, in the Old Bailey, and down to the office of the London *Times*. It is, as I expected, a little, insignificant-looking place in Printers' square, and no one could imagine that such a "thunderer" could find its electricity in such a small battery. However, they are building a much larger edifice, and we must excuse them. The front of the old building is very much like the first page of the *Times* itself, even to the frontispiece; and men who wield such an influence can afford to live without any attempt at display.

I then visited the rooms of the British and Foreign Bible Society, which has issued the Bible in two hundred different languages, and where I bought for one shilling a Bible that would cost with us seventy-five cents. I then started on up the Thames to the Temple Gardens. Here I hired an escort at sixpence, who conducted me to the Middle and Inner Temple, where I saw the great dining-hall where the judges and barristers have a dinner four times a year, during term-time, at which kings are sometimes present. The hall itself is very finely carved, and adorned with most excellent portraits of the most distinguished jurists and kings who have been benchers in the Temple.

Winding around through various old courts and lanes, we entered the old Knight Templar Chapel, where Vaughan is now the chaplain, saw the tombs of some of the most distinguished Crusaders who were buried here, and then went to the grave of Oliver Goldsmith. I do not know that I have had sadder and at the same time more grateful feelings anywhere, than when standing over the dust of the author of "The Vicar of Wakefield." I gathered a few leaves of ivy and picked up a few stones, and then looked in at the very window out of which he for the last time looked at that nature which he so much admired. I thought of Johnson and Garrick, and Reynolds and Burke, until memory itself was weary; and going out upon the Strand, I went into the former palace of Henry VIII. and Cardinal Wolsey (as the sign asserts), and had my head shampooed by machinery. "To what base uses," etc. That is one difficulty about England, in contrast with other countries that we have visited: in Paris every memento of antiquity seems to be preserved with the greatest veneration; but here they are all turned to some practical use, or else pulled down, to give way for some modern edifice. I suppose the difference is somewhat due to the difference of nationality; and while the glory of France is in the past, in England they are constantly advancing, and hence have no especial use for these memorials of a past which is now eclipsed by the living present.

Washington Irving describes his hunt for the old Boar's Head Tavern of Dame Quickly, and states that, after a long ramble through the narrow lanes of the old city, he found nothing but the original "boar's head," and this was built into the wall of a modern building.

And here, in my case, remember I have taken a bench in the banqueting-room of Crosby Hall, have sipped some wine at a house where Queen Elizabeth took a lunch on her way from the Tower, and have capped the climax by having my hair shampooed in the original palace of Henry VIII. and Cardinal Wolsey! I think I shall get a "boots" to shine my gaiters on the foundation of old Blackfriars, and then close my visit to London by repeating Mark Twain's soliloquy at the grave of Adam, if I can find where old Bishop Hooper was buried, and then return to Scotland and America.

I hope that your printers may do better in the way of deciphering my manuscript in this than they did in my first three letters which I have seen, and that soon after this appears I shall meet you "at home."

Letters from the Rev. A. B. Whipple, President of Lansingburgh College, N. Y.

ON BOARD THE VICTORIA, August 29, 1873.

Once more, kind readers, in the cabin of this good ship, I take the pen to while away the hours of a rainy day. Some are singing "Homeward Bound," and some "A Life on the Ocean Wave," and all are being "Rocked in the Cradle of the Deep"—a sentiment, by the way, more beautiful in song than in sensation, and more than sensational enough for those whose inner life heaves responsive to the sea. Some are playing cards, some chess, some checkers, some lie reading, some are writing, and many are in their berths longing for land. We are a part of the Educational Party, returning to our friends, who have all along been interested in our passage and welfare; they will expect something, and some will ask this, others that. "What did you see in London?" "O, ever so many things." "Well, what? Did you see the Crystal Palace?" "Certainly." "Well, tell us something about it." "Will you have it in mathematics, geography, history, manufactures, or the fine arts?" "Just as you will." Altogether, then.

Architecturally the palace is modern English, a style unlike any thing ancient, made so by necessity of materials used, and the object of the structure.

The materials are iron and glass; the object, a permanent palace of art and education. Above the basement floor is one grand central nave, two side aisles, two main galleries, two transepts, and two wings, made wholly of iron and glass, save a little wood paneling on the west front. In length the main building is 1,508 feet, each wing 574, and a colonnade from the railroad station of 720, a total of 3,476 feet, or nearly three-fourths of a mile long, 380 feet wide, and, in central transept, 200 feet high, covered with a roof of glass. The iron columns, if placed end to end, would reach over sixteen miles, and the glass would cover twenty-five acres, and, if the panes were laid endwise, would reach 242 miles; add 30,000 superficial feet of glass and sixty tons of iron for the colonnade, and you have the materials above the basement. It is built on a side hill, leaving the lower side as a basement story, fronting the gardens; while the back side is tunneled by a horizontal brick shaft twenty-four feet wide, connected with the railroad, and used as a roadway to take into the palace heavy materials. Leading out of this tunnel are passages for the furnaces, boilers, coal-bins, engines, and the heating apparatus, whereby the enormous area of the palace is made to have the genial heat of Madeira through all the damp English winter—thus tropical plants have a living home. In front are two hundred acres of gardens and walks, uniform in structure with the palace; *i. e.*, the width of the walks, the width and length of the basins of the fountains, the length of the terraces, and the breadth of the steps, are all multiples or submultiples of eight. So you will see that mathematics has much to do with the artistic harmony of palace and garden. Though you ask me to describe the palace, let me pause a moment on the broad flight of steps of the first turret, and glance at the prospect. Below are lower

terraces, bordered by stone balustrades. Along
these, at intervals, are placed statues, and, in front,
the broad central walk, doubly lined with plant-
trees. On the next terrace the green turf is filled
with richly-tinted flowers, watered by fountains jet-
ting high in the air. Central is the large circular
fountain, surrounded by white marble classic statues
of heroic size. On the left, or north, stand cedar
trees; below are the water temples, with rushing
cataracts on either side, down to the vast basins of
the great fountains, lying like lakes in the green
turf beyond. Right and left are pleasant, sloping
lawns, dotted here and there with trees and shades;
and far away in the distance is the great garden of
nature herself, in rural loveliness unmatched by any
skill of man. From all this out-of-door beauty let
us turn and enter the very center of the palace, and,
looking around, find that it is not, like the Industrial Palace of Vienna, a place for the exhibition of
modern fabrics and modern arts, but rather what a
teacher prefers, a progressive view of civilization
for more than 3,000 years, as shown by the restored
specimens of architecture, sculpture, and mural
decorations. To these let us turn our attention,
noting at the outset that a nation's religion has
much to do with its architecture and art. Oldest
here is the Egyptian, and interesting because of its
connection with Bible history, as well as the perfect
condition of the remains. We find here, recon-
structed, an Egyptian court, giving us an insight
into the manner of life thirty centuries ago. We
find the style of structure simple, gigantic, and
with massive solidity, almost entirely of stone.
This solidity, suited to their requirements, seems a
permanent feature, because their religion forbade
any change in the representations of those gods and
kings so frequently carved on temples and tombs.
In the restored court before us, we have the outer

walls and colonnades of a temple constructed 300 years B.C., during the Ptolemaic period. On the walls we see colored sunk-reliefs of a king making offerings or receiving gifts from the gods; on the capitals of the columns palm and locust leaves, some showing the papyrus in its various stages of development, from the simple bud to the full-blown flower. The frieze above the column has a hieroglyphic inscription, which, when translated, reads: "In the seventeenth year of the reign of Victoria, the ruler of the waves, this palace was erected and furnished with a thousand statues, a thousand plants, etc., like as a book, for the use of the men of all countries." On the outside of the court, on the cornice, is engraved in character the names of her majesty and the Prince Consort, while within, on lintels and sides, are engraved the different titles of King Ptolemy; and the decorations of the inner walls, in coloring, are taken from actual remains in Egypt. Here we see a large picture copied from the great temple of Rameses III., near Thebes. It represents the counting of 3,000 hands of warriors slain in battle. On the left we see eight gigantic figures of Rameses the Great, of date 1300 B.C. Passing on, we enter a dark tomb, copied from one at Beni-Hassan. This is the oldest architectural work in the Crystal Palace—1660 B.C. We come out to find ourselves among scattered statues, among which we see two circular-headed stones, copies of the celebrated Rosetta stone, from which Dr. Young and Champollion obtained a key for deciphering the hieroglyphics. The stone is engraved in three characters—that of the priests, hieroglyphic; that of the people, enchorial; and the last in Greek; the whole is an address to Ptolemy V., the Greek king of Egypt, setting forth his praises. All this represents customs 200 B.C. Farther on is a model of the Temple of Aboo Simbel, cut in the side of a rock in

Nubia. Immense sitting figures represent Rameses the Great; and smaller ones his mother, wife, and daughter. The models are one-tenth in size of the original; hence the columns and statues were forty-seven and sixty-two feet in height. Without being more minute, one can learn that in the Crystal Palace we can go to Egypt and see it as it was in its best days. The impression made on our minds is favorable, and henceforth Egypt will suggest pleasant thoughts. We have been in her royal palaces, and seen their cheerful surroundings. Like modern cities full of art, there doubtless was much of ignorance and slavish toil; and sun-burnt brick, full of straw, recall the labors of the Israelites. We next enter the Greek court, to find that architecture and sculpture have greatly advanced. No priestly religion fettered its progress, and so we pass from shadow into sunshine. A religion deifying the intellect of man stimulates that intellect to the utmost, and imagination seeks in every realm the highest type of beauty. The court that we enter is of the Doric order, taken from the Temple of Jupiter, at Nemea, 300 B.C., the highest period of Greek art. We enter first the forum, used as a market and for political assemblies, and see around the frieze the names of poets, artists, and philosophers. We see Greek monograms, formed of the initial letters of the Muses, Graces, the good, and the wise. We behold walls of blue, red, and yellow, blazoned with gold, and causing a beautiful effect. But we may not describe all the beautiful works of art, as we should need a full knowledge of Greek mythology and a whole book to do the subject justice. Suffice it to say, we visited Greece—the Greece of ancient history—better than the traveler of to-day. In like manner we enter the palace of ancient Rome; this, too, after we had been among its ruins, and could the better appreciate Rome as it was in its palmiest days. We notice one thing noteworthy—it is the use of the *arch* in architecture, a feature found susceptible of the greatest variety of treatment; though known by Greek and Assyrian, it seems not to have been much used till by the Romans. The use of the arch produced a marked change in Roman buildings. Leaving the Roman, we enter the Alhambra, or Saracenic court, an offshoot, or graft of the parent stem, wonderful for its novelty, and exciting our highest admiration by rich and splendid decorations within, while the external structure is plain, simple masonry. Moorish architecture is rich with arabesque work in colored stucco, mosaic pavements, marble fountains, and sweet-smelling flowers. The Alhambra—the red—was of the thirteenth century, the scene of luxurious pleasures, and of many fearful crimes. The portions here reproduced are the Court of Lyons, Tribunal of Justice, Hall of the Abencerrages, and the Divan. Outside these courts are diaper-work, consisting of inscriptions in Arabic, representations of bowers and of flowing decorations, over which the eye wanders, pleased with harmony of color and variety of ornament. The Hall of the Abencerrages is most noteworthy, the splendid fringe of the stalactite roof composed of 5,000 separate pieces, keyed into and supporting each other. These are variously colored and very beautiful. Over the columns in the Court of Lyons we read in Cufic characters, "And there is no Conqueror but God." Lingering here, however long, we discover no statue or paintings of bird and beast; for Moorish religion forbade the representations of living objects. Despite this law, the Moorish mind has evoked enough artistic skill to arrest and enchain our pleased attention. But I may not prolong these descriptions, for I should have to take you through the Romanesque, the Byzantine, the Mediæval, English, French, German, and Italian varieties, together with the *Renaissance* and Elizabethan styles, thus giving the world's progressive architecture. I spent the day alone amid all these; yet they are only part of the studies of this wonderful palace of art and education, costing already $7,500,000, and still to be increased. There are industrial compartments of cutlery, porcelain, paper, etc.; collections of pictures, photographs, and casts of medallions; illustrations of mechanics and manufactures; botany; ethnology, or illustrations of national characteristics, including our own American Indians; palæontology, or extinct animals; geology; hydraulics, as seen in the fountains; musical facilities of an unprecedented kind; also, a Technological Museum, with collections of home, colonial, and foreign products; and finally, the Marine Aquarium, three hundred feet long and fifty wide, with many thousands of sea creatures, vertebrate and invertebrate, in thirty-eight tanks, requiring one hundred and fifty thousand gallons of sea-water. Crabs, lobsters, star-fish, anemones, corals, in all their beauty of coloring, radiation, and motion, catch the eye and stay the footsteps of the many thousand visitors who gaze into the clear and quiet waters, and thus behold the wonders of the deep sea, on whose heaving surface we are tossing homeward.

LANSINGBURGH, March —, 1874.

MY DEAR DOCTOR:—You ask of me—"the quiet man"—for some thoughts not yet in print. Stored away in my note-book I find little seed-thoughts, labeled "odds and oddities." I send you a few at random; may others do likewise!

Under July 9th I find in my book the word "Pacific." It has its lesson. That day we (the Italian party) left London for Harwich; thence, on the

"Pacific," across the German Ocean; a good supper before we started. On deck your "quiet man" took to reading his Italian volume, with its double alphabet of pages. Such a school-book you never saw. At first it seemed all !!!; soon these changed to ???; next ,,, followed by ;;; then :::, and finally came a full. The fly-leaves indicated a threatening calm. The full moon was watching us. Gently then began to play the mirthful waves of the German sea. Some of our quiet teachers could keep silence no longer. They seemed to have caught the intonations of the German language, and made some matter-of-fact ejaculations, directed rather to dolphins than deities. I think there was as much solidity of utterance as is often expressed by "schoolmasters abroad." The "poetry of motion" seemed exhaustive, while the tones sank lower and lower, till in the "*ingentes cavernas navis*" they died away in moanings and groanings, to the music of which your quiet man "paced along the deck upon the giddy footing of the hatches."

Under Friday the 11th — unlucky day — I wrote "Penny for a chair." We had been doing Brussels all day; and, just as the sun was setting, a fellow-traveler and myself, walking along the Boulevard de Waterloo, espied a couple of chairs. We thought fortune favored us, as we seated ourselves. Presently a little German boy appeared before us with a paper. Not being able to read, we shook our heads, and said "*Nein.*" He stuck by like a good boy, as no doubt he was, till we had said "*nein*" at least ninety-nine times, when he disappeared, and soon reäppeared with about three hundred pounds of mother, red in the face and arms, the hands of which were entreatingly extended toward us. She talked away impatiently, as I should judge from her appearance and the appearance of a crowd at the same time about us, a couple of foreigners. She did not seem to understand our "*neins*" any better than we did her "*kreutzers.*" We seemed to be very attractive—to the crowd. A new thought seemed to be born just then; for, darting across the street, she shook her fist in the face of a man who wore a sword, and then pointed at us. He immediately surrounded us, and talked beautifully—I presume—though we did not know a word. We were getting rested, and enjoyed the sights and sounds. Indeed, we did not know till then how much we were thought of. Growing calmer as the army was preparing for a *coup de* something, we bribed the *frau* with two cents to open a way of retreat, and, escaping to our hotel, pondered long on the fashions around, especially that of leaving chairs in the streets to entrap the wandering schoolteacher.

Under July 13th I find "Pendulum Pumps"—to the traveler in Cologne suggesting a curious way by which the tall pumps are made to discharge water. The word itself explains the manner. Where so much beer and wine are used, hydrants are numerous, and human ones in public places are far from being infrequent. On our way to the grand old cathedral, these water-works often seemed a bar to our farther progress, till some encouraging D.D. would strengthen the wavering footsteps of the erubescent creature beside him with the remark, "In this country we must walk by faith, and not by sight," and so the Americans "move on."

Friday, 18—another unlucky day—has the word "Brandy." We—friend Tift and myself—had looked down upon Vienna from the lofty dome of the Exposition building, and wandered among its inside wonders, and by mistake had wandered into a strange part of the city instead of our own hotel, and we could not make ourselves understood, and so left the horse-cars. We sought instruction in saloons; no one spoke English or French. Despairing as night drew on, we tried again. I tried my French: "*Parlez-vous Francais?*" "*Oui, Monsieur.*" "*Où est l' Hotel de Ville?*" She smiled, called a little boy, who at her command disappeared for a moment, and then came smiling toward us with a server, on which were two small glasses of brandy. What could two good temperance men do? We looked at the woman, the boy, the brandy; thought what we could, and departed, leaving the "*dame*" and "*garcon*" greatly astonished; and I seem to hear her say, "What did they come in here for, if not to drink?" Sure enough, how could they get "*Hotel de Ville*" out of my "*eau de vie*"? I stopped talking French to Austrians.

Saturday, 19—"Paid for." Again we had roamed through the Industrial-Palace, seen the goods and the emperor. We were tired, and wanted to be relieved; were ready to be relieved of something more than blood and money. By searching, we found what the Italians call a "Retireta," and the French a "Palace d'Alsace." In a central place we found it—a beautiful architectural design, concealed and well watered. We enter, to find a comfortable room, with a table, and two not over-beautiful Austrian ladies seated thereat. They rise to receive us, and do us personal favors, inquiring our necessities, even to the utmost, and for a sixpence allow us to depart, greatly relieved and amused at Austrian customs. They gave us their cards, which you may translate at your leisure:

Funt Kreuzer. Contr.

7315

Die Cassierin ist verpflichtet, nur gegen Uebergabe dieses Billets den hierauf bezeichneten Betrag in Empfang zu nehmen.
Es wird höflichst ersucht, dieses Billet, nachdem es von der im Innern aufgestellten Controlls-Person con rit ist, bis zum Austritt aus der Toilette behufs weiterer Controlle aufzubewahren. 6

Droud von T. B. Ballishauffer.

July 30. Rome—"Extras." In the matter of eating we have had but little to say. Breakfast at eight, and dinner at six, with ten intermediate hours for digestion, gave us generally a good appetite, and, perhaps, the wonder of the waiters. We also wondered at some of their ways. Almost the first thing they would ask us at table was this: "What is your number?" Every thing is charged to the number of the room we occupy; hence, sometimes good temperance men find extras for wine, etc., which they have not had—a plan by which some one has imbibed at another's expense. Such a plan was tried on us at Lucerne; but we would not pay the bill. Well, on the morning of our departure from Rome, we had the usual continental biscuit and one piece of meat. Friend Tift sat at my right; he had taken his allowance. "Number, sir?" inquired the waiter. "Number one," answered the hungry man. Having a good appetite, he called for another piece of meat. Waiter brought it, saying, "Extra, sir; number, sir?" "Number *two!* Extra, is it? Glad of it." Soon No. 2 was buried with its predecessor, and he called for more. "Extra," said the waiter. "Glad of it; bring it on, then; hurry up!" said the excited man. Soon it came, with the usual question, "Number, sir?" "Number *three!*" growled the still busy eater. While admiring friends were on the watch, meat No. 3, morsel by morsel, sank to rise no more, and "Waiter!" rang out clear and authoritatively. He came. "More meat! I want one square meal before leaving this eternal city." "Extra, sir." "I know it, sir; so bring it on." "Number, sir?" "Number FOUR!" thundered our hero, as the astonished waiter departed. Soon he returned, saying, "Last piece, sir." Amid his admirers sat our man of *muscle*, unperturbed, and with an inflexible determination "to have one square meal, extra or no extra." He had "seen every thing in Rome he wished, except meat—enough for once." While we all gloried in his zeal, he bravely attacked his last extra. One enthusiastic admirer of his maxillary power, shouted, "Bully for you!" as he redeposited upon his plate a morsel that had already been in his mouth; and, looking sadly at the last speaker, replied, "Altogether too much so." He was satisfied. "Now let us leave Rome in peace," he said. For all this *extra* entertainment, our friend of the Buffalo Dairy paid, over and above his regular bill, in gold, $150, while our *extra*ordinary enjoyment cost us many—a laugh at his expense. To this day there are some fifty living witnesses who would like to see the man who once had enough at Rome.

Homeward bound—From London to Edinburgh—Interesting sights in the Scottish capital—Castle Rock—Burns's grave—Mary Queen of Scots—Dr. Chalmers—Bunyan.

STEAMSHIP VICTORIA, August 30, 1873.

Omitting, for the present, several places visited in London, I will sketch our route from that city to Edinburgh, Scotland. We left the Midland Grand Hotel early on Thursday morning. This depot, being the largest in the world, is connected with the hotel claiming the same relation. The span of the shed is 243 feet from wall to wall, length 700, height 100, length of roof 690 feet, with a span covering four platforms and eleven lines of rails, and occupying a site of nearly ten acres. Highgate stands 450 feet higher than St. Paul's Cathedral. We pass a picturesque village, in which Lord Bacon lived in 1226. The Bishops of London resided there in succession. Hendon is the highest point within ten miles of London. Lord Byron and the late Robert Peel were scholars here. Near this is St. Alban's, at the foot of which flows the

15

river Bev. It was remarkable as the scene of battles in the time of Julius Cesar, and subsequent periods of history. Also, the place of the first recorded English martyrdom, in the third century, when St. Abenus was beheaded by pagans. Portions of the old Roman walls of St. Alban's still exist. Tutan and Bourne are near each other. At the former Bunyan preached; at the latter Dr. Wm. Dodd was born in 1729. Bedford is the place where Bunyan preached for seventeen years, when he was imprisoned, and where he wrote the "Pilgrim's Progress."

We now enter the manufacturing district. At Derby the first silk-mill was erected in 1718.

Sheffield is the place famous for cutlery, and the manufacturing of all kinds of iron and steel goods, plated ware, and metallic instruments. It was here cast steel was first wrought. It was, indeed, "grand, gloomy, and peculiar," to see the hundreds of chimneys of immense height, belching forth flames and smoke, darkening the whole country round, and the roar of the engines driving the machinery and forges of these establishments.

From these we pass on to the linen manufactures. Their "bleaching fields" resembled snow-covered grounds. Here also, are wire and needle manufactories. One can have but little idea of the extent of these manufactories without seeing them. Just think that there are three hundred and fifty trains of passengers, goods, and minerals arrive and depart in twenty-four hours. This will give a better idea of the extent of the business done in this vicinity. It was in this vicinity—Huntingdon—that Oliver Cromwell was born, April 25, 1699, and was baptized four days afterward, as appears from the parish register. The house is now called the Cromwell House.

Miss Nightingale.—Lea Hurst, the home of Miss

Nightingale, is in this vicinity. This was her father's residence and estate. She was born in Florence in 1820; hence her name, Florence Nightingale. She went to the Crimea with a staff of voluntary nurses at the time of the war. In honor of her noble conduct, a testimonial fund was raised of $250,000 by the people of England, and, at her request, the money was donated to a hospital for training nurses.

Here at Crawford was the first cotton-mill, built in 1771, by Richard Arkwright, the inventor of the "spinning-jenny." The old frame is still preserved in the present mill as a curiosity. The invention was followed by various improvements for which an enlarged patent was obtained in 1775.

This was one of the most important inventions ever made. Only one hundred years! What wonders have been effected by it! Cotton, though not a crowned monarch, governs a large portion of the civilized world. Much of England's greatness has been produced by its extensive manufacture. Most of the material prosperity of our own sunny South land has been from its production, and here its manufacture first commenced. No wonder we looked at this place with much interest.

The country from London, for near two hundred miles, is rich, and in a high state of cultivation. It then becomes more undulating, and more sparsely settled. We see some fine old castles, on which are windmills, performing a different kind of a service than was originally designed by their founders. Though we travel four hundred miles, we see no soldiers—nothing warlike—only a few cannon at one of the foundries. The railway officials are the only uniformed gentry we find here. Our train runs from fifty to sixty miles an hour. Two large saloon-carriages are assigned to our party—only fourteen now—on which Mr. Thos. Cook has a fine lunch served to us. In the evening we reach the Highlands of Scotland, around which cluster so much historic interest, with which your readers are familiar.

We arrive at Edinburgh on time, and we soon domicile at a good hotel, kept by a genuine old Scotchman. Early in the morning we start out to see this venerable old city. I notice every house of every kind is built of stone. The door and window-frames are stone. The city consists mainly of heights, hollows, acclivities, and ravines, in much diversity of character. It is a gem of a landscape, exquisitely beautiful. Castle Rock surveys one of the most gorgeous panoramic views in the world. It is a rugged mass of green stone, about seven hundred yards in circumference, and breaks down on three sides of the castle's ramparts—north, west, and south—in faces of bare rock, all precipitous. It is the most interesting natural object in the city. A garrison of soldiers keep the castle. An old State prison surmounts the archway, which has kept many illustrious captives. The armory is capable of storing 30,000 stands of arms. The old Parliament Hall (80 by 33 feet) occupies the south side of the palace yard. This was long the residence of the kings and queens of Scotland. From this castle you have a most magnificent view of the city and its surroundings. In front of it stands Scott's monument, erected in 1840–44. It is 200 feet high, and contains a marble statue of Sir Walter Scott, which cost $10,000, and was inaugurated in 1846. Here is where the great reformer, John Knox, lived and labored, and where his remains rest. His house is resorted to as one of the most interesting objects of antiquity, of which there are many. This is the great center of Scotch Presbyterianism. From all I can learn, they are doing more than any other Protestant Church in the missions. We took the street-car, and went to see their docks and shipping.

These were more extensive than I had supposed. We then took another car through the principal streets and around the city.

Edinburgh.—It is, perhaps, the most substantially built of any city we have visited. Its population, including the suburbs, is about 200,000. Nearly all the people you see here have a similar Scotch appearance. I have never seen any place where there was such a marked family likeness. Their Scotch brogue seems to be universal. They are pictures of fine health, with vim and activity in their movements. They are the most universally educated people (Germany, perhaps, excepted) that we have seen on our tour. There are many things of interest in this city. Nelson's monument, on Calton Hill, and Burns's monument, Regent Road, commemorate two men who moved in very different spheres, both honored by this people. Here, too, the immortal Rev. Dr. Chalmers labored, and here his mortal remains sleep, while his noble moral heroism lives in the hearts of his countrymen. Here Mary Queen of Scots figured during her eventful life, yet her body sleeps beside her sister, Queen Elizabeth, whose jealousy caused her to be beheaded in the Tower of London. When our guide showed us the two sisters, sleeping side by side in Westminster Abbey, I remarked to him that they were more friendly in death than they had been in their lives. Such is the fate of womankind, as well as mankind, in high places. But I will not moralize.

The steward moves us all from the table to prepare for dinner. So I will close this disconnected scrawl, written while the ship is being tossed by the rolling waves, and most of the passengers are suffering from sea-sickness.

The rolling deep—Leaving Glasgow, the prosperous city on the Clyde—The pleasures and misfortunes of a life of ten days on the ocean wave.

STEAMSHIP VICTORIA, September 1, 1873.

I closed my last letter rather abruptly. I was writing relative to Edinburgh. While it is a fine old city, abounding in historic interest, it looks to me as though it has attained its growth. There seemed to be but little business being done, only in a small portion of it. I observed several streets, with magnificent buildings, with but few persons to be seen on them. Glasgow, I suppose, has taken a large portion of the business formerly done here. The country between those two cities is very fine, and made to yield all that it can by the high cultivation it receives.

Glasgow is the second city of the United Kingdom. Its population, in the city proper, is only about four hundred thousand; but, with what properly belongs to it—with streets extending as one continuous city—it has nearly a million. The Scotch characteristics are not seen here, as in other parts of this country, and especially in the city we had just left. It looks more like New York than any place we have seen. It owes its rapid increase to its ship-building. It was here that the first steam-vessel was built on this side of the Atlantic. It is now the most important place for building steam-ships in the world. It is said that there are more steam-ships built here than in all the world besides. We saw a vast number of them in process of building, on the stocks. The River Clyde is a very small affair; but they have deepened its channel until vessels of the largest class can come up to its docks. Here may be seen representatives from almost every nation among trade's rough sons.

Glasgow has its great thoroughfare more distinctly marked, perhaps, than any city we have seen.

Along that not only run its 'buses, but a number of street-railways, running out to every part of the city, concentrate here. Here we see, as in Broadway, New York (only more so), the dense crowds of humanity passing each other in every direction. The streets intersect this great thoroughfare at right angles, so that a stranger is soon able to understand them, which is a very uncommon thing in European cities. This is more like an American city in several respects than any other we have visited. We went out at night to see the vast crowds that pass along this, their Broadway. A large amount of business is done after night in their stores and shops. Returning to our hotel, we happened to pass their fish-market. There we met with a larger number of the lower class of humanity than we have ever seen together at one time. It extended between a quarter and half a mile. The street was filled with women, a large portion of whom were bare-footed, coarsely clad, and seemed to be of the very lowest order of womankind.

Saturday morning the scattered fragments of our party met at the steamer. At noon our noble ship is loosed, and slowly moves down the Clyde, passing the docks, where many vessels were delivering and receiving their cargoes. On both sides, for miles, we see ships in various stages of progress toward completion. The hills rise in picturesque beauty on both sides. We keep on deck to see the last of Scotland as it fades in the distant horizon from our view.

Sunday morning finds us at Moville, on the coast of Ireland. Here we met the last of our party, who had come through from London to see Ireland. Here, also, we add about one hundred and fifty to the list of steerage passengers. I was very much interested, here and at Glasgow, in the parting of these people from their friends, from whom they were separating, perhaps, forever. It was, indeed, very affecting to see and hear how they gave vent to their feelings—many waving their handkerchiefs and expressing in various ways their interest in their friends, while others, unable to restrain their grief, poured forth lamentations that brought tears from those who were observing the affecting scene.

We are now fairly out from *terra firma*, with our bow toward the setting sun. The beautiful hills of the Emerald Isle loom up for miles as we pass along the Irish coast. We gaze with intense interest upon this land, which has furnished so many noble hearts and strong arms to develop the vast resources of our native America.

We also take on board two Irish ministers, going over to attend the meeting of the Evangelical Alliance, which meets in New York the 2d proximo. Dr. Thompson, of New York, preached in the forenoon, and Dr. Gregory in the evening. We have prayers every night in the dining-saloon, and grace, or rather a short prayer, at each meal. The petition offered for "appetites to enjoy the food before us," no doubt, met with a hearty response from most of the passengers who were able to fill their seats at the table.

We have had near a week of bad weather, just the reverse of what we had when we went over in June. The sea has been rough most of the time—no very high waves, but enough to stir the stomachs of most of the passengers. Some of them were not out of their rooms for nearly a week, while some of those who were promptly at their meals had to cast them into the ocean soon after.

Many years since I was very anxious to be seasick, believing it would be conducive to my health. I have several times seen most of the persons on board sick, while I had not the least symptom of it. I think, now, that the virtue of sea-sickness is more in the fasting than any salutary influence it has upon the system. My curiosity and anxiety on this subject have been fully satisfied.

While this is one of the finest and swiftest ships of the Anchor Line, or any other line, they have studied the most rigid economy in their rooms. At least, we have found it so in the one that has been assigned to four ministers. The Revs. Mr. Baker, Mr. Richardson, and Mr. Witherspoon, of Virginia, and one from Boston, were given a room less than eight feet square. As I am in the berth which was to have been occupied by my old friend, Witherspoon, I can speak more of that than any other. To get into it you must stretch yourself out on the railing, and roll in. On arriving at your destination, you find a tolerably close fit all around, your head reaching very near the bottom of the apartment or bin just above you, which is just the same size. There is, however, one advantage in these close quarters. When the ship rolls we have but little room for this unpleasant exercise. These Presbyterian brethren think it rather strange that a "Scottish line," from the land of Presbyterianism, should put them in such a room, especially as they have first-class tickets, and their passage had been engaged for nearly three months. At their request I mention these facts. Our Irish Presbyterian brethren have the room next us, which, I presume, is of the same dimensions. The room we had on the Canada, coming over, was one-third larger, with a number of conveniences which we have not here. Two more nights will terminate our occupancy of quarters, and when we cross the ocean again we will know more of the place we are to occupy before leaving port.

We see several vessels to-day. One came near crossing our track. She had been out from England thirty-six days. We see some whales, and many

15*

porpoises tossing themselves about. Our sick passengers are nearly all well, and are making up for lost time at the table.

Our ministers preached in the morning and evening yesterday. We have a missionary from Turkey, who has spent several years there. He has given us two very interesting talks about that country. This ship is steered by steam, so that the labor of the pilot is very trifling. They raise the sails, as well as load and unload the ship, by steam.

The most interesting thing is a little machine fastened to a long rope, and thrown out into the ocean. As the ship moves, the machine turns over, so that it tells correctly the distance the ship has sailed every day. This is a very ingenious and important invention; for a ship's navigation is now done with as much precision as if you saw just the place to which you were going. Science has enabled the seaman to strike out from one port to the other in a direct line. After the ship is out at sea, they go direct to their destination. We are making good time, and will be the first of the eight ships that sailed on the day we did to reach New York. We learn the Olympic, which left three days before this ship, is only about twenty hours in advance of us. We have a gentlemanly and careful captain and officers, and as clever a set of cabin passengers as could be desired.

September 2, 1873.

A pilot-boat is seen in the distance, and as no signal is given that we have one engaged, it steers for our ship. We had several hundred passengers on board who had never seen a native American at home. These crowded around to see him come on board. He has some New York papers, which are eagerly devoured by those who had known nothing of the outer world for ten days.

In the evening we see along in the dim, distant horizon some hills on Long Island. Such rejoicing I have never or rarely seen among so many persons. After prayer and thanksgiving for our safe and speedy passage, there was a very interesting speaking meeting held in the dining-saloon. The Irish ministers, being called on, gave some very interesting facts in regard to their country. The emigrants on board were mostly Scotch-Irish, and many of them were members of the Presbyterian Church.

The condition of Ireland has been greatly improved within a few years. In 1841 the population was over eight millions. Now it is less than six millions. So said the preacher in his speech. I thought to myself that all the countries of Europe might be greatly improved if a large portion of their people would seek homes on this American soil.

One of our party said he had heard it said several times that America needed whipping worse than any people in the world. He heard the same thing said the other day in Paris, where there were several nationalities represented. One said that, as the world could not whip the Americans, they had concluded to whip each other, and had thus demonstrated the fact, now acknowledged by other nations, that we cannot be whipped by the world.

The silvery queen of night gives a most lovely view to the rippling waves of the dashing blue sea. We are all out on deck, watching with deepest interest as we pass around Sandy Hook. Away in the distant west are seen the lights from Long Branch. The noble ship, without erring from a direct line, has run its three thousand five hundred miles in less than ten days; and we are safely moored at quarantine, some eight miles from the city, at 11 P.M., to wait for the health-officer to pass us into port, while we retire for the last time to our narrow quarters below.

In the morning, after the health-officer permits, we steam up to Gotham. The examination of baggage by the United States officers is much more strict than any we had in Europe. I believe, however, they passed free of duty nearly all our party except those who had silk. The friends of the tourists met them gladly, thanking us for the attention given to their lady friends on the tour.

I cannot close these sketches without bearing my testimony to the complete fulfillment of the agreement by Messrs. Cook, Son & Jenkins. Those of us who went on the Canada were met at Liverpool by their agent, Mr. Anderson, who took charge of us and our baggage, and gave us every attention required on our way to London. Mr. Plagge, our conductor of the Italian section, discharged his duty faithfully, and relieved us of many annoyances necessarily attending those who take such tours without having some one who understands the languages of the different countries. Every thing was first-class—railroads, steam-boats, hotels—all ready at the right time to accommodate us in the best style of the country. I voluntarily and most cheerfully recommend all who visit Europe to go under the direction of Messrs. Cook, Son & Jenkins, 261 Broadway, New York.

I take pleasure in copying and indorsing the following, from the Rev. C. W. Cushing:

"The entire expense of this trip was five hundred dollars in gold. This included first-class traveling by railway and steam-boat throughout the entire journey; omnibuses, where necessary, from stations to hotels; porterage and transportation of baggage; gondolas and guide in Venice; carriages, and other expenses, such as admission-fees, etc., while under the direction of Mr. Wood in Rome. In Great Britain, hotel provision included room, lights, and service, meat-breakfast, dinner at *table d'hôte*, and plain tea. On the Continent it was the same, except that the breakfast was a plain breakfast of tea, coffee, or chocolate, and bread-and-butter, with the addition of honey in Switzerland, dinner at *table d'hôte*, and additional coupons to the amount of one franc and a half per day, which could be used for a plain tea, or for a meat-breakfast.

"The hotels selected were intended to be first-class, and were good, though not always the most stylish and expensive in the place. This was particularly true in Paris, while in London the whole party was kept at the best hotel in Europe.

"Our conductor, who was a well-educated German, and who met us in New York, and returned there with us, as a rule took the entire charge of our tickets, luggage, etc. Our hotels were engaged days in advance, so that our rooms were assigned us before we reached the hotel, or immediately after, thus saving all annoyance from that source. Carriages were always awaiting when we reached a station, so that there was no delay. Then our conductor was familiar with every place we visited, and knew what was of most interest to see, so that no time was wasted in experimenting. So far as was practicable, the Messrs. Cook had anticipated all our wants, and provided for them. Our money was deposited with them, and we were allowed to draw upon our conductor as we wanted it for purchases or other purposes, always receiving it in the currency of the country in which we happened to be.

"Many of the party made more purchases than they had anticipated. Mr. Cook had told us, before we left London, that it would probably be so, and that we might draw on him for whatever we might want, and remit it when we returned home. This was done by many of the party, in some instances to the amount of several hundred dollars.

"And now, looking back upon this most delightful and profitable trip, the memory of which is worth many times its cost, it is my impression that, for a party of six or more who want to make the most of their time and money, such an arrangement is a saving of considerable expense, an indefinite amount of annoyance, and at least about one-third of the time. If one has plenty of money and plenty of time—which only very few have—he may possibly suit himself better, though this may be doubted. The name of Mr. Thomas Cook is like a household word all through Europe, and will often secure for a man what he would be unable to get without it. He is a noble old Christian gentleman, and worthy of the respect and confidence he has; and his sons are in a fair way to make his place good. There are not enough of these Cooks yet to spoil the broth."

OUR TOUR.

BY A MEMBER OF THE EDUCATIONAL PARTY OF 1873.

The last farewells are sadly said, each lingering clasp of hand
Is loosed, and we have turned our backs upon our native land.
Afloat upon the watery waste, her fluttering canvas spread,
With tossing, white-capp'd waves beneath, and blue sky overhead,
Our noble ship moves proudly on; we tread her decks in glee,
And revel in the joyous thought that we are out at sea.
To watch the dolphins at their play, or scan the passing sail,
Or rush with one accord when some one shouts, "A whale!"
To walk and talk, to read or write, to hear the sailors sing,
Or mark the airy, graceful flight of sea-birds on the wing;
To look for phosphorus at night; the ever-changing play
Of ocean in his many moods, is new from day to day.
But now, these days, so long, so short, so full of charm, are o'er,
And in the soft gray light of morn we see a foreign shore.
We test fair Erin's generous heart, upon her emerald strand,
The first, with hearty greeting, to welcome us to land.
We've looked on Scotland's misty hills, and castles old and gray,
And lakes, of fame in many lands, Lochs Katrine and Achray;
Through Trosachs' wild, romantic glens of heather and of fern;
From Stirling's battlements look out on Teith and Bannockburn.
"Fair Melrose," and its ruined walls, with ivy overgrown,
Where names and dates of long ago survive upon its stone,
While they who builded sleep below, with all their hopes and fears;
Their sculptured work has braved the storms of twice three hundred years.
With loving hearts we seek the spot where trod the noble bard,
Whose genius lives and breathes and moves in lovely Abbotsford.
From Calton Hill and Holyrood we wander up and down
Among the old historic scenes of "Edinboro' town."
And England's summer sun has beamed with welcome as we stood
Mid gardens rare, and fountains grand, and gently-rolling wood,
Where Alton's generous Lord shall win a more enduring name
Than they who tread the battle-field for empire or for fame.
We stand within her crowded mart; we traverse street by street;
Amid the things of olden times we go with busy feet—
The Tower, St. Paul's, and Westminster, where lie, enthroned in state,
The monarchs of the world of mind beside the earthly great.

We view them all with sated eyes; and when we next advance,
It is among the sunny slopes and vine-clad hills of France.
Among her ruined palaces, her splendid works of art,
Where kings and emperors, by turns, have borne their fitful part.
We leave *her* glittering scenes to tread the henceforth hallowed
    ground
Where England and America with white-winged peace were
    crowned;
While far, yet near, an emblem meet, robed in eternal white—
Mont Blanc, in hoary majesty—looked down upon the sight.
Our eyes beheld the glory of the Brunig and the Thun,
Where hazy, cloud-girt, snow-capp'd peaks seem stretching to the
    sun.
We slowly climb the mountain-road, then thunder down its side;
We sail upon the dark-green lake, with softly-rippling tide;
We look from lofty Alpine heights on beauteous valleys green,
Where Swiss *chalets*, and harvest fields, and gentle-winding stream,
Have landscapes made so fair to see, that years of change and care
May not efface from memory's page the pictures painted there.
We've gazed on Jungfrau's lovely head, where shadows come and go,
As sunlight breaks or fades upon her crown of purest snow.
A peep at Lauterbrunnen's Fall we have from wayside ridge,
Because our guide, with wearied brain,* slept at the turning bridge.
But mountain glacier tempts us on, mid summits grim and bald,
Where lies, upon the lofty plain, long-looked-for Grindelwald.
Fair Griesbach, in her highland nest, has welcomed one and all
To pure, sweet air, and native woods, and gorgeous waterfall.
Again, upon the placid lake, our eyes we fondly turn
To where the sunset bathes in gold the beautiful Lucerne.
On Rigi's bold and rugged top with reverend feet we've trod,
And felt that in His glorious works we nearer drew to GOD.
We watched the sunset's fading glow, and in the early morn
Our slumbering ears are sweetly waked by winding Alpine horn.
O glorious Alps and lovely lakes! ye pain our happy band;
For sadly we shall bid farewell to thee, fair Switzerland.
And though we have before us still Vienna and the Rhine,
Their tempting shapes and loveliest hues shall not outrival thine.
But when we leave these foreign scenes to seek each distant home,
We'll give three cheers, with hearty will, for Thomas Cook & Son!

LUCERNE, July 22, 1873.

---

* The design was to have gone direct to Grindelwald, omitting Lauterbrunnen; but the conductor was taking "forty winks" at the junction of the roads, and the driver had the party near to Lauterbrunnen before the mistake was discovered.

THE END.

www.ingramcontent.com/pod-product-compliance
Lightning Source LLC
Chambersburg PA
CBHW030255240426
43673CB00040B/975